SEX AS BAIT

SEX AS BAIT: EVE, CASANOVA, AND DON JUAN

S. GIORA SHOHAM

WITHDRAWN

University of Queensland Press
St Lucia • *London* • *New York*

© University of Queensland Press, St Lucia, Queensland 1983

Typeset by University of Queensland Press
Printed and bound by The Dominion Press—Hedges & Bell, Melbourne

Distributed in the United Kingdom, Europe, the Middle East,
Africa, and the Caribbean by Prentice-Hall International,
International Book Distributors Ltd, 66 Wood Lane End, Hemel
Hempstead, Herts., England.

National Library of Australia
Cataloguing-in-Publication data

Shoham, S. Giora (Shlomo Giora), 1929–.
  Sex as bait.

  Includes index.
  ISBN 0 7022 1703 4.

  1. Sex (Psychology). I. Title.

155.3

Library of Congress Cataloging in Publication Data

Shoham, S. Giora, 1929–
  Sex as bait.

  Includes index.
  1. Sex. 2. Love. I. Title.
HQ21.S481 1983 306.7 82-17386
ISBN 0-7022-1703-4

Giora: Love is ephemeral except for the departed.

Contents

Figures

Acknowledgments

The author wishes to acknowledge with thanks the expert editing of the manuscript by Gill Sher, who also prepared the index; as well as the devoted secretarial work of Sheila Bahat and Rene Wide. Anthony Grahame was responsible for the earlier editorial work of this volume and his help is hereby acknowledged.

Gratitude is also extended to the publishers granting permission to quote from the following.

The Making of Man ed. V.F. Calverton, Random House Inc., excerpts from pages, 162, 487–88; *The Sources of the Doctrine of the Fall* F.R. Tennant, Schocken Books Inc., 1968, "Introduction" copyright 1946 by Mary Frances Thelen; *The Biological Bases of Sexual Behavior* by G. Bermant and J.M. Davidson, Harper & Row Publishers Inc., excerpts from pp. 9 and 253; *Mourning and Its Relation to Manic-Depressive States* by Melanie Klein in the volume *Love, Guilt and Reparation and Other Works* by Melanie Klein, The Melanie Klein Trust and Hogarth Press Ltd and Seymour Lawrence Inc.; *Selected Papers of Karl Abraham* by Karl Abraham, The Author's Literary Estate and Hogarth Press Ltd and Brunner/Mazel Inc.; *The Sociology of Georg Simmel* trans. Kurt H. Wolff, The Free Press, a division of Macmillan Publishing Co. Inc.; copyright 1950, renewed 1978; *Essays on a Science of Mythology* by C.G. Jung and C. Kerenyi, Princeton University, copyright 1949, 1959 and 1963 by Princeton University Press, and copyright 1951 by Routledge & Kegan Paul Ltd.

The Great Mother: An Analysis of the Archetype by Erich Neumann, trans. Ralph Manheim, Bollingen series 47, Princeton University Press, 1955, excerpts from pp. 42, 307 and 171; *Dialogues of Plato* trans. B. Jowett, Random House Inc., 1937; and *Iphigenia in Aulis* trans. F.M. Stawell, Bell and Hyman Publishers.

Editor's Note

Rather than refer to the action of the child and neonate as an "it", a rather dehumanizing form of address indicated by the example, "the mouth ego receives a dual image from its breast-mother", the author explains his ideas by continuous use of the masculine form. Arguments presented in this way are equally valid for the feminine. Any differences in the action/reaction of the child due to gender are specifically mentioned in the text.

Similarly, instead of cluttering up the presentation of "ego-alter" arguments, with he/she, the text usually refers to ego as he, and alter as she. For example, "Where the separant ego achieves the participant submission of alter, he loses interest and seeks other conquests". Arguments presented in this way are equally valid for cases where ego is feminine, and alter masculine. Where gender is not reversible, it is specifically mentioned in the text.

SEX AS BAIT

Introduction

Therefore shall a man leave his father
and his mother, and shall cleave unto his
wife: and they shall be one flesh.

Genesis 2:24

The present volume is the fifth in a series of works which has resulted from the author's preoccupation over the last two decades with the breakdown of human communication.[1] Although this work is self-contained in both content and form it utilizes some concepts of the previous works.

The two major conceptual vectors are "participation" and "separation". If we envisage love as an affective longing of the lover to fuse with his beloved into an ecstatic unity, the two personality core vectors, which were also postulated in the previous works, respectively enhance or impede the realization of the lovers' aim. Participation means the identification of ego with a person (persons), an object, or a symbolic construct outside himself, and his striving to lose his separate identity by fusion with this other object or symbol. Indeed, love is one of the manifestations of ego's quest for participation. Separation, of course, is the opposite vector. These opposing vectors of unification-fusion and separation-isolation are used as the main axis of our personality theory in conjunction with three major developmental phases. The first phase of separation is the process of birth; the second is the crystallization of an individual ego by the molding of the "ego boundary"; and the third phase of separation is a corollary of socialization when one reaches one's "ego identity".[2]

The strain to overcome the separating and dividing pressures never leaves the human individual. The striving to partake (participate) in a pantheistic whole is ever present and takes many forms; if one avenue towards its realization is blocked it surges out from another channel, although actual participation is unattainable by definition. The objective impossibility of participation is augmented by the countering separating vectors, both instinctual and interactive. At any given moment of our lives is a disjuncture, a gap between our desires for participation and our subjectively defined distance from our participatory aims. We have denoted this gap the Tantalus Ratio which is the relationship between the longed for participatory goal and the distance from it as perceived by ego.[3]

We define love as the participant quest for the melting down of partitions between individuals. This participation through affect has been considered by Sartre as an ontological impossibility. Buber, however, considered this fusion of souls as possible for some time, through a meaningful dialogue between ego and alter.

Another basic premise which has a direct bearing on ego's quest for love as expounded in the present volume, is the fixation of the separant and participant personality types. These are related to the crystallization at later orality of a separate self out of the pantheistic mass of totality at early orality. This is the ontological base-line by which the self is defined by the non-self (the object). The coagulation of the self marks the cutting-off point for the most basic developmental dichotomy: from birth and early orality to the phase where the ego boundary is formed around the emerging individual separatum and from later orality onwards. In the first phase, any fixation that might occur and imprint thereby some character traits on the developing personality, is not registered by a separate self capable of discerning between the objects which are the source of the fixation-causing trauma and himself as its recipient. The experiencing entity is a non-differentiated pantheistic totality. On the other hand, if the traumatizing fixation occurs at the later oral phase after the objects have expelled the self from their togetherness by a depriving interaction with it, the self may well be in a position to attribute the cause of pain and deprivation to its proper source, that is to the objects that are the source of the fixation-causing trauma. We have previously proposed a personality typology anchored on this developmental dichotomy of pre and post-differentiation of the self, and we rely on this typology in the present work.[4]

The moulding process is the nature and severity of the fixation which determines, in turn, the placement of a given individual on the personality type continuum. However, the types themselves are fixated by developmental chronology: the participant at pre-differentiated early orality and the separant after the formation of the separate self. The participant core personality vector operates with varying degrees of potency on both these personality types but the quest for congruity manifests itself differently with each polar personality type. The participant aims to achieve congruity by effacing and annihilating himself, by melting back (to so speak) into the object and achieving thereby the pantheistic togetherness and non-differentiation of early orality. The separant type aims to achieve congruity by overpowering or "swallowing" the object. We have denoted the congruity aims of the self-effacing participant as exclusion, whereas the object devouring separant wishes to achieve congruity by inclusion, that is by incorporating the object in his out reaching self.

The application of this terminology to the present context is that if the lover's personality is closer to the separant pole of the personality-core continuum he would strive to "include" (to engulf and overpower) his beloved. Conversely, if the lover tends to be a participant he would tend to exclude himself and long to be engulfed by his lover and incorporated in his (the lover's) person. However, both the inclusive and exclusive aims of the lover can never be achieved in actual relationship with the beloved. We may denote, therefore, the separant lover's longing to engulf his beloved as Sisyphean and the participant's aim to be immersed in his beloved as Tantalic. Indeed, sex, especially when not accompanied by the emotional infatuation of love, is Sisyphean in the original sense of the myth: one is aroused by sexual excitement onto the plateau phase in intercourse culminating in the crescendo of orgasm and followed by momentary satiety.[5] Love is also tantalizing in its mythical sense in so far as an intersubjective emotional communion between lovers cannot be realized. Its fulfilment seems to be evasive however ardently one may long for it and pursue it.

Love is Sisyphean when a separant Casanova aims to court, seduce and conquer a woman. But when he succeeds he loses interest in his conquest and pursues the next female silhouette to gain another short-lived Sisyphean triumph. On the other hand, a participant Don Juan longs for the grace of the Absolute Woman. He is intoxicated with womanhood and is in love with love itself. His endeavours are Tantalic because his romantic affairs only seem to — but do not — convey him nearer to his ever receding ideal woman.

Sex and love more than any other dynamic of life, strive to implement the core personality vectors. The separant lover fixated on the object craves to overpower, "swallow" and absorb his beloved within himself, whereas the participant fixated on pre-differentiated wholeness longs to be incorporated and absorbed by his lover. These quests are again Sisyphean and Tantalic because, irrespective of the intensity of the lovers' longing and the number of their attempts, they can never satisfy the core drives of the personality. Sex and love are the most primary and potent manifestations of the personality core vectors, and their Sisyphean and Tantalic nature stems from their corresponding core dynamics.

We have demonstrated in the *Violence of Silence* that the possibilities of attaining a meaningful dyadic dialogue are lowered by two major processes. The first is that ego and alter's different bio-personal configurations and sociocultural experiences make for their different expectations from the encounter. As there cannot be an effective intersubjective link between them to convey their mutual expectations from each other — they are liable to be frustrated to varying degrees (depending on the nature of their expectations) from the outcome of their encounter. Secondly, the deeper the level of encounter expected the higher are the chances of frustration. If the encounter is on a shallow and routine level, for example a client cashing a cheque at a bank counter or a housewife shopping at a supermarket, the aims of the encounter are usually achieved but if the expectations from the encounter are a meeting of minds, emotional rapport and a meaningful dialogue, the chances of its attainment are inversely related to its expected depth. Because ego and alter are liable to expect different things from an encounter as well as different depths and intensities of dialogue, ego has the greatest difficulties to convey to alter his love-motivated expectations.

Ego and alter might, of course, be raised to the heights of euphoria by their mutual longing for the communion of love. In this case the differences of their expectations from their amorous encounter would be temporarily repressed and anaesthetized by the crescendos of repeated orgasms. However, when the excitement wanes and the novelty wears off, ego may feel as if he emerged from a psychedelic trip. Then his longing for love *qua* love and his pursuit of the hedonistic excitement of sex would not be enough to gloss over the unfulfilled expectations he had from his love affair. It may dawn on him/her that their that their (ex)beloved "does not understand" them and come to think of it they never did to begin with. Also, how was it they did not notice that their beloved had a crooked smile, bad teeth and keeps repeating himself with the same shallow clichés. We shall try in the following chapters to substantiate our claim that the participant longing for love of both partners to the emotional dyad temporarily blunts the perceived differences in their mutual expectations from each other.

At the height of excitement ego feels as if all his expectations from alter have already been fulfilled and vice versa. However, after the initial peak experience subsides ego may suddenly realize that the expectations he projected on his (ex)lover were not really fulfilled. He is, of course, not aware that in the heat of passion and love he projected on his partner qualities and attributes which the partner never had. When the halo of love vanishes and takes with it the hazy glow from around the person and personality of the beloved alter, ego sees that alter has *lost* the ability to fulfil the expectations of his (ego's) love. This ability has not been lost, it was never there to begin with. These fulfilled expectations were mere refractions of ego's longings bouncing back from the glowing aura projected on the beloved by the lover himself. After the infatuation subsides, which it invariably does, ego may ask himself "What did I ever find in this person", not realizing that he was deceived by his own projected expectations. Why should this be so? Why cannot Jack and Jill live happily ever after in the same, or even in an ever increasing passion and bliss as in the first few months of their love story?

One of the main theses of this present work is that this linkage between our temporary illusions of perfect harmony and fusion of souls inherent in love, is effected by our basic programming to procreate. We are not concerned whether this linkage and basic programming is metaphysical, stems from the Darwinian dynamics of the survival of the fittest or is ordained by the "selfish genes" of the sociobiologists. We are interested in the mechanisms and dynamics by which this programming has implanted in love and sex the Sisyphean and Tantalic craving and longing inherent in our personality core vectors, to lure us to reproduce. After a while, deemed long enough by our basic programming to consummate the reproductive function, the charm snaps and the illusion of rapport, participation and communion fade away. It seems as if this basic programming loses interest after its reproductive aims seem to have been achieved. Flowers wane and shrivel after fertilization; the head of the male praying mantis is eaten by the female after copulation; and the human animal usually ends his euphoric trip of love (if he ever had it) some time after marriage. Our programming baits us by temporarily reinforcing our sex and love with short-lived feelings so that the aims of our personality core vectors, both participant and separant, may be fulfilled through them. This bait is necessary to induce us to reproduce. This is true to varying degrees for most flora and fauna but with Man this linkage between love and his personality core vectors becomes a central pivot for his personal and social existence. One of the objectives of the present work is to try and examine the centrality of love and sex within the dynamics of the human personality core vectors described earlier.

The Violent Separations

Definitions convey an illusion of exactness. Those who indulge in them suffer from the scientistic occupational hazard of imputing to language qualities it cannot have. The diffuse boundaries of the connotative meaning of words are not meant for exact definitions. Of much greater use are inspired descriptions of what sex does. One such description is the following by Bermant and Davidson:

> Sex is separateness: A division of reproductive labor into specialized cells, organs, and organisms. The sexes of a species are the classes of reproductively incomplete individuals. In order for a sex member to contribute to the physical foundations of its species, to reproduce part of itself into the next generation, it must remedy its incompleteness. The remedy is found in the union of incomplete parts from complementary incomplete organisms: sperm and egg unite. The accomplishment of this union requires energy. The animals must locomote, gesture, posture, vocalise, display, or otherwise behave if union is to occur. Any behaviour that increases the likelihood of gametic union may reasonably be called sexual behaviour.[6]

This fits our conceptual matrix of the dialectical interplay between the core vectors of separation and participation as the basic dynamic of human and animal behaviour. Sexual reproduction involves first of all the havoc wrought by the separation of meiosis in comparison with which the less violent cell division by mitosis is a divorce by mutual consent. Meiosis reduces by half the number of chromosomes in the cell. The process of "crossing over" tears the chromosomes apart and recombines them in order to achieve greater genetic variation which amounts to a virtual pogrom within the cell. The meiotic separation which is bound to be registered as a shattering event by every particle of the cells and every coil of the double-helix molecules of the genes, leaves the haploid gametes with half the number of chromosomes. This implants, apparently, in the gametes, the drive to regain their previous wholeness and full diploid number of chromosomes. Consequently the sole *raison d'être* of the gametes is to regain a participant union of fusion between sperm and ovum which effects the *restitutio in integrum* of diploid cells and starts thereby the generation of a new organism. The participant union of the gametes which recreates diploid cells seem to be the biological "bait" offered to the violently separated haploid cells in the same way that the whole organism is baited by sex and love to court, mate and reproduce.

We intend to substantiate our claim that the quest of union following some violent processes of separation is the basis of the biological processes of reproduction as well as sexual behaviour. This brings the present work into the wider theoretical framework which we have postulated elsewhere: that Man's personality core dynamics as well as much of his social interaction is motivated by his quest to overcome the catastrophic separation of birth, the ejection from the pantheistic wholeness of early orality and the expulsion from the protection of the family fold.[7]

For the first two billion years of life on earth reproduction was asexual. Flora and fauna divided, produced buds and propagated by offshoots. This was the relatively calm, Edenic period of growth when except for occasional mutations the offspring generation resembled very much the parent generation. Sometime at the beginning of the third billion years of life on earth eukaryotes (i.e., cells and membrane-bound nuclei with gene arrangements within chromosomes) developed and prepared the evolutionary background for sexual reproduction and the vast population explosion of life on earth.[8] The more advanced a species is on the evolutionary scale the more likely it is to reproduce sexually. Sexual reproduction makes a species more adaptable to environmental changes. The greater variability and reshuffling of genes involved in sexual reproduction makes for a greater variety of the genotype and phenotype of the individuals in a species, so that some would prove to be adaptable to the adverse environmental changes in which others perished. The evolutionary password seems to be: "The versatile − not the meek − shall inherit the earth".[9] There is a fair amount of evidence and it is also logical to assume that sexual reproduction evolved in times of hardship, changing conditions and environmental hazards, so that the greater variability of offspring would increase their hardiness and raise the possibility of survival of some of the individuals in the species. "As soon as cloning was possible in the history of life", says Williams, "sexual reproduction would be confined to times of change or stress."[10] Later we shall mention instances of fauna and flora which reproduce asexually in favourable environmental conditions, but when the weather turns bad and food becomes scarce these specimens start reproducing sexually. It seems that sexual reproduction is linked to adverse conditions, to stress, want and environmental catastrophes.

We shall elaborate our thesis that sex is linked to the phases of separant growth by the manifestations of change, variability, stress, upheaval and adverse conditions on the group and on the environment. It is also accompanied by violence, pain and suffering on the biological and personal levels. These stressful manifestations of sex precede the separation of birth which signifies the violent transition from a blissful existence in utero to the harsh exposure to want and to a deprivational interaction with the environment. We shall try to substantiate our hypothesis that given these circumstances, there would be no sexual reproduction without the participant bait provided by our programming in the form of some moments of blissful visions of union in orgasm and temporary feelings of communion with our beloved. We assume by inference without being able to prove it, that similar forms of participant baits motivate other fauna and flora which engage in sexual reproduction.

The mechanisms of sex and reproduction are both prior and subsequent to the separant developmental processes of birth, the oral coagulation of the ego boundary and the rites of passage from childhood to puberty. As these separant processes of birth and growth are registered by the organism as catastrophes, the individual strives all his life to overcome these catastrophes by reverting back to the previous states of familial togetherness and forgiveness, to the pantheistic wholeness of early orality and to the bliss of self-sufficiency *in utero* and of non-being. It is expected that no individual would engage in reproduction and subject his offspring to the catastrophes of separation unless he is baited by the most intense sensation of fusion and togetherness which are precisely those inherent in orgasm and longed for by love. The paradoxical or rather the dialectical outcome is that another separant cycle is initiated by such a participant "trigger" and the baits used to set it off. These baits are the personality core incentives to reproduce which are, no doubt, related to our genetic programming to procreate. We shall try and examine further the relationship between this core personality incentive to reproduce and the other biological, interactive and cultural motivations of reproduction, in the subsequent chapters of this work. An etymological sideglance which is rather interesting to the present context is the statement by Capellanus that "Love gets its name (Amor) from the word hook (Amus) which means 'to capture' or 'to be captured' for he who is in love is captured in chains of desire . . . just as a skillful fisherman tries to attract fishes by his bait . . . "[11] Rarely does an etymological source of a word fit its function as in the present case of sex and love.

Another premise with which we shall be concerned in the present work is the fact that sex dichotomizes our developmental continuum of separant growth/participant non-being, an idea also referred to in previous works.[12] The mythological symbolics and archetypal sources in some of the myths of creation and the fall with which we shall deal later, depict woman as the temptress, the seductress and as the evil channel through which human beings are expelled into this world and exposed to its vicissitudes. The male, on the other hand, is depicted as the baited − the one who was lured by sex to reproduce. We shall try to show that sex as the basis of reproduction was one of the mythological foundations of the Original Sin because the word ידע (*yada*) in Hebrew is both to have sex and to know, so that there is a mythological relationship between having sex and the myth of the Fall. However, at the later developmental stages there is a diametrical change of the mythological male/female roles. Abraham and the male in the Kabbala become the source of authoritarian stern judgement whereas the image of the adolescents' mother is depicted as the source of grace. This meta-

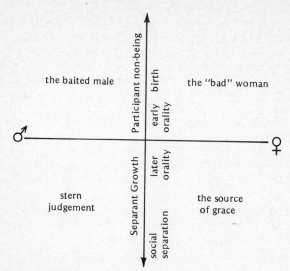

Figure 1 Development Continuum of Participation/Separation

morphosis of parental roles from the earlier developmental stages to the later ones, which is apparent in mythological literature and rites of passages in many societies, will also be dealt with.

Both the separant phases of development and their participant counterparts have sexual manifestations. For instance, the birth through the vagina has its participant Tantric rituals in which sex is performed as a symbolic regression back to the womb. Sexual differentiation may be related even in the oral phase to the differential attitude of the mother towards her suckling baby. Finally, after the rites of passage from childhood to puberty, the participant graceful image of the mother quite often manifests itself in the boy's desire to court and marry a girl resembling his mother; while there is a tendency in girls to prefer boys who remind them overtly or symbolically of their father.

The human animal unlike most fauna and flora can be and is constantly aroused and even obsessed by sex. He is also in a carnivorous mood even when not hungry. Homo sapiens has made a ritual, a pastime, an art and a status symbol out of feeding so that many people do not eat in order to live but live for eating. This inflated importance of the basic drives which transcends their physiological functions is especially apparent in sex. Sex is the main, and with the higher forms of flora and fauna, the exclusive mechanism of reproduction and hence, the prime manifestation of separant growth. Yet sex is also the anchor of participant longings and Tantalic quests because of the short-lived yet intense sensation of union in orgasm and the craving for communion of the lover with his beloved. Because reproduction is the main aim of our genetic programming sex is the main manifestation of our core vectors both separant and participant. We differ here from Freud who saw in sex the motivational fuel of our existence. For us the dynamics of life are expressed by the dialectical interplay between the separant and participant core vectors, sex being one such dynamic albeit the most primary and central one. Freud bases his personality theory on sex and denotes the developmental stages of the personality as psycho-sexual. We, on the other hand, see sex as one phase or segment on the continuum of being/not-being which is subject to the core dialectics of separation and participation. Freud also saw in sex the primary instinct which impels the human being to function biologically, develop its personality, reproduce and through sublimation to create culture. Freud relates:

> we believe that civilisation has been built up, under the pressure of the struggle for existence, by sacrifices in gratification of the primitive impulses, and that it is to a great extent forever being recreated, as each individual successively joining the community, repeats the sacrifice of his instinctive pleasures for the common good. The sexual are amongst the most important of the instinctive forces thus utilised: they are in this way sublimated, that is to say, their energy is turned aside from its sexual goal and directed towards other ends, no longer sexual and socially more valuable. . . . These sexual impulses have contributed invaluably to the highest cultural, artistic, and social achievements of the human mind.[13]

We regard the vector of separation and growth as being programmed from outside the organism. (We are planning to devote a volume length exposition to this programming but at this stage it is enough for us to observe that the programming of our separant propagation and growth, even if partially apparent in the codes of our genes, has been initiated outside our organism.) For us, sex is an instrumental manifestation of this programmed vector of separation and growth. The vector of participation, on the other hand, aiming to reverse and annul the effects of separation, operates from within the organism and interacts with the opposing separant vectors. Our conception of sex differs from Freud's, both in relation to its biological function and its role within and outside of the personality structure. Sex and love are also not really subject to socioeconomic differentation. The Victorian anecdote tells about a lord and a lady who make love and after orgasm the lady asks if the lower classes do the same and the lord retorts that "It's too good for the lower classes". Yet sex and love seem to be equally available to the landed gentry, the jet set, the Russian members of the Politburo, Indian beggars and Amazonian cannibals. Because of the social norms and proscriptions which enmesh the manifestations of sex and love in all human societies, sex has become the subject and object of an enormous range of human Sisyphean quests and Tantalic longings. For the same reason sex and love, more than any other human dynamic, are subject to psychic defence mechanisms of projection, repression, selective perception and distortion.

Love as Dialogue

The conception of the dyad of love as an unattainable dialogue has been expressed by Georg Simmel as follows:

> The fact that male and female strive after their mutual union is the foremost example or primordial image of a dualism which stamps our life-contents generally. It always presses toward reconciliation, and both success and failure of the reconciliation reveal this basic dualism only the more clearly. The union of man and woman is possible, precisely because they are opposites. As something essentially unattainable, it stands in the way of the most passionate craving for convergence and fusion. The fact that, in any real and absolute sense, the "I" can *not* seize mutual supplementation and fusion seem to be the very reason for the opposites to exist at all. Passion seeks to tear down the borders of the ego and to absorb "I" and "thou" in one another. But it is not they which become a unit: rather a *new* unit emerges, the child.[14]

Simmel's ingenious observation which is not very far removed from our own conception of the unachievable aims of core vectors, is that the impossibility of union between man and woman leads to the dialectical synthesis of the child. This seems to us as too mechanistic a concretization of dialectics. We envisage that man and woman are induced by shifty visions of participation emanating from sex and love to mate and breed not unlike the way racing dogs are lured to win by an every receding plastic rabbit running in front of their noses. Male and female do not directly intend to perpetuate the species by their sex and love. They are tricked into it by their programming. They are driven to mate by the quest of an orgasm which is meant to be a quick glimpse of participation, and by the Tantalic visions of eternal love which is a surrogate image of the unattainable aims of our participant core vectors.

The agonies of love described by the myriads of lovers from the pulp magazines to the *Song of Songs,* stems from ego's feelings that "he opened up" towards his beloved alter and that he/she did not respond to him as expected. This is the inevitable gap between ego's amorous expectations and alter's response. Ego many times experiences the chagrin of the disenchanted lover for having invested so much emotion in such an unworthy person. Ego would rarely have the inclination or the ability to realize that he projected on alter his inner craving for participation and expected him to fulfil this core longing by their love. As intersubjective communication is an ontological impossibility alter cannot perceive ego's expectations and is even less able to fulfil them. "That love is suffering", says Capellanus, "is easy to see, for before love becomes equally balanced on both sides there is no torment greater, since the lover is always in fear that his love may not gain its desire and he is wasting his efforts."[15] Love, however, cannot be "equally balanced on both sides" because ego's amorous expectations from alter and vice versa are determined by their differences in gender, neuro-endocrinology, personality core vectors and cultural imprints. Furthermore, ego's expectations are bound to change with time and place so that alter's ability to meet these expectations are diminished further.

What characterizes love at its peak is that the lover, spurred on by an intense longing for participation, claims the exclusive attention and time of his beloved. Ego desires (sometimes accompanied by overt demands) to share all the thoughts and all experiences of alter. At that very place and time, alter may not be able or willing to be totally attuned to ego and match his staccato display of emotions. Alter may have reached his own emotional crescendo at another time or place and he cannot or will not match his emotional peaks with those of ego. The pangs of love and the romantic agonies stem from the disparity of expectations between lover and loved. Love is either Sisyphean or Tantalic because we tend to project on our beloved expectations which we ourselves are not aware of so that the beloved cannot be expected to be aware of them. If we aspire for our love to be what it cannot be, we make this love impossible. Consequently the impossibility of love is related to ego's projection of his personality core longing for participation. As alter cannot fulfil this longing in the form, contents and duration expected by ego, love is bound to be a temporary and many times a lonely trip of ego brushing occasionally and tangentially with the emotional orbits of alter.

We shall deal extensively in the present work with the continuum ranging from the Sisyphean separant lover who aims to include, subjugate and "swallow" his beloved, to the participant Tantalic who longs to be immersed, excluded and, so to speak, consumed by his love. The latter has been depicted in literature and art as *l'amour sacre*: the spiritual and sacred love for a person who stands for and symbolizes an archetype such as the Great Mother, the Virgin Mary, an absolute value, the Divine Presence or God Himself. This love of an ethereal purity is tailor-made as a surrogate participation dynamic: by immersing oneself in the spiritual love of an unattainable woman one enacts the longing of the core participant vector to partake in the absolute. The Tantalic nature of these sacred loves calls for their partial, at least, impossibility. The less attainable they are the more pure, spiritual and sacred they become. Temporary blindness and selective perception is of great help in these cases. Without them a Don Quixote can hardly be expected to sing odes of love and worship to a Dulcinea the way she really is. The main function of the beloved in a Tantalic participant dyad is to trigger and reflect the lovers' own longing to partake in an omnipresent absolute and melt into an all engulfing wholeness.

The prototype for the Tantalic lover is Don Juan whereas the characteristic Sisyphean lover is Casanova. In chapter 8 we intend to analyze as illustrative case studies the poetry, drama and literature of Don Juan, and the memoirs of Casanova. This brings us to the main thesis of the present work which may be stated tentatively as follows: both the form and contents of the participant expectation of the lover are determined by his biological parameters including gender, his participant or separant personality structure and his socialization in a Sisyphean or Tantalic culture.[16]

For ego's amorous expectations as determined by his bio-psycho-cultural configuration to be met by alter, the latter's expectations as determined by his configuration have to be exactly complementary, which is a statistical improbability. Secondly, we have stated in the *Violence of Silence* that meaningful communication is more feasible on shallow and routine levels of encounter, whereas on deeper levels of encounter communication is hardly possible.[17] The expectations of love are for the deepest level of encounter and for the most complete fusion of bodies and souls, yet communication between the lovers as to the intricate nuances of their mutual expectations are almost impossible. Consequently the more a couple are in love, the less able are the partners to convey to each other the depths, range and intensity of their emotions and mutual expectations from each other.

Thirdly, we know that an extreme need dulls all the other functions of the body and personality. It generates biased perceptions and even hallucinations. For example, hungry subjects perceive food-related stimuli and ignore a wide range of other stimuli.[18] In like manner a sex hungry subject or one who is emotionally infatuated by love cannot evaluate the stimuli and expectations of his beloved except in the context of his turbulent emotions. Ego the lover is bound, therefore, to twist his perception and expectations of his beloved alter according to his emotionally biased perceptions which are twisted in turn by his own intense motivated expectations *de capo*. The more intense the love is the more the impossibility of a meaningful communication between the lovers to enable them to realize their participant aim. Love seems to be dominated by a self-defeating negative feedback cycle.

Finally, the investigators of the Least Interest Principle have shown that when ego is very high in his emotional involvement alter seems to cool off and vice versa.[19] Although this phenomenon is well documented, as far as we know no-one has yet offered an aetiological explanation for the phenomenon. We, however, are able to do so: a separant ego who aims to gain and conquer alter will lose interest once he achieves his aim. This is especially so when ego's desire to overpower alter is dominated by his separant core personality vector which is not satisfied by an intermediate conquest but is every craving to subjugate and "swallow" more bodies. A participant ego with his ever-ready submission will be taken and had by the separant alter only to be rejected immediately afterwards, as just another item in the conqueror's log book. If both ego and alter are separants (or participants) an amorous encounter between them would be quite unlikely from the outset. As their expectations are diametrically opposite, they are more likely to be repelled by each other than attracted to each other.

If sex is bait, and the exclusive communion through love cannot be attained, what reinforces the torrents of emotions invested by couples throughout the world trembling with desire for each other? What sustains the furtive longing glances of girls and boys in societies which forbid public manifestations of love? What makes a Tristam and Isolde so turbulently immortal, or the death for love of a Romeo and Juliet so intensely and continuously relevant? What makes Solomon's love song ever fresh and the cliches of Segal's *Love Story* sell millions of copies? The answer is that the longing in itself for the communion of love, and not its attainment, is the necessary and sufficient reinforcer. Moreover in many cases some amorous longings should not be quenched in order to ensure their viability: Solomon of the *Song of Songs*, after trying to fulfil his amorous longing with a thousand spouses, reached the abysmal despair of Ecclesiastes. Ephraim Kishon, the Israeli satirist, had the ingenuity of continuing the story of Romeo and Juliet who have been saved, married and have sunk into the nagging life of a bourgeois boredom. Kierkegaard, on the other hand, renounced the realization of his love and freed it, thereby, from the bonds of its fulfilment. By making his love independent of its fulfilment Kierkegaard assured its continuity.

The quest of participant union by sex and the grace of communion by love as spurred by our core vectors are unattainable. Yet the common longing for them by people in love creates a bond and a frame into which their different participant cravings might be expressed. Love encloses the lovers within a common boundary in which their separate and disparate visions of union seem to each one of them as if flowing in unison.

The Method

The present work, like its four predecessors which we have mentioned earlier, is interdisciplinary but not ecclectic. We hold every manifestation of the human soma and psyche as well as every human endeavour to be relevant to the understanding of the aetiology of behaviour. We shall avail ourselves with research results in the human sciences as well as with theoretical expositions in biology, works of fiction and drama, to structure our models and illustrate our expositions. We shall compose them into paradigms and interrelate them within levels and hierarchies to demonstrate our notion of an aetiological hierarchy of behaviour which synchronizes many levels of analysis into an interdisciplinary synthetic whole.[20] It is necessary, of course, to study the relationship between some factors on one level of analysis with a given phenomenon, but such study must be regarded as a process within a whole and not as an independent process. The current fallacy of over-specialized atomism may claim that our genetic code determines sexual behaviour or that a high level of testosterone accounts for aggression in males; the synthetic holistic view, on the other hand, acknowledges the relevance of both genes and hormones but only within the wider integrative context which also includes personality parameters and cultural imprints. The core vectors of separation and participation may serve then, as a dialectical scaffolding within which the various levels of observation may be integrated.

Our macro-synthetic approach is indeed strictly deterministic because we envisage every pattern of behaviour (even the most minute), every myth, every pattern of culture and every work of art, to be an expression of the human bio-psycho-cultural configuration and hence aetiologically related to it. The problems of correlation and measurement of these links are, of course, enormous. At the present state of our knowledge these links are not yet solvable, but without these assumptions of full deterministic interrelationship we cannot proceed with our synthetic inferences.

One of our basic claims in the present work is that the dialectical interplay between the participant and separant core vectors operates on each level of the aetiological hierarchy of sex as well as between the levels. This book is essentially a description, a documentation and an interdisciplinary synthetic exposition of this interaction between the aetiological hierarchy of sex and the personality core vectors. Our aim in the present work is to construe a theoretical framework of sexual behaviour based on the core personality vectors as an external frame in which various models, hypotheses and research findings are fitted as in a jigsaw puzzle. We shall link our theoretical structure to some empirical anchors and illustrate it by two case studies: the separant Sisyphean Casanova who tries to overcome the rift between himself and the object by the continuous conquest of female bodies; and the participant archetype of Don Juan longing to partake in and be possessed by the ultimate woman, by being in love with love and chasing love affairs in a Tantalic succession.

Before proceeding with our argument, we will briefly recap some of our basic concepts. Separant and participant denote the core vectors. Sisyphean and Tantalic relate to personality components. And inclusion and exclusion are the corresponding attitudes and modes of behaviour of the respective personality types.

1
Why Sex?

The sexual instinct. What is this instinct?
On the one hand it is the ultimate
expression of nature and, on the other,
the blind force which demands
the total subjection of human beings,
even at the price of their destruction.

A. Camus: *The Rebel*

The Violence of Sex

The long range of advantage of sex is deemed to be the more effective
distribution and transmission of favourable mutations; whereas its
short-term advantage is related to the greater variability of the genotype and phenotype of sexually reproduced offspring and hence their
greater adaptability to changing and adverse environmental conditions.[1]
We are concerned with the translation of this evolutionary programming
to the core dynamics of the sexually interacting individuals. The first
premise in this context is that sexual reproduction is the most effective
separating agent insofar as it creates unique genotypes and phenotypes
with each individual which, except for the anomaly of monozygotic
twins, are as genetically unique as fingerprints. The enormity of the
separating potential of sexual reproduction may be surmised from the
fact that a single human couple is capable of producing 64.000.000-
000.000 genetically different offspring.[2] Sex is the ideal means to
realize the separant core dynamic aims of apartness, variability and
discrepancy, which coincide with the biological aims of growth and
evolutionary adaptation. For our present theoretical purposes it is
sufficient to point out the link between the variable aim of sexual reproduction inherent in evolutionary adaptiveness, and the separating
core dynamic pushing towards maximum difference and plurality.

The sexual mechanisms which may be related to the participant
core dynamic, which induces individuals to mate with other individuals
of the same species, are the reproductive isolating mechanisms (RIM).
These isolating mechanisms are the main ingredient of the definition
of a species. "A species", says Mayr, "is a population of actually or

potentially interbreeding individuals that is reproductively isolated from other populations under natural conditions."[3] These RIM mechanisms operate on many levels: the well known hybrid sterility of the mule is a physiological RIM, as is the gametic and zygotic mortality following heterospecific mating. Anatomical RIMs are related to non-compatible sex organs which prevent insemination. Differences in seasons and locations of breeding also prevent heterospecific mating.[4] Finally, there are the most widespread behavioural RIMs of different courtship displays and mating calls attracting only species-specific mates. Crane has shown that the semaphore-like wavings of the front claw of the fiddler crab are meant to attract females to their species-specific mates and chase away competing males from the courting pair.[5] In like manner, Lloyd has demonstrated that the flash patterns of fireflys are different for each species and are meant to attract only species-specific mates.[6] Similar RIMs are effected by mating calls, and the chemical and tactile stimuli of a wide variety of fauna.[7]

We hold that with all his behavioural and cultural pecularities Homo sapiens is still on the same continuum with the other fauna. Although all human beings belong to one species there are many behavioural RIMs which are based on participant criteria of likeness and together-ness: ethnicity, caste, religion, socioeconomic and political status have all been used as bases for inducing like to court and mate with like. On the other hand, incest taboos and their widest possible manifesta-tions of exogamy are separant mechanisms for preventing inbreeding and enhancing variability of offspring.[8] Here again we see the dialecti-cal dynamics between the separating vectors of growth, variety, plurality and genetic uniqueness of the individuals, with the participant vectors of likeness and togetherness manifested by the reproductive isolating mechanisms.

The aim of growth and survival inherent in genetic variety is, no doubt, served by the separant diversity of sexual reproduction whereas the quest of participation and the attraction of like to like inherent in the RIMs seem to be participant "baits" to induce mating and diver-sified reproduction, thus ensuring better adaptation to changing and adverse conditions. Any particular species seems to comply with the motives of the core vectors of the individuals which comprise the species. Their quest for partaking in the togetherness of the group and the solidarity of likes triggers another cycle of separant reproduction. The participant "baiting" of sexual reproduction seems to hold true not only on the individual level but also for the species. Moreover, we shall later try to show that the more violent sexual reproduction (in comparison to non-sexual reproduction) may have a collective motivational force, to use a Jungian term, not unlike the separating of the distinct individual ego from the pantheistic togetherness of early orality.

Sex and Catastrophe

There is no clear evidence as to how and when sexual reproduction evolved with most of the higher organisms. We may infer, however, that in times of adverse environmental conditions those organisms that developed genetic diversity through the evolution of sexual reproduction survived the catastrophic environmental changes; whereas those which continued their homogeneous asexual reproduction perished. There are, of course, many organisms which still carry on their thriving asexual reproduction by mitosis and parthenogenesis – the assumption being that they have not encountered environmental changes and adverse conditions which were fierce enough to induce them to evolve sexual reproduction. There are also some organisms which change from asexual to sexual reproduction due to environmental circumstances. Such occurrences are highly relevant to our present context. The Daphnia, for instance, reproduces parthenogenetically when food is plenty and the temperature is cosy. But when the temperature falls and food becomes scarce, the parthenogenetic profusion of female offspring crowds the pond. The water becomes polluted, males develop and the Daphnia starts reproducing sexually. Of special interest is the fact that males may develop when only some of the environmental conditions become adverse, but if the situation is not really bad the females will carry on reproducing parthenogenetically and the males will die out. Only when the climatic conditions become really tough and the pollution and overcrowding in the pond become unbearable does the reproduction of the Daphnia become fully sexual.[9] Sex for the Daphnia is a survival technique in the face of catastrophe.

The hydra reproduces asexually by budding but when the concentration of carbon dioxide in the water rises above a certain level the hydra starts reproducing sexually. The concentration of carbon dioxide in the water, which Loomis called the hydra "sex gas", is an index of overcrowdedness and hence of adverse conditions in the habitat of the hydra which induces it to shift from budding to sexual reproduction.[10] Here again sexual reproduction is linked with adverse conditions. Another example are the Aphids (greenfly) which multiply parthenogenetically in spring and summer but in the unstable weather of autumn begin reproducing sexually.[11]

There are many other instances of flora and fauna which reproduce asexually in times of stability and plenty, but shift to sexuality in times of turmoil and stress. Reproduction in itself is a separant dynamic of growth. Our programming to produce offspring seems to be the main *raison d'être* of our existance, yet sexual reproduction seems to be an additional defence mechanism of life against the violence of the elements and of other organisms. Our hypothesis is that sexual reproduction evolved in catastrophic conditions so that the wider range of genotypes and phenotypes of the offspring enhanced survival. The earlier modes of non-sexual reproduction, which presumably occurred in times of relative stability, are registered by the collective memory of the species as Edenic bliss in comparison with the violent upheavals linked with sexual reproduction. The notion of a collective developmental memory is not too wild a conjecture because the developing ovum and embryo pass through all the evolutionary phases of its species in a very accelerated and concentrated manner.[12]

The above examples of the adverse environmental conditions associated with the transition from asexual to sexual reproduction are just initial empirical anchors to illustrate our present premise. One important inference is that sexual reproduction with its greater variety of offspring is more violently separant than the homogeneous similarities and cloning of parthenogenesis, budding and mitosis. For conceptual clarification we may compare asexual reproduction to the pantheistic phase of the development of the individual in early orality and *in utero*; whereas the separant upheavals linked to sexual reproduction may be likened to the violence of the separation of the developing individual from the togetherness of early orality and the cushioning of the family fold. Our analogy between the processes here is not related to any similarity between their form or contents but to their dynamics of participation and separation. Non-sexual reproduction is much more participant than sexual reproduction which is not only more violent in its dynamics but is also linked with adverse external conditions. The analogy here is between the participant motivation of the individual to revert back to the tranquillity of early orality and *in utero*, and the "bait" inherent in orgasm and love of participant bliss and togetherness.

The gist of our present premise is that there is an increasing level of separation from non-being through asexual to sexual reproduction. Because the developmental memory in the Jungian sense of the collective subconscious links sex to catastrophes and adverse environmental conditions,[13] the organisms might not be willing to engage in reproduction unless lured by visions of orgasmic blissful union and by the longing for the communion of love. The participant "bait" of sex and love thus has a dual reinforcement function for reproduction. First, it provides the individual with an image of bliss and union as motivations for sex and love which lead presumably to reproduction. Second, the ecstatic peak experiences of sex and love may blunt the stressful developmental memories related to sexual reproduction so that the individual engages in it and reproduces as ordained by its programming. It should be stressed that our theorizing is quite speculative in relation to non-sexual reproduction. Later on we shall deal with the dynamics of sexual reproduction and the feelings of those who engage in sex and love, but we can only infer that asexual reproduction, although a separant mechanism of growth, is more peaceful and tranquil than the internal violence of meiosis and the adverse environmental conditions linked to the genesis of sexual reproduction. We certainly do not know how a Daphnia feels when it multiplies parthenogenetically or how a hydra is "baited" to clone and bud its young.

The mitotic divisions of cells as well as the asexual reproduction by budding and parthenogenesis involve no doubt, strenuous dynamisms of separation. Meiosis, which is necessary for the formation of the haploid gametes and is instrumental for sexual reproduction is, in comparison, fiercely violent.[14] This increase in separateness with evolutionary development from asexual to sexual reproduction may be likened to the dynamics, but not to the form and contents, of the developmental phases of the individual. The separation of birth, the crystallization of the separate self and the social rites of passage from the cushioning family fold to the loneliness of adulthood are countered by the participant quest of reverting back to the pantheistic grace of early orality and the non-differentiated bliss *in utero*. In similar manner the evolutionary separation is also countered by a quest of participation. The more violent the separation the more ardent is the quest for the participant *restitutio in integrum*.

Indeed, the participant fusion of the haploid gametes by sexual reproduction following the violently separant meiosis is the only instance in nature of a successful participant fusion. Lovers may long to melt into each other; Proust may dream of reverting back to the protecting grace of mother in childhood; and an individual may be unconsciously motivated by his desire to regain the togetherness of early orality — yet none can actually achieve participation. Contrarily the diploid gametes do achieve actual participant fusion into a diploid embryo, through sexual reproduction. This is the only instance where a participant quest is actually reinforced. The less violent forms of asexual reproduction would seem presumably to generate a lower quest of participation because their initial separation was not too fierce to begin with. The offspring are identical with their mothers. Buds and offshoots form usually rather close and tighty knit colonies. The Elm for instance is actually one organism with many interconnected trees. Asexual reproduction is linked, as we have seen, with more tranquil and peaceful environmental conditions. It is, of course, a matter of wild conjecture as to where the evolutionary developmental memory of separation is stored so that the organism would be motivated to regain participation. One possible hypothesis is that in their own development the gametes and embryo flash through the evolutionary phases of their species. The genetic code which stores the programming for the separant meiosis evidently stores also the participant quest of the haploid gametes to fuse into a diploid embryo. This very same quest manifests itself with the whole organism by courting, mating, love and sex. We risk a sweeping generalization by stating that the dialectics of the participant and separant core vectors, as manifest both in the evolutionary development of the species and the growth of individual organisms, seem to be of such wide application in the sciences of life as $E=MC^2$ is in physics.

It should be noted that our discussion centres on sexual and asexual reproduction, but there are also intermediate cases, for example, the recombination of escherichia coli when two bacteria cells form a bridge of cytoplasm through which genetic material is exchanged. Also, there are many instances of hermaphrodites which have both male and female gonads and gametes. However, recombination has many elements of sexual reproduction and most plants and animal hermaphrodites fertilize not themselves but other plants and animals. Consequently, we did not err much in confining our macro theorizing to "pure" sexual and asexual reproduction.

Sexual Aggression

The basic gender of most animals and especially of mammals is female. The spurting of androgen (male hormones) into the developing embryo "masculinizes" it.[15] These very same male hormones (especially testosterone) which effect the primary sexual differentiation are also responsible for the higher aggressiveness of males. The relevance of this to our wider theoretical context is that the primary differentiation of sex is effected by an aggression related hormone.

The more aggressive males are able to ward off other males more effectively which compete with them over females. The aggressive male is also better equipped to guard his territory, the females in it and eventually the offspring. Aggression related hormones are not only the first differentiating correlate between male and female, but aggression itself is a favourable trait for the male offspring to inherit because it enhances the chances of survival. The logic behind this is that if a male baboon has a higher level of testosterone he would tend to be more dominantly aggressive and display more sexual prowess. Dominance and leadership would, therefore, be linked to prowess in sex not only among primates but also among humans. A traditional Judaic source states that: "He is great whose (sexual) passion is great". The greatness of Solomon and contemporary Bedouin sheikhs is sometimes measured by the number of their wives and especially of their progeny.

The relationship between male aggressiveness and the better survival of its progeny was noted by Darwin.[16] In practice, however, inter-male aggression is much more elaborate and has more of a display function in courtship than a serious fight leading to injury and death. The defeated wolf, for instance, shows its jugular vein to its opponent and then the fight ends.[17] Inter-male fighting is full of bluff and ritualistic threats to impress the females who watch the display of muscle so that they may choose a stronger and hence a better father for the children. This brings to mind the mediaeval knights fighting in front of the ladies who wait for the winner in order to accept his advances with proper coquetry. In like manner girls at the college football match will be glad to date the football stars but only as an atavism because usually they will prefer to marry boys with brains or money, which are the contemporary human equivalent to the coveted genetic traits of brute force of mediaeval knights and male mammals. Evidence that inter-male aggression and violence is sex related has been demonstrated experimentally by the castration of male mammals from various species which were notorious for their fierce inter-male fighting. After their castration these males hardly fought their male peers.[18]

The higher mobility and motile energy of the male is already apparent with the spermatozoa which are provided with an energy generating system which propels them towards the ovum.[19] The initial structure of the sperm and ova, and the relationships between them, reveal a participant urge of the sperm to reach the ovum and be absorbed by it; whereas the ovum is separantly structured to "swallow" the sperm and incorporate it within her. Right after the ejaculation a competitive race starts among the male sperms. The more energetic and the quickest amongst them gets to the ovum, melts its surrounding membrane with the enzymes on its head cover and merges its haploid chromosomes with those of the ovum. Once an ovum is fertilized it is covered with a protective membrane to prevent other sperm from entering it. The trophy of the "best" and quickest sperm who won the race is the only successful participant union in the cycle of growth and development. In all other developmental phases an individual may long for a participant union with objects and with other people, but will never achieve it. Only the rush of the sperm towards an ovum is terminated by an actual participant union. We have to bear in mind that spermatozoa are living organisms carrying with them a genetic heritage yet our programming is wastefully cruel and violently ruthless towards all but one of the spermatozoa (in cases where the ovum is fertilized) in its frantic efforts to achieve reproduction.

Males may often display a separant tendency to possess the female and prevent other males from inseminating her. The inclusionary techniques of the male to assure his exclusive rights to inseminate a female range from the bizarre to the macabre.[20] The Bruce effect makes pregnant female mice abort when they smell the odour of a new male, thus making themselves ready to be inseminated; a male lion in competition for a female against other male competitors will kill the progeny of the female so that the new progeny will be entirely his; the male *nitida* fly is eaten by the female but its genitals are left in the female genital tracts as mating plugs — in this case the *nitida* male achieves exclusiveness of mating at the price of his life; the male dragon fly attaches itself to the female's abdomen to prevent other males from copulating with her — not unlike a man dancing all the time with his date at a party so that no other man is able to court her. Finally, total exclusiveness of re-insemination is achieved by the fish *viridis*, the male of which spends all his life in the female's vagina inseminating her whenever necessary. The males are baited by their quest for the exclusive insemination and hence domination of the female in order to achieve a diploid mixture of genes and a resultant greater genetic variety of offspring. The baiting of the male's quest of unity leads, therefore, to a greater variety of the genotype and a greater diversity of the phenotype of offspring.

Sex is also linked to aggression in mating. Many animals are quite violent in their sexual intercourse. Briffault in his classic essay on the origins of love states that:

> The male animal captures, mauls and bites the female, who in turn uses her teeth and claws freely, and the "lovers" issue from the sexual combat bleeding and mangled. Crustaceans usually lose a limb or two in the encounter. All mammals without exception use their teeth on these occasions. Pallas describes the mating of camels: as soon as impregnation has taken place, the female, with a vicious snarl, turns around and attacks the male with her teeth, and the latter is driven away in terror. Renegger remarks that the sexual union of a pair of jaguars must be a formidable conflict, for he found the forest devastated and strewn with broken branches over an area of a hundred feet where the fierce "love-making" had taken place.[21]

Sex is not only violent but is also related to restlessness and increased nervous tension which is linked to courting, mating and copulation.[22] Mating is a tense, anxious and many times disruptive and painful activity.

The male praying mantis is mortally afraid of the female when he approaches to copulate with her. His anxiety is apparent from his movements and general behaviour. His dread is fully justified because many times the female starts munching his head and upper thorax immediately after the copulation has started. Roeder explains that this cannibalism of the male's head is functional for reproduction. The decapitation removes the male's subesophageal ganglion which inhibited the males copulatory movements. The headless male performs his mating more effectively with a higher probability of sperm transfer.[23] This highlights a theme which we shall elaborate further, namely the relative disregard of the welfare of the organism and its focusing on the process of reproduction.

It seems as if our programming has a desperate need to bring about the reproduction of flora and fauna for reasons known only to itself, with the process of reproduction being the aim of the exercise while the reproducing life forms seem to be tools or secondary instruments to the process of reproduction itself. Moreover, we have seen that sex is a very consuming activity both bodily and mentally. It involves some violent conflicts with other males and some cramped, painful and sometimes dangerous positions during mating itself. No life form is likely to engage in reproduction which seems to be the target of our programming unless we have been "baited", as indeed we are, by short-lived experiences of participant bliss in orgasm and non-realizable visions of the communion of love. Our programming seems to be indifferent to the fact that the Tantalic *fata Morgana* of love cannot be fulfilled so long as it helps to blunt the violence and stress incidental to courting and mating, and brings the life forms to reproduce successfully. We are being anaesthesized by sex and love to carry on reproducing in circumstances which are at best repetitive and at worst violent and painful. The name of the game is reproduction. Yet our programmer did not divulge why it is all so important to him or to us. Moreover, it seems to offend our sense of fair play that the baits of sex and love, although effective, have not been construed with more sophistication so that they would seem, at least, more credible and viable.

Reproduction seems to be the *raison d'être* of life. Animals stop their fighting and courting after mating, flowers wane after fertilization and pregnant women lose their eagerness to flirt. In most cultures especially in separant ones, youth is worshipped as a corollary of fertility whereas sterile old age is dreaded and considered non-aesthetic.

Only in some of the more separant cultures in the Far and Middle East, which anchor on transcendence and other worldliness, is old age revered as wise and sacred. In similar vein, the infatuation of love seems to wane with marriage and childbirth as if the bait of love takes one up to reproduction but becomes superfluous after it. Also, with sexual arousal and during intercourse the body of the mate and its odours feel and smell attractive, but right after orgasm some parts of the mate's body might seem repulsive and disgusting.

After reproduction the bait of sex and love has fulfilled its purpose. The rose petals fall off the swelling of the fertilized hips; pregnant women lose their expectant freshness; and the queen ants after their mating flight are shorn of their wings and the drones are chased away. Love has fulfilled its purpose. The time for play is over and the nest should be prepared for the young. The centrality of reproduction to life may be apparent in the frantic efforts of injured or sick plants which muster their last vestiges of energy to flower prematurely and produce seed. Lastly, the worst blow to a human being is the death of his offspring because it deprives him of his programmed *raison d'être* of reproduction.

Sex and Hormones

In the beginning was the female. The original hypothalamic disposition is towards the female sex. Only the spurting of androgenes through the tissues around the third or fourth months of pregnancy masculinize the gonads by developing the Wolffian duct and regressing the female Mullerian duct.[24] The secretion of androgenes also fixates the brain gender-wise and hence the masculine predisposition of behaviour. It is important to note that testosterone, the hormone which is primarily responsible for the change into masculinity from the basic feminine nature of the embryo and hence for sexual differentiation, is also related to aggression. This relates sex, even if in a roundabout manner, to a violence-linked hormone.

The female sexual typing, as well as her sexual and a great deal of her general behaviour, is influenced by her menstrual cycles effected by the secretion of the female hormones. This cyclicity of the female is so pronounced and pervasive that her whole biology and behaviour is influenced by it from her moods to the operation of the neurotransmitters in her brain. The female's hormonal cycles are related to ovulation, fertilization and reproduction, so that her whole being is related both directly and indirectly to her fertility linked cycles. Her pregnancies and births make her, and not the male, the prime agent of reproduction and growth. Mrs Navon, the Israeli First Lady, once said in an interview that during the long time she could not become pregnant she was profoundly jealous of pregnant alley cats she used to watch in the streets. This more than anything else expresses the essence of femininity, namely the core role of reproducing and rearing off-spring. Woman is programmed to form, create and rear new essences and this dominates her being. All her other roles seem secondary to her even if some feminist movements may argue to the contrary.

Even the sexual baiting of woman is cyclic. They seem to be more sexually aroused and receptive at ovulation, in the middle of their menstrual cycle, so that fertilization would be more likely. This might be one of the reasons for the many taboos against intercourse in the infertile days of menstruation as well as for the traditional Judaic norm to have intercourse in the mid-cycle fertile days.[25] The sexuality of the female is therefore related to ever undulating cycles between the expectancy of ovulation and fertilization and the waste of menstruation. Finally, sexual puberty during and after adolescence is effected in males by spurts of testosterone and in females by corresponding spurts of estrogenes. Sexual maturity is thus linked with the conflicts, physiological changes and behavioural upheavals of adolescence. The endocrinological message here is clear : the basic sexual differentiation is effected by an aggression linked hormone. Feminine sexuality is marked by cyclic agitations, and sexual maturity of both sexes is linked to the violent upheavals of adolescence.

To sum up the present chapter we note that the female is the primary sex both developmentally and in its more prominent role in reproduction. The female is biologically the more separant sex in so far as she absorbs the fertilizing sperm. This is obvious in heterogamy where fertilization is effected by the fusion of gametes differing in size, but even in isogamy where fertilization is effected by the fusion of like-sized (yet physiologically different) gametes. The female is instrumental for the growth and separation aspects of reproduction (i.e., pregnancy, laying eggs, initial care and rearing of offspring), whereas the male is usually more participant because he seeks union with the female by the absorption of his gametes by the female ova and their incorporation within them. Biologically there is a complementarity of roles between the separation of the female and the participation of the male. Without this complementarity no successful reproduction could have taken place. In later chapters we shall deal with the social roles of man and woman and with the cases of conflict between their biological and social roles.

The creation of maleness and hence sexual dimorphism is fixated by the secretion of testosterone which is also linked to male-aggressiveness.

However, this outwardly exhibited tendency towards violence is less separantly domineering than it seems at first sight. We have seen that the inter-male aggression is more playful than serious. It has more of a display function so that the winner is chosen as a mate by the watching females. The female seems to have the manipulative trump card because the more powerful and dominant males would presumably possess the more durable genes. The female baboon, for instance, with the maximal perineal swelling which signifies ovulation and hence prime fertility, will tend to give in to the most aggressively dominant male in the troop so that it may absorb more powerful and viable genes.[26]

Biologically males are much more expendable because one male may impregnate a vast number of females. This might be linked to the fact that males are more aggressive and hence are more engaged in defending territories, hunting and fighting wars. Their greater mortality is not such a great loss to the biologically dominant females because only a few males are needed to impregnate them so that they may carry on their all important task of reproducing and rearing their offspring.

2
The Models

Rabbi Nachman Bar-Shmuel said:
"And all that is very good is the
Evil Passion. But how can the Evil
Passion be very good? Because without it
Man will not build a house or marry a wife."

Genesis Raba 16A

For Freud sex is one of three basic instincts, yet for the development of the personality the Freudian conception of the Libido is the juice of psychic energy, much more central to psycho-sexual development than Eros or Thanathos. Freud regarded sex as axiomatic, as something which cannot and need not be explained or interpreted other than by biological premises: "We are faced here" says Freud, "by the great enigma of the biological fact of the duality of the sexes. It is an ultimate fact of our knowledge, it defies every attempt to trace it back to something else. Psychoanalysis has contributed nothing to clearing up this problem which clearly falls wholly within the province of biology."[1] We, however, envisage the core dynamics of separation and participation utilizing sex as a means to achieve their ends so that it can be "interpreted" within the framework of the interplay of these core dynamics. We shall, therefore, reexamine our three developmental phases of the individual within the framework of the core dynamics as related to sex.

In the introduction we described the first ontological phase of separation which is the "thrownness" of birth. This transitional catastrophe as registered by the neonate is related by some myths and religions to the "bad mother" who is instrumental in expelling her children from the cushioned bliss of the womb to the struggles and strife of life. Existentialist philosophy and psychology also expounds its basic premises in terms of Man being "thrown into this world unto death". The participant counterpart to the separant "bad mother" is the Judaic Shechina and the Gnostic Sophia, both of which are female and signify the perfection, wholeness and the pre-being partaking in unity.

The second existential phase of development, which culminates in the coagulation of a separate self, differs distinctly between male and female. This phase which is effected in early orality is not only related to the child's basic developmental fixations but, according to our hypothesis, also to the proscriptions against incest which are implanted by the mother or her surrogate. This, no doubt, involves formidable sexual conflicts and dialectics between the mother and her male and female children. We shall examine these conflicts in the following chapters. The participant equivalent of this developmental state is the sexless "pure mother", like the Virgin Mary and her equivalents in other cultures and creeds, who gives birth to a holy "pure" son through immaculate conception without the pollution of sex. The third social phase of separation has the father as a stern doctrinaire presiding over the rites of passage of puberty. At this stage the mother is the participant image of the forgiveness of childhood and the grace of the family fold. Elements of sex are inherent in the identifications and complementarities between daughter/son and mother/father.

Woman: The Instrument of *Geworfenheit* and the Fall

If birth is registered by the organism as a separant catastrophe then the birth-giving mother may be archetypically conceived as evil. Indeed some myths, religions and cultures do express this. In *Salvation Through the Gutters*[2] and the *Myth of Tantalus*[3] we related the ontological separation of birth to the catastrophic transition from the womb to the trials outside it. In the present volume we shall concentrate on the sex related pregnancy and birth effected by the mother. The birth-giving mother is depicted as evil by myths and religions as a projection of the neonate's experience of his disastrous expulsion into the world. The participant counterpart may be related to the quest of the pre-birth wholeness of non-being and to the seeking of the all embracing goddess-mother who takes in and reabsorbs in her cosmic womb the stranded souls who have been rejected from the womb of the "bad" birth-giving mother. This longing for ontological participation may be expressed by the romantic agony of *mourir d'amour*, and the interchange of love and death.

In *Salvation Through the Gutters* we described the existential phase of the coagulation of the separate self from the pantheistic mass of early orality in terms of the mythical fall from the Edenic grace.[4] We related the process of the individuation of the newly formed self impelled from its togetherness in the Genesis account of the Fall as interpreted by the church fathers, the Gnostics and some rabbinical sources.[5] In the present work we shall focus on the seduction and sexual elements of the Fall myth as depicted by the interaction between the archetypes of Man, Woman, fruit-breast and snake-phallus. We shall also try to show how the Fall myth may be related to the dialectics between mother and child at early orality, which are in turn linked to the imprinting on the child of anti-incestuous norms, and their cultural and moral correlates. If the general phase of existential separation tears away the individual from the One, the sexual aspects of this phase of separation relate to the need for a sexual partner and hence the dependence on him/her. The individual separatum becomes subjugated to his partner through sex for biological reproduction, emotional involvement and social interaction. We claim that the most basic patterns of sexual identification are crystallized as a corollary of mother-infant deprivational interaction at this stage of existential separation. Of special importance in this context is the finding that mothers tend to tolerate more proximal relations with their infant daughters than with their sons.[6] This could mean that males have a higher chance of being fixated at early orality than females. As a result males would tend to have more initial Tantalic personality characteristics whereas females would have more of a Sisyphean personality base line.[7] Males would tend to anchor more on abstractions and ideas whereas females would be more concerned with the concrete management of their surroundings and the routines of daily life. This brings to mind the anecdote that in the average occidental nuclear family the husband is responsible for the important things such as the pros and cons of the SALT treaties, the world energy crisis and the future of mankind; whereas the wife is entrusted with such trivialities as where to buy the new family home, how to educate the children and how to spend the monthly salary.

The object relationship of the neonate with his mother and his early and later oral fixations predispose him/her to some core sexual characteristics and attitudes. In order to better expound this premise we have first to present the dynamics of the crystallization of the separate self. At the very early oral stage described by Freud as primary narcissism, by Fairbairn as "mouth ego with a breast" and by us as omnipresent pantheism, the mouth feeds (empties) the breast and is temporarily content. However, disturbances in feeding and other related irritations generate the agony of want and pains of anxiety. Fairbairn says that the infant infers that this feeding destroyed the nourishing and comforting breast.[8] This is not tenable to us. At the very early oral stage the "mouth entity" is not capable of problem solving. Moreover, the me/object dichotomy does not yet exist at this pantheistic stage. Any pain, anxiety and want that occur are in me and *only in me*, because I am omnipresent and except for the mouth-anchored me there

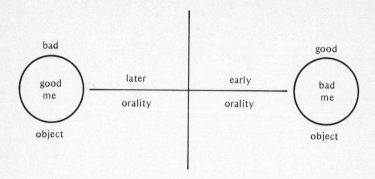

Figure 2 Crystallization of the Separate Self

is nothing. A fixation at the early oral phase would result in the registration of a painful wanting (bad) me where the nourishing (good) something is somewhere in the vague unchartered outside of me which, at this stage of awareness, is outside of everything. What is present is a painful aching me and the nourishing and soothing goodness that was previously me is absent, hovering out of my reach. An early oral fixation is therefore a "bad me" surrounded by the good (nourishing) object.

At the other extreme of the child axis of our model in figure 2 we have the good self surrounded by the bad object (mother). The later oral stage of development is characterized by a partial differentiation of the infant from the mother and the development of ambivalence towards her, which is manifested, among other things, by the biting of the breasts by the child in its moments of aggression.[9] Here again we may add our own observation on the nature of later oral fixations. The emerging separation of the self due to the deprivational interaction with the mother creates an easily accessible source and a sequential explanation of the frustrations, deprivations and anxieties of the infant. The occasionally non-caring, non-feeding mother, who is already separate from the suffering (good) me, is all-apparent and very often in front of the child's mouth. This location of responsibility is accentuated by the vengeful bite. An early oral fixation would predispose an infant to seek the participant image of a pure and immaculate *amour-sacre* sexual object; whereas the later oral fixated Sisyphean type would tend to regard sex in a conflictual frame of reference — its object to be manipulated, "swallowed" and overpowered. It must be stressed that at this stage the core sexual patterns of children are fixated irrespective of their sex. The differentiation between the sexual attitudes is effected later in a manner which we shall describe in the following chapters.

Man: The Authoritarian Doctrinaire

At the first stage of ontological separation, the father does not play any role at all. At the second existential stage he is barely present in the background. In the third socionormative phase of separation, however, the father plays a central role. He presides over the rites of passage from childhood to puberty and is instrumental in transferring, actually or symbolically, some repressive norms of society to his preadolescent children. At this stage the differences of the normative dynamics of separation between boys and girls are extensive. We have presented elsewhere the Isaac Syndrome which is the symbolic sacrifice inherent in the encapsulation of youth in the normative system of society by paternal authority.[10]

The Iphigenia myth is the corresponding archetypal sacrifice of the daughter to the normative demands of the group. The participant counterpart to the normative separation of the boy by parental authority is the longing for the irresponsibility and forgiveness by the mother within the family fold. In mythical archetypal terms this is expressed in the female image of the angel representing Sarah who forbids Abraham to slaughter his son, and by Demeter rescuing her daughter Kore from the (normative) hell to which she was banished by the connivance of her father Zeus. Schematically, these familial dynamics at the normative stage of human development are presented in figure 3.

In this third phase of normative separation the father stands for stern judgement and authoritarian indoctrination for both son and

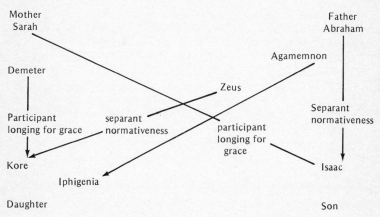

Figure 3 Familial Dynamics of Normative Separation

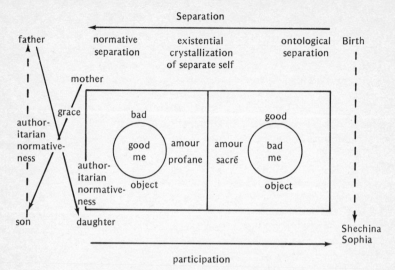

Figure 4 Master Model of Participation/Separation

daughter; while the mother represents for both genders of her children the grace and forgiveness of the family fold. For adults, the longing for mother is to yearn for the maternally cushioned and sheltered childhood. In ancient Greek the word nostalgia is νοστεο ∝λγΙς, which literally translated means the pains of longing to return home. The master model which will guide our deliberations is presented in figure 4.

The continuum which serves as the scaffolding for our model ranges from the separant birth-giving mother; through the bad/good alternating mother at the transition from early to later orality; to the grace-bearing mother of preadolescence as contrasted with the authoritarian separant father represented by the broken line at the extreme left of our model. On the extreme right we have the participant longing for the feminine all embracing pre-being which is represented by a broken line in contrast to the extremity of separation of the birth-giving mother which represents the ontological "thrownness" from non-being to being. In the centre we have the early oral fixated child who is situated in the participant "good object" part of the continuum, predisposed to ever seek a "pure love". On the left hand side the later oral fixated type will be predisposed in a separant manner to view sex as a power play, as a dialectic of flesh and as a conflict of desires. Finally, our scheme describing the dynamics of normative separation as related to the core attitudes of parents towards their children is integrated in the far left of our master model.

Myths

In the present work we shall be utilizing myths not as illustrations for our theoretical premises but as their empirical anchors. Students of myths have always regarded them as reliable records of events before written history. Bachofen says: "The mythical tradition may be taken as a faithful reflection of the life in those times in which historical antiquity is rooted. It is a manifestation of primordial thinking, an immediate historical revelation and consequently a highly reliable source."[11] Eliade further claims that because myths faithfully reflect the occurrence of events on a high level of abstraction they also reveal the principles or designs underlying the events and their sequences. Eliade says: "The myth discloses the eventful creation of the world and of man, and at the same time, the principles which govern the cosmic process and human existence . . . the myths succeed each other and articulate themselves into a sacred history, which is continuously recovered in the life of the community as well as in the existence of each individual. . . What happened in the beginning describes at once both the original perfection and the destiny of each individual."[12]

This brings us to Jung who regards myths not only as the archetypal contents of the "collective human unconsciousness" but also as a means for individual psychic expression.[13] Our stance is even more extreme. In *Salvation Through the Gutters* we have stated that:

> Our methodological anchor is the conception of myths as projections of personal history. The individual is aware of his personality as the sole existential entity in his cognition. Myths cannot therefore, be divorced from the human personality. This awareness of existence is the only epistemological reality. Whatever happened to us in the amnestic years and even later is projected towards cosmogony, magic and other human beings. The events that happened in the highly receptive amnestic years have been recorded by the human brain. Events that happened after the amnestic years may be recalled cognitively, but whatever happened within these first years of life would be played back, *inter alia*, by myths of cosmogony. Myths as personal history may, therefore, be regarded as the account of some crucial developmental stages in the formative years.[14]

Moreover, as we have mentioned earlier in this work, human development in the early formative years passes in an accelerated manner through the whole evolutionary phases of the species. Myths are a projection of the development of the species as inherent in the development of the human individual. It is interesting to note that this conception of myth as a projection of personal history may be inferred from the *Apocalypse of Baruch* which stated that "Every man is the

Adam of his own soul", meaning that every human being experiences in his development the original sin so that the myth of the fall is indeed a projection of individual yet universal human developmental experience.[16]

Myths become archetypal projections of human experience only when they are widespread. The more common a human developmental experience is the higher its chances of becoming a mythical projection. The inverse is also valid: the more widespread a myth, the higher are its chances of being a projection of a universal phase of human development. The universality of the Fall myth, for instance, points to the fact that its corresponding developmental phase of the expulsion of the separate self from the pantheistic togetherness of early orality is indeed experienced by every human being.

Furthermore, myths have many layers. The Lurianic Kabbala, for instance, utilizes the myth of the breaking of the vessels to depict cosmogony, yet some vestiges of the same myth may be interpreted as a projection of the neonate's experience of the "thrownness" of birth. In similar vein the Fall myth may be taken as a projection of the crystallization of the self at early orality but some of its components may be linked to the proscriptions of incest and hence to the vicissitudes of sexual desire.

Myths are so many and diverse that any exhaustive treatment of them even in relation to one single topic is well nigh impossible. As we intend to deal with a wide range of subjects relating to sexuality and development we shall avail ourselves of one single myth to serve as an empirical anchor to our theoretical premises relating to each of our focal concerns. We denote this method as "mytho-empiricism". With all their divergencies in views and theoretical conflicts, Bachofen, Jung, Briffault, Claude Levi-Strauss and Eliade are all mytho-empiricists because they rely considerably and many times mainly on myths for the empirical validation of their theories.

3
The Disastrous Ejection

What youthful mother, a shape upon her lap
Honey of generation had betrayed,
And that must sleep, shriek, struggle to escape
As recollection or the drug decide,
Would think her son, did she but see that shape
With sixty or more winters on its head,
A compensation for the pang of his birth,
Or the uncertainty of his setting forth?

W. B. Yeats: *Among School Children*

Our mythical anchor to the "thrownness" of birth is the Lurianic Kabbala doctrine of breaking of the vessels. This cosmic catastrophe brought about the reification of existence, the straying of divine particles into the mires of spatiotemporality and the introduction of evil into the world.[1] The analogy here is that the sparks of divinity are strewn in the shells of the broken vessels which are denoted by Lurianic Kabbala as *Kelippot* meaning evil. This evil is the way the soul (which is a particle of Divinity) is embedded in the stultifying and delimiting body through the "thrownness" of birth. The fiercely participant and mystical Kabbala regards birth and spatiotemporality as a catastrophic flaw in Creation. The duty of Man is to effect a *Tikkun,* a mending of the cosmic catastrophe by returning the dispersed sparks of Divinity to their origin which in our context could be taken as the participant quest for the reversal of each separatum to its perfect origin. Of special importance is the fact that the mythological Kabbalist totality in which one longs to partake is the feminine Shechina. This free-floating participant longing for the annihilation of the separate self to the totality of non-being could express itself by a self-destructive romantic agony about which we shall deal later.

Boundlessness and Vile Creation

Man's inability to grasp infinity may be taken as our metaphysical programming against the knowledge of God of whom infinity is an essence. This could be the meaning of the myth in Genesis proscribing the eating from the tree of knowledge. In the Lurianic Kabbala the continuum from the participant infinity of non-being to the separant spatiotemporality of creation has three dynamic phases.[2] First, the boundless light of immanent infinity (*Olam Ha'atzilut*) embeds itself into the first phase of condensation (*Akudim*).[3] The second phase of the creation of the cosmic vessels (*Nekudim*), which is closely linked to the creation of the human limbs, culminates in the catastrophe of the breaking of the vessels which we interpret as the mythical projection of birth. This catastrophe is described by the *Zohar* as "The Death of the Kings" because they died to Divinity and were thrown by the breaking of the vessels into the profane, Godless world.[4] The analogy with birth here is evident by the expulsion, through this breaking of the vessels, of the divine sparks embedded in dirt and profanity which brings the fallen souls "thrown" into this world amidst the blood and pollution oozing out of the woman's womb at birth. This is typical of the Gnostic and Lurianic Kabbalist conception of the profanity of spatiotemporality in contrast to the purity and boundless radiance of the pre-created non-being of infinity. Consequently, the creation of spatiotemporality, which was incidental to the breaking of the vessels, calls for the third "mending" phase (*Olam "Ha'tikkun" Berudim*) in which Man strives to return the particles of Divinity scattered by the cosmic catastrophe to their divine origin, and effect thereby a salvation of the world, Man and God. When all creation and Man return to their divine origin not only the objects, flora, fauna and Man are saved, but also God is "mended" because He regains His original wholeness.

Although the Kabbala, following some Gnostic premises, constructs a graded continuum between the boundless infinity and the delimiting fragmentation of spatiotemporality, it actually expounds a dualism: participant pure nothingness of the divine world of *Atzilut* (*Olam Ha'atzilat*) and the separant, strife-laden world of creation. Moreover, the more concrete and visible are the vessels of creation, the more they are the embodiment of vileness and the less imbued they are with divine grace.[5] Both the Lurianic Kabbala and the *Zohar* equate matter and corporeality with evil and thus share the general *Weltanschauung* of Gnosis, Neoplatonism and Existentialism that temporal existence is a "thrown" exile from the bliss of non-being.[6] It is interesting to note that the Kabbala calls the "lower worlds" of concrete existence the "worlds of separation".[7] This seems to be a semantic vindication for the name of the separant core vector of our theory. This striking similarity of terms was brought to the attention of the author by a Jerusalem Kabbalist who came across the author's theory describing the dialectics between the separant and participant core vectors of the human personality and their parallels in Kabbalist cosmogony.[8]

The God of Lurianic Kabbala is a less than perfect God: the catastrophe of the breaking of the vessels seems to have been out of his control and beyond his ability to prevent.[9] Moreover, He needs the help of Man to "mend" this catastrophe so that Man and God become partners in the business of each other's salvation. This theologically absurd conception of Divinity becomes viable if we regard the breaking of the vessels as a projection of the separant vicissitude of human birth and the subsequent quest of the Man–God to annul his "thrownness" and revert to the plenitude of non-being. Another solution to this paradox of an imperfect God displaying pettiness, weaknesses and inconsistencies as evident from His creation, is the Gnostic Marcion's attribution of spatiotemporality to a miserable erratic God of Creation (the Demiurge) who is contrasted with the pure "unknown", "unperceivable" and perfect "alien" God.[10]

In the more recent Chenoboskion discoveries of Gnostic texts the theme of the erring Sophia and her son, the Demiurge, is fully developed. The guilty Sophia suffers because of her misdeed, and as a result boundless pain, darkness and misery were created.[11] In our context this could mean that the errant birth-giving Sophia-mother is responsible for the trials of being "thrown" into this world whereas the good Sophia-mother, like the Kabbalist Shechina, symbolizes the participant perfection of non-being with whom exiled Man longs to reunite. A dramatic illustration of the dialectics between the good and bad mother, and the good and bad son is presented by the Gnostic text of the *Hypostasis of the Archons*: the errant Sophia tries to create a heavenly creation but she fails. Her efforts result in the creation of base spatiotemporal matter in which a monstrous male/female man-god named Ialdabaoth who boasts that "I am God and there is no other God but I". This could be interpreted as the mythical hubris of the separant forces of creation revelling in their illusive omnipotence within the material world. Sophia then reprimands Ialdabaoth and proves to him, by introducing divine light into matter, that wholeness of noncorporeality existed before him. Ialdabaoth is not convinced and still claims that he is the god of the universe. Zoe, the daughter of Sophia, untainted by her mother's error, drives Ialdabaoth to the hell of Tartarus; and Sabaoth, the repenting son of Ialdabaoth, is installed in the seventh heaven just below the veil which separates the lower world from divine light.[12] This again could be interpreted as the mythical dynamics depicting the separant birth of the base Ialdabaoth as the result of the error of the cosmic Sophia which has much in common with the Kabbalist doctrine of the catastrophe of the breaking of the vessels which brought about the vile creation. The participant counterpart is portrayed by the non-erring Zoe, the blameless daughter of light who reveals to Sabaoth the lights of wholeness and non-material perfection to which he can belong while he is lodged just below the veil which separates him from the perfect non-corporeal light-mother. The dichotomy of this mythological account, which is relevant for our premise, is that there are two opposing dyads. The dyad of the separant birth-giving mother, the errant Sophia, and the vile creature Ialdabaoth; and the dyad of the participant longing for perfection of the daughter of light, Zoe, and the repentant son who has "seen the light", Sabaoth.

The particles of Divinity (*Reshimu*) which have been scattered by the catastrophic breaking of the vessels are embedded in each separatum of spatiotemporality. The vile shells (*Kellippot*) of the body encase and circumscribe these divine sparks which are, so to speak, splinters from the boundless infinity of pre-being. Ibn-Tabul describes this containment of the sacred particles of light by the temporal bodies as follows: "And the *Reshimu* of light remained there with the powers of stern judgement (the symbol of temporal evil in Lurianic Kabbala) ... But the powers of measurement (regulation) went down and selected each separate particle of light and stern judgement (vileness), and formed a container like a body for the soul and embedded each particle in a container."[13] In mythical terms the particles of light represent souls which are splinters of Divinity embedded in profane temporal bodies. But in our context this represents the projections of the longing of the participant core vector of Man to return to the boundlessness of non-being, and liberation thereby from the confines of the temporal body.

There are some arguments among the students of Lurianic Kabbala whether the transition from good to evil is by a Neoplatonist continuum or more like a Gnostic dualism.[14] There is no doubt, however, that the Kabbala sees this world as dominated by the forces of evil and that birth is to be viewed as the expulsion of some particles of divine light into the profane world of existence. This is conceived as the death of the seven mythical kings whose severance from the wholeness of Divinity (*Olam Ha'atzilut*) was tantamount to death. "The death of these seven kings", explains the Kabbala, "was because the branches by themselves were severed without the roots. These branches were unable, therefore, to receive (divine) light and consequently died."[15] In like manner the Gnostics considered the creation of Man as a devilish design and the human body as a satanic substance.[16] The soul of fallen Man does not belong in this world. It is "alien" because it belongs to the extraterrestrial Divinity.[17] It should be noted that the participant longing to reunite with the Perfect Divinity is much more pronounced in the Kabbalist and Gnostic myths than the separant "thrownness" into this world. The ontological expulsion into this world is actually experienced and mythologically projected as a fact, but the participant craving to escape the deprivational interaction with objects and other people is more strongly projected onto participant myths of union with boundless grace.

The gist of our premise about the Lurianic Kabbalist and Gnostic conceptions of Man's expulsion into this profane and vile world is that both woman and sex, which are instrumental in effecting the catastrophe of birth, are also conceived as vile and depraved. Indeed, we shall see later that some of the Gnostic sects advocate asceticism, celibacy and the cessation of reproduction as a way of combating the Demiurge and His evil creation. As for the similarity between the Gnostic (especially the Mandaean) conception of the soul being "thrown" into a vile body, and the Heideggerian concept of *Dasein,* that is being-in-the-world as *Geworfenheit zum Todt* ("thrownness" unto death), we have the rather intriguing exposition by Jonas of existentialism as modern Gnosticism.[18]

Birth and the Lures of Participation

The basic premise which guides our present deliberations is that man cannot but see himself as the source of his ontological awareness and as the sole object of his immediate existential experiences. This is even more so in the pre-differentiated phases of early orality and *in utero* in which the foetus and neonate feel a pantheistic togetherness with their surroundings and an omnipresent uniqueness. We have pointed out elsewhere that the foetus and neonate are able to register their basic experiences *in utero*, at birth and immediately after it.[19] We are therefore justified in inferring that some layers of the cosmogonic myths are projections of the human ontological experiences at birth and *in utero*.

Prior to the birth-like breaking of the vessels the Kabbala envisages a *Tzimtzum* which is a condensation or a congestion of the divine lights into the cosmic vessels which could not have otherwise contained the boundlessness of the lights. (Literally, it is the contraction of boundless infinity into a delineated space.)[20] This *Tzimtzum* is the beginning of cosmogony and we shall try to show that it may be interpreted as a projection of the beginning of life (i.e., pregnancy). The *Tzimtzum* is conceived by the Kabbala as the beginning of the flaw in the cosmic infinity which culminated in the coagulation of material evil. This *Tzimtzum,* which is both a contraction and a congestion, first brought about a delimitation of infinity which is conceived as "stern judgement" and hence as evil in the Kabbalist jargon. Second, the *Tzimtzum* was linked to the making dense and thickening of matter which is related in turn to the substance of evil which fills the world.[21] The contraction of the *Tzimtzum* caused the boundless divine light to dim and diminish, and the cosmic vessels to materialize. This transition from boundless infinity to the formation of concrete vessels was the beginning of the exile from Divinity because in the boundless infinity (*Olam Ha'atzilut*) no profane matter or concrete vessels can exist or even be mentioned.[22]

The process of pregnancy is described in detail by the Lurianic Kabbala. It envisages the foetus as a core of divinity surrounded by the vile refuse and pollution which sprouts forth from the womb at birth.[23] This description of pregnancy is almost identical to the description of the *Tzimtzum*, that is the formation of the material vessels and the mixing therein of the sacred particles (*Reshimu*) with the elements of profanity.[24] Rabbi Haim Vital, who is the Plato of Rabbi Isaac Lurie's oral teaching, states categorically that there is no temporal being without the congestion of *Tzimtzum*. As this *Tzimtzum* can be equated with "stern judgement" and hence evil, it is tantamount to saying that no temporal being is without evil.[25] This initial congestion which we hold to be a mythical projection of pregnancy (because it is conceived as a flaw in sacred infinity) is syllogistically related by the Kabbala to both being and adverseness. The gist of the premise here is that the *Tzimtzum,* the condensation of a bounded something out of a boundless infinity, led to the congestion and materialization of the vessels. These vessels are expressly portrayed by the Kabbala as containers for the particles of light which have been separated from divinity. The metaphor used by the Kabbala is that the vessels to the divine particles are like bodies to souls.[26]

In another instance the Kabbala compares the emanation of divine lights into the vessels to the "secret of the pregnancy of children in the entrails of their mother".[27] This indeed justifies our mytho-empirical interpretation of the anthropocentric Kabbalist description of the congelation of being out of nothingness, as the projection of the process of pregnancy. To substantiate our claim there is nothing better than to cite from *Etz Haim*, the main text of Lurianic Kabbala, which describes the process of divine condensation (*Tzimtzum*) as follows: "And when He contracted Himself a line like a thin pipe of light was formed from one side of the space and this pipe led from infinity and filled up the space. By this line the light of infinity leads to the round space which is the emanant, and thus the emanating and the emanant are tied together."[28] This is a plastic description of a womb-like roundness being filled up by an emanation from an umbilical cord.

If the *Tzimtzum* is the beginning of the profane congelation of formless infinity into matter, the breaking of the vessels is the full-fledged catastrophe of the expulsion of the divine particles into the exile of being. We shall try in the following pages to substantiate our claim that the Kabbalist myth of the breaking of the vessels is a mytho-empiric anchor to Man's disastrous transition from the cushioned bliss *in utero*, to the *Geworfenheit zum Todt* of being-in-the-world.

The breaking of the vessels as expounded by the *Zohar* recounts that when the containers of divine light were shattered a flow of waste materials and refuse (*Kelippot*) together with some divine sparks (*Reshimu*) came into being. These *Kelippot,* which in the Kabbala are synonymous with evil, are a direct outcome of the breaking of the vessels. The *Zohar*, in its tradition of plastic imagery, expressly compares the breaking of the vessels to the process of birth.[29] We may proceed then from this basic comparison of birth to a cosmic disaster, and its being instrumental to the creation of evil.

The breaking of the vessels has been traced by Vital to a disaster, to an accidental flaw in the process of creation.[30] This would mean that God is not really omnipotent and omniscient because His supreme task, the creation of the world, has been riddled by accidents and unforeseen catastrophes. This concept has led to endless controversies and difficulties in interpretation among students of the Kabbala.[31] A theological and scholastic system of cosmogony cannot easily come to terms with the image of God, who is at best a partial failure in what should have been his *magnum opus,* the creation of the world. Precisely this theological dissonance in the Kabbalistic cosmogony is of great value in the interpretation of myths as personal histories.

The interpretation of the breaking of the vessels as a random disaster might well represent the traumatic anomalies, injuries and pressures experienced during birth. The chance element in birth traumas is rather high. Some complications in the process of birth are predictable but most of them are not. To impute randomness to birth anomalies is feasible, but to allege random catastrophes in the act of creation is to curb the omnipotency of divinity, which borders on heresy. This is a prime illustration of the reality of myths. It records the events of early personal history, the way it actually happened, even at the risk of inconsistency with religious dogma. The breaking of the vessels, which is an evil event in itself, throws into the world the fragments of divine light mixed with pollution and waste. The analogy with birth seems to be obvious. The divine spark of a pre-existent unity is separated and "thrown" into this world surrounded by waste and dirt.

"The root of evil", says Vital, "is the broken vessels, without them the eternal goodness would have reigned supreme in the world."[32] More specifically, the mythical kings fell down to the lower spheres as a result of the breaking of the vessels. This degradation of the divine kings amounted to their death.[33] Before the breaking of the vessels these kings were part and parcel of Divinity. The cosmic catastrophe forced them to crystallize into material and separate existence, whereas before the breaking of the vessels they were partaking in the infinite wholeness.[34] Moreover, this metamorphosis effected by the cosmic disaster from a non-differentiated unity to a finite vulnerable existence, is not only death but also burial. For the Kabbala the genesis of cosmic evil is through the separation and particularization of fragments from the blissful bosom of infinity. "This death", says the Kabbala, "is not real death, it is a degradation, if you wish it's like a woman giving birth and emitting thereby refuse and pollution."[35] This striking imagery relates the genesis of evil to the breaking of the vessels, which represents birth and signifies a process of separation. The crucial point here is that the coming into being as a separate entity from the boundless non-being seems to be the primal cause of evil.[36] This conception of evil as separation from an engulfing whole is a rather central theme in Buddhism. The Buddhists trace human suffering to the separate existence of the individual. Goodness is equated with the emptiness of non-being. Good reality is the undifferentiated not-self. On the other hand individual cognition and a distinct self are bad and painful.[37] Birth may also be considered as a symbolic death. Death to the divine non-being amounts to birth — birth leads to the "death" of separate existence. Eliade also brings forward instances where separation was considered a spiritual death.[38]

The Kabbalistic conception is shared by many other mythologies and cosmogonies. The Buddhists, for instance, regard the moulding of the individual self out of the eternal non-awareness as a painful misfortune which the individual must train himself to overcome. In Greek cosmogony the separation of heaven from earth by the sickle of Kronos was regarded as essentially evil; and Gnostic cosmogony, the similarity of which to the Kabbala is fairly established, regards the existing world as a prison.[39] The here and now is surrounded by barriers which separate it from Divinity. Archons guard the stranded souls who wish to escape from this world of strife and pain, and prevent them from reunification with the boundless Divinity.

As the existence of the individual is evil, the Kabbala extends this vileness to the initiation of human exile by the separation of the newborn from his mother. For similar reasons the Zoroastrians regarded fertility cults as evil.[40] Jeh, the archetypal whore as well as the first woman in Zervanite mythology, stems from the evil spirit.[41] This is related to the evil nature of sexual desire symbolized by femininity. It could, however, mean more than that: namely that human existence, per se, is evil. One of the Zervanite texts elegizes: "I come into this world, I receive evil, I am content with death."[42] The individual's coming into this world (i.e., birth) is a disgrace, one yearns to reverse this disaster and flee from life. It would follow that woman, the harbinger of this catastrophe, is one of the prime sources of evil. This would also explain the Gnostic aversion to women that breed the young of the species and thus expose more human beings to the squalor of this world.

The intrinsic similarity between the separation of birth and the Heideggerian *Geworfenheit* is quite clear. As the agnostic existentialists have chosen to ignore Divinity, they have sanctified this "thrownness", and made the estranged and alienated state of man the basic dogma of their secular religion.

The Kabbala is rather blunt in its description of human existence in this world. Following the breaking of the vessels, this earth is pure waste and dominated by evil and scoundrels who are for ever victorious. Human life is dominated by Satan. The Kabbalist's conception of the vileness of temporal existence may stem here too from Gnostic sources, which regarded the here and now as a creation of sinister forces.[43] This view of creation as evil is rather widespread; from the ancient Messopotamian cosmogony visualizing the world as sprouting out of the vile Tiamat, to the Buddhist Yoga, that laments, "All is painful, all is transient, all is pain, all is ephemeral".[44]

It is interesting to note that in many cultures woman is symbolized by a vessel because it contains the foetus in pregnancy and gives birth.[45] Erich Neumann says:

> For obvious reasons woman is experienced as the vessel par excellence. Woman as body-vessel is the natural expression of the human experience of woman bearing the child "within" her and of man entering "into" her in the sexual act. Because the identity of the female personality with the encompassing body-vessel in which the child is sheltered belongs to the foundation of feminine existence, woman is not only the vessel that like every body contains something within itself, but, both for herself and the male, is the "life-vessel as such", in which life forms, and which bears all living things and discharges them out of itself and into the world.[46]

This supports our interpretation of the Kabbalist myth of the breaking of the vessels as the traumatic experience of birth.

Woman: The Vessel of Pollution

In Greek the word woman γυνε and the word genesis γενεσις (generation) are of the same root. Consequently, the myths which hold the creation of Man to be evil spread the halo effect of vileness to the female of the species which is the most proximate cause and clearly the primary instrument for the initiation and perpetuation of man's vile existence. The Zervanites who gloomily worshipped an evil Ahriman who dominated an evil temporal creation, regarded Az (sexual desire) and Jeh (the woman-whore) as the main pillars of Ahriman's reign.[47] Although the Zoroastreans did not expressly link femininity and desire with the evil essence of procreation, in Buddhism this is clearly postulated. The Buddha fights Kama (sexual pleasure) because it "is the seducer of men, for through pleasure men are reborn and so chained to the wheel of existence".[48] The same view in a different garb was expressed by the Kabbalists who equated evil with temptation and sex.[49]

The traditional attitude towards Uranus in Greek mythology was that his prevention of the birth of his children was an evil deed. But a deeper examination of Hesiod's *Theogony* reveals that he rejoiced in his deed because there would be no other entities in the cosmos except himself and the earth locked in eternal embrace.[50] This could well be an archetypal rejection of the catastrophic separation of birth and the safeguarding of the primordial participation in unity.

Gnosticism of the Manichean brand regarded Eve as evil not so much because she seduced Adam to carnal lust but because she gave origin thereby to reproduction and the continuity of the race. As a core of exiled divine light is embedded in every individual the continuity of procreation prolongs indefinitely the exile of the divine particles which is precisely the scheme of the devil.[51] Neumann tries very hard to contrast the birth-giving mother which he considers to be "good", with the terrible devouring mother.[52] (This is in line with the Jungian theory of the positive and negative maternal archetypes.) To us this is untenable because Neumann's mythical birth-giving goddesses and mythological females display their wombs as symbolic tombs and graves. How is it that the "goodness" of birth is described with such grim morbidity? It is because the womb is a grave signifying the cessation of the individual's participation in unity and his "thrownness" to the vicissitudes of being-in-the-world. We shall substantiate our claim later that the mythical birth-giving mothers are not really portrayed as positive.

Fertility rites range from the guilt-ridden necessity to be promiscuous in order to induce nature to enhance the processes of procreation of plant, beast and Man (but the sinfulness of which may lead its participants to hell); to the consciously promiscuous orgies which are meant to be promiscuous not because they are normatively legitimized but because they are meant to worship promiscuous gods (in a manner which would presumably please the gods as well as enhance the normatively prescribed mandate to procreate). The really pure mother of wholesome goodness is a contrast to the birth-giving mother. The Kabbalist Shechina weeps over her children (the particles of light who left her to the exile of temporal existence). The Shechina as well as the Gnostic Sophia are the original archetypal females of the divine wholeness of pre-being because they did not give birth to the separata of particles in spatiotemporality. Yet they long to reunite with them in the boundless folds of infinity. In contrast to promiscuous fertility indulging feminine goddesses and mythical figures, is the Virgin Mary and her mythical equivalents who give birth by immaculate conception. We shall elaborate this point further in chapter 4 where we shall discuss the significance of fertility rites.

Lurianic Kabbala sees the breaking of the vessels as the doings of the devil and hence the source of evil.[53] It also describes the refuse and pollution which ooze out of the birth-giving woman and gives this as an illustration for the cosmic catastrophe. This again lends further support for our interpretation of the Kabbalist myth of the breaking of the vessels as the source of both evil and the expulsion of man into the vileness of temporal existence. The birth-giving mother (the broken vessel) is, therefore, bad from the beginning. In Hebrew, the word *Kellipot* means the broken shells of the vessel and is common, colloquial usage denoting bad women. The destructive womb replete with deathly teeth or macabre masks is quite widespread among African and American Indian goddesses, and feminine mythical figures.[54] It should be stressed here that the "devouring" wombs mentioned by Neumann relate to the inclusive separant function of the womb "swallowing" the male penis.[55] In the present context the dead womb symbolism relates to its function as the vessel of death expelling the neonate from participant unity to the trials of temporal existence.

The Greek myth of Pandora is also in the category of the evil birth-giving mother. Pandora, like Eve, was created by the Gods to entice Man. She was given as a present to Epimetheus who married her. Then Pandora opened her cask, which is equivalent to the Kabbalist and Gnostic vessel-womb and out of this cask-womb streamed misery and strife. Pandora the all-giving, programmed by the Gods to bait mankind to carry on reproducing, thus perpetuates the vileness of temporal existence. Greek mythology recounts that Prometheus warned his brother Epimetheus not to accept any gifts from the Gods because he knew what "strings" are invariably attached to such gifts. Epimetheus, however, was dazzled, lured and baited by the beauty of Pandora. He hastened to marry her and was hence trapped into the design of the Gods. This lends support to the notion that separant reproduction was the design of the Gods, a metaphysical programming to which man is a helpless guinea pig.

The parallels between Eve and Pandora are obvious.[56] A third century alchemical text "Upon the letter Omega", states that the Light-Man, which is the metaphoric boundless Man-God similar to the Kabbalist *Adam-Kadoman*, was enslaved by Pandora, "she whom the Hebrews call Eve".[57] Eve to was responsible for the separant propagation of Man and hence according to the Gnostics, instrumental in the sinister design of the powers of darkness to enslave more and more particles of divine light in the profane limits of temporal bodies.

The Stranded Sparks

In the first chapter of *Salvation Through the Gutters* we showed that the foetus at birth is fully capable of registering the enormity of the shock of its expulsion from the womb both bodily and mentally.[58] In a recent publication on the psychology of childbirth Leboyer describes the infernal experiences of the neonate during birth and just after it: "Hell exists, and is white hot. It is not a fable. But we go through it at the beginning of our lives, not the end. Hell is what the child goes through to reach us. Its flames assail the child from every side, they burn its eyes, its skin, they sear its flesh; they devour. This fire is what the baby feels as the air rushes into the lungs. The air, which enters and sweeps through the trachea, and expand the aveoli, is like the acid poured on a wound."[59]

The transition from the womb to the world outside it is violent in all respects. The breathing of oxygen instead of receiving it directly from the blood stream of the mother, the need to seek food and digest it, and the exposure to changing temperatures and hard objects instead of the constant warmth and cushioned resilient walls in the womb are all severe shocks. The expulsion from the womb is also accompanied by a period of being squeezed and pushed into the rather narrow and inflexible birth canal which inflicts on the freshly born baby a painful stupor. The shock of birth is mercifully not remembered by us as a necessary defence against its intense bodily pains and psychic traumata, but it is undoubtedly registered by our sub or pre-conscious and projected by myths. The myth of the breaking of the vessels relates to the birth-giving mother and the ejection from the womb, whereas the myth of the scattering of the divine sparks relates more directly to the neonate himself. The new born feels himself as a precious particle of Divinity omnipresent and hence omnipotent because at this stage of his life he cannot be aware of anything or anybody except himself. Yet he experiences in his omnipresent eccentricity a disastrous catapulting from blissful self-sufficiency into painful troubled and hostile surroundings which are not far from the mythical characteristics of hell.

Lurianic Kabbala postulates that at birth the forces of evil embed a divine spark (*Reshimu*) in the profane body.[60] This exile of the spark from its sacred origin is denoted by the Kabbala as "the descent of creation" and is equivalent to death to its former participation in boundless light.[61] It is important to note that the sparks that were exiled into spatiotemporality were not chipped off from divinity at random but that the worst sparks, those which were tainted or less than perfect, were sent to "do-time" on the cosmic Devils' Island of spatiotemporality. This is a rather difficult theological doctrine because it assumes a differentiation in divinity, some parts of which are "better" and others are "worse". A possible wild hypothesis is that this differentiation is the basis for Divinity's plight and its need of "mending" by man as expounded by the Kabbala. This topic, however, is outside the domain of our present interest although we intend to pursue it in a volume length exposition of the metaphysical implications of human behaviour. Another important premise is the pantheistic nature of the *Reshimu* doctrine. "There is nothing in the world," says Vital, "and in all the worlds and in all parts of creation; the inanimate plants, living and talking that does not have in it sparks of Divinity which are embedded in their profane shells."[62] All creation, not only Man, was thrown into spatiotemporality. All flora, fauna and inanimate objects are in this respect equal to man with exiled cores of Divinity encased in every created separatum and every vestige of spatiotemporality.

Sex as Disaster

If birth is a catastrophe then sex, which is instrumental to it, is also a disaster. Indeed, the breaking of the vessels is related by the Kabbala to some form of intercourse between two divine spheres which represent father and mother.[63] The Gnostic *Secret Book of John* is even more explicit on the topic of sex. Ialdabaoth, the evil First Archon of Darkness, emanated from the pernicious desire (*Prunicon*) of Sophia. This vile First Archon was responsible for marital intercourse. "He planted in Adam a desire for sowing, so that it is of this essence that women produce a copy from their imitation (spirit). And he set the two Archons over the principalities, so that they might rule over the grave (i.e., the body)."[64] The sequence here is : pernicious desire produces Ialdabaoth who implants sexual desire in man and woman, which produces and perpetuates the body graves of human beings. Zervanism also regards sexual desire and woman as evil because they are instrumental in the continuous exile of humanity in the temporal world which is in the domain of the evil Ahriman. In Buddhism, sexual desire (kama) is one of the attributes of Mara the lord of the temporal world. It is the evil seducer of humanity because through it human beings are reborn and thereby chained to the profane Samsara wheel of existence.[65]

Finally, we integrate our present premise into the main thesis of our work by stating that sexuality, being the prime tool of reproductive separation, is projected by man's participant core into myths and religions as evil, subjugating and profane. By some wild conjecture we may envisage the mitosis of cells as a microcosmic breaking of the vessels. However, as stated in the introduction and first chapter of this work, the reproductive separation of mitosis is orderly and mild in comparison with the violence of sexual meiosis which is virtually a disruption of the vessel on the microcosmic level. The separant function of sex is displayed in the interaction between separatum whose dialectics of desire are a condition precedent for further reproduction, the result of which is to bring forth another separata to suffer the pangs of birth and undergo the vicissitudes of Man's deprivational interaction with his surroundings. This lends a novel hue to God's curse on Eve: "I will increase your labour and your groanings and in labour you shall bear children."[66] The curse is inherent in the pains, sorrows and vicissitudes of separation through sex and reproduction.

The Craving for the Good Mother

After the neonate has been expelled by the "bad" mother and exposed to the trials of being-thrown-into-the-world, he is immersed in the omnipresence of early orality. Although the neonate suffers during this period, there is at the same time an amorphous "goodness" around him which feeds him and eases his painful contacts with hard objects and uncomfortable temperatures. As the infant's violently separant experience of birth is countered by an equally potent quest for participation in pre-differentiated blissful wholeness, the amorphous "goodness" of early orality (which is mythically projected as the good-mother) becomes the object for the infant's participant longing.[67] The mythical longing for participation as expounded by the Kabbala is the quest of each particle which was expelled to the mires of temporal existence by the breaking of the vessels to reunite with the holiness of pre-differentiation. Indeed, Salvation is effected by the mending (*Tikkun*) of the broken vessels through the return of the strewn divine particles (i.e., the return of the souls to their perfect holy origin).[68] This quest of exiled souls to return back to their origin is not only their main motivation but also their temporal *raison d'être* as ordained by

Divinity. The *Tikkun,* the Kabbalist mending of the catastrophe of the broken vessels, is a symbiosis between Man and Divinity. By returning back to its origin the exiled soul not only saves itself but also mends some of the blemishes of injured Divinity. This Divinity is the Kabbalist Shechina and the Gnostic Sophia, the mythical good-mother to whom the stranded soul-particle wishes to return and undo the "thrownness" of birth caused by the "bad-expelling mother". The wish to return back to the fold of the Shechina means in our context to return back to non-differentiation and to non-being. Moreover, the longing to partake in the good-mother, if fixated at early orality, will effect a tendency to link love with non-being, a premise on which we shall elaborate later.

Both the Kabbalists and the Gnostics regard temporal existence as an incarceration of parts of divinity in profane bodies. The quest of participation is a longing for a more benign and boundless reality in contrast to the separant profane creation. It should be stressed that the longing of the exiled separatum to be reunited with the "good mother" is not a Rankian quest for *regressus in uterum.* This is because the "good mother" object at early orality is an amorphic, ethereal and diffuse entity hovering somewhere around the pantheistic awareness of the neonate, and not a cushioned, womblike shelter to crawl into. Consequently, the early oral quest to partake in the totality of the good, mother-like holy presence (the Shechina) is more of a longing to merge with the non-corporeal grace of non-being. An early oral fixation would also entail, therefore, a tendency to be involved in spiritual loves with improbable and unattainable objects. This rather self-defeating infatuation may be linked to the longing for grace by partaking in the goodness of the perfect mother irrespective of the sexes of the partners in the love dyad. We have to remind ourselves that both the mythical archetypes of the "bad" and "good" mothers are projections of the developmental memories of the human organism and psyche. This is clearly apparent in the Gnostic myths of exiled Man's striving to be reunited with Sophia. Man is being instructed on how to overcome the various aeons of separation from boundless light. Sophia finally instructs him and laments: "You see, O child through how many bodies (elements), how many ranks of demons, how many concatenations and revolutions of stars, we have to work our way in order to hasten to the one and only God."[69] The participant aim of the strewn particle is to achieve union with unity: "It is by means of Unity that each one shall receive himself back again."[70] And unity in this context means being reabsorbed within the pulsating totality of Sophia.

Some variations on this theme may be found in the story of Rama-krishna the 19th century Indian mystic who lived all his life in the temple of the White Goddess Kali. He married a fellow mystic who helped him to prove the possibility of a purely spiritual and non-carnal union of the sexes. As a consummation of his "sense of uniqueness as the Goddess's child and (spiritual) lover . . . he followed Kali's image into the Ganges until the waters closed over his head".[71] This is the epitome of an early oral fixation on the "pure mother" with whom Ramakrishna aimed to reunite. This absolute "purity" of participant devotion to his good-mother-goddess excluded any possibility of pro- fanating this immaculate longing by having (filthy) carnal sex with a wife.

Another instance of longing to reunite with the pure good-mother, which has actually been mythologically fulfilled, is the case of the Gnostic Jesus who managed to escape from the profane earthly passion just after his birth. A Manichean text recounts that right after the birth of Jesus, while he was still an infant, the Holy Spirit came to visit him in Mary's house and merged with him.[72] This is a mythical projection of the longing of Jesus, the archetypal divine splinter of God, to reunite with his perfect and immaculate "good-mother" (the Holy Spirit) and not with the mother who actually gave birth to him. It should be men- tioned that the whole idea of Gnostic salvation is centred around the return of the divine stranded sparks (i.e., the return of all the born individuals to their origin in perfect unity).[73] The reversal of birth and the return to pre-differentiated non-being seems to be the gist of the Gnostic religion. The Gnostics and the Lurianic Kabbalists are collectively fixated on early orality. Their wish to be reunited with the Shechina and with Sophia is the mythical projection of their participant craving for non-being.

The purification by a plunge both prevalent in Judaism and the practice of baptism in Christianity is highly relevant to our present context. If myths and their ritualistic correlates are projections of Man's developmental phases then the central place of baptism in Christianity signifies the importance of purifying the neonate from the vileness of the polluted "sinful" womb from which he has just been expelled. He is submerged into a pure baptismal vessel-womb filled with holy water. Indeed, Neumann states that "the pre-Christian plunge bath signifies return to the mysterious uterus of the Great Mother and its water of life".[74] This completes our theoretical cycle: the abhorrence of the perfidious womb of the "bad mother" and the longing to be re- united with the good-mother/Shechina/Sophia leads to the ritualistic dialectical compromise of being submerged into the whole (i.e., into the unbroken vessel-womb of the good-mother filled with Holy water). The purifying function of baptism is also important here: one aims to be pure, that is to return to the pre-birth state of wholeness and boundless- ness and not just to return to the womb. The Rankian neonate longs to return to the coziness of the womb but our expelled separatum aims at nothing less than partaking in unity and regaining the infinity of pre-being.

The Romantic Agony

We claim that an early oral fixation on the pure good-mother may predispose a person, irrespective of gender, to seek the impossible ideal and perfect loves which cannot be attainable so that the quest for the impossible becomes a painfully sad, self-destructive and Tantalic via Dolorosa. The Tantalic romantic agony needs a love which is unattainable so that the self-defeating, self-debasing and tortuous quest of it may involve annihilation of the self and a consequent absorption by the perfect beloved one which is a surrogate pure good-mother. The less attainable a love is the more appropriate it is for a Tantalic romantic agony. Moreover, if a seemingly unattainable love becomes or seems to be attainable it is discarded for an impossible love, the accessibility of which is safely remote or non-existent. The painfully sad romantic longing for an unattainable love involving self-destructive behaviour or phantasy as a surrogate participation in the perfection of pre-being is so abundant in literature, drama, cinema and pulp magazines that one is overwhelmed by the embarrassing richness of choices. One may begin with a heavily drunk Edgar Allan Poe moaning for a Lenore who can nevermore be reached or maybe never existed. Or take Gautier's story of a young, beautiful and chaste lion-hunter who falls in love with Cleopatra precisely because she was unattainable.[75]

We should stress that at this stage we are dealing with the romantic agony of longing for non-being; with the elegiac sadness and despair because of a Tantalic quest of a love which can never be reached. The Sadique or Masochistic equation of painful pleasure and sexual passion is a totally different premise. Our romantic agony is a quest for a love which may lead us to the purity of non-being. This is the search of a Moreau for "The Beauty of Inertia", and a Baudelaire seeking "Les Gracieuse Melancolies et les Noble Desespoirs".[76] The greed here is for a spiritual, not a carnal, communion with our unattainable love because it is a surrogate quest for an even less attainable participant communion with the early oral "pure" mother. Indeed, Flaubert forcefully describes the hallucinatory craving of St Anthony to unite with his impossible love Ammonasia, the beatified martyr: "J'aurais pu être attaché a la colonne pres de la tienne", elegizes St. Anthony, "face a face, sou tes yeux, repondant a tec cris par mes soupirs et nos douleurs se seraient confondues, nos ames se seraient melées".[77] We stress here the longing for spiritual communion with the "pure" love and not the actual death or suicide because of it. We have pointed out elsewhere thar romantic suicide is usually motivated by a *ressentiment* wish to gain the sympathy of the beloved or by a separant wish of magic repossession, or an act of ritualistic vengeance towards the non-complying beloved.[78] Our participant romantic agony longs for non-being as a Tantalic aim in itself for which the infatuation with an impossible love is a means. Martyrdom and soldiers dying for the motherland may, therefore, be surrogate means for sacrificing oneself to the love of the great good-mother. The private martyr in love who has to feel martyred for or by her/his beloved in order to feel happy, will provoke their paramours or mates to persecute them so they can achieve their participant feeling of martyrdom. In like manner some vestiges of the romantic agony are apparent in the parents who "sacrifice" themselves for their children.

In *Salvation Through the Gutters*[79] and the *Myth of Tantalus*[80] we described the Tantalic quest of the mystic to partake in divinity. With regard to love, the lover aims to be debased spiritually as a symbolic or ritualistic annihilation which may enhance a corresponding melting into or merging with the early oral good-mother. At early orality the nascent self is fixated on the good object mother while having an overall sense of a "bad" me. Consequently, the longing for a spiritual union with the "perfect" mother is sublimated into a romantic agony in ego's love relationships and coupled by a martyred self-debasement of the "unworthy" me. Romantic agony is also the longing to leave the nauseating dirt and horrors of this world and be reunited in the eternal embrace of a pure-woman-Shechina-Sophia. There is a trace of this Tantalic longing in the sometimes sincere sometimes halfhearted promises of eternal love. The lovers may feel that they are deluding themselves, yet they cannot help but long for the eternity of community in pre-being through their time-bound love.

4
Replenish the Earth and Subdue It

Reish Lakish said: "Let us be beholden to
our parents because if they did not sin
we could not have come to this world."

Talmud Avoda Zara 5:1

Da Capo: The Next Generation

Both the neo-Darwinists tracing the dynamics of natural selection and
the sociobiologists describing life with a science fiction aura as being
dominated by the DNA in our genes, deal only with growth. They
confine themselves to what we denote as the separant expansive core
vectors of life. To our mind, these are necessary but not sufficient.
As with the individual personality, the evolution of species is subject
to the dialectical interplay between the separant forces of growth and
propagation, and the participant vectors of striving to unite with the
object, other people and with the pre-birth totality of boundlessness.
Indeed, we shall try to establish our claim that no growth and no reproduction is possible without the dialectic interplay between the separant
and participant core vectors.

The basic rule which we have formulated elsewhere is that the more
potent the separant vector, the more expressive would be the participant vector in its efforts to counter it.[1] If we apply this rule to reproduction we have evidence that the main development which led eventually to sexual reproduction is the evolution of a membrane bound
cellular structure (i.e., eukaryotes out of the amorphic mass of pro-
karyotes which had no membrane bound nucleus).[2] We may compare
this formation of the membrane surrounded cellular structure as the
formation of the ego boundary around the nascent self at early orality.
This again is an instant of the wider rule we have mentioned earlier that
the human organism seems to undergo in its development, in an
accelerated manner, all the evolutionary stages of its species up to the
very first life forms. This eukaryote formation of a cellular ego
boundary is, naturally, a process of individuation and a delimiting
separation which confines the previously amorphic mass of cellular
matter into clearly defined boundaries. However, the separant processes

are not forceful enough because the mitotic division of cells produce identical new cells which are exact replicas of the parent cell. These new monads, which are identical in genetic material with their parent monads, did not undergo any intrinsic or discernible process of change or separation for the participant vector to counter with a corresponding vigour. In meiosis and sexual reproduction, however, the processes of separation are not only brutal and violent but also radical. They effect an irreversible and, except for monozygotic twins, a unique change in the genetic structure of the cells. Sexual reproduction is thus linked to a violent separant disruption which is countered by a corresponding strong participant reaction.

Because of the violent and shattering nature of sexual reproduction a very strong incentive should be built in the organism to engage in it. We have stated in the introduction and chapter one of this work that sex and love are these built-in incentives; they are the participant baits to lure the organism to engage in its programming to reproduce. Here we wish to add that the participant lure also operates on the evolutionary level, seducing the organism by memories of earlier developmental phases to engage in courting and sex. Lovers are attracted to the sea, to the meadow and to the woods to engage in their courting, love and sex (although beds are much more comfortable), because the participant memories of their earlier evolutionary phases are linked to woods, meadows and seas. This rather bold hypothesis has yet to be substantiated but without it there is no functional reason for the accelerated passage of the developing organism through the evolutionary phases of previous life forms unless it was meant to implant in it a participant urge to revert back to its earlier developmental phases and forms. These were less complex, less hectic and in the organism's very early forms reproduced in the less disruptive non-sexual form. In love and sex the participant baits are maximized on all possible levels as if nature went to great lengths not to take any chances in the most important goal of the organism, namely to reproduce. These baits are as follows. First, on the biological level the rather short-lived (alas) feeling of fusion with one's mate in orgasm; second, the longing of the lover to achieve a merging of souls with his beloved on the socio-psychological level; and third, the lure of nature, the wilds and the participant oceanic feeling on the evolutionary level.

The cardinal importance of our programming to reproduce is apparent not only in the strong participant baiting to engage in mating which is otherwise uncomfortable and sometimes painful, but also in its rather abrupt loss of interest after fertilization has presumably been consummated. We have already mentioned the rather sad wilting of flowers after fertilization, the loss of glamour of women at pregnancy and for some time after it, and the momentary weariness of sex and the sex mate right after orgasm. The crucial importance of reproduction is also apparent in the rush of the organism to flower and reproduce in times of stress, danger and adverse conditions. We have already pointed out that some species which reproduce parthenogenetically in times of peace and stability change to the genetically more viable sexual reproduction in adverse environmental conditions. Non-sexual reproduction too is also more imminent when the plant feels threatened or in danger. Horticulturists know that a pampered spider-plant will not produce its offshoot stolon (its spiderlets); only when its soil is not rich and fertilizer is withheld (i.e., the spider-plant feels starved and threatened) will it start producing stolon in profusion. There is some evidence which indicates that in times of stress human beings tend to be more promiscuous. An extreme example was recounted to the author by a friend who served in the British army during the Second World War and fought on the Italian front. After his unit had occupied one of the villages with the help of heavy artillery bombardment, he entered the house of one of the peasants and found the owner copulating vigorously with his wife.

The separant programming to reproduce has been adopted and sanctioned by institutionalized religions. Judaism, for instance, has taken literally God's command in *Genesis* to reproduce so that any sexual intercourse which is not intended for reproduction is deemed sinful and promiscuous.[3] A direct corollary of this premise is that intercourse in the non-fertile days of menstruation is forbidden and sinful.[4] The pollution of menstruation may also be interpreted in conjunction with the polluted blood which sprouts forth from the womb at birth. According to our interpretation the breaking of the vessels results in the expulsion at birth of a divine particle encased in the profane body and surrounded by the polluted *Kellipot* and blood. In menstruation, however, there is no divine particle to attenuate the pollution of the menstrual blood.

Fertility

As we have specified earlier, our mytho-empirical method consists in anchoring on a single myth as an illustrative instance with occasional side-glances to other myths for contrast or analogy. We shall illustrate our ideas on fertility by focusing on the Greek myth of Demeter, Mother-Earth, the Goddess of Fertility, and her daughter Kore/Persephone. The gist of the myth is that Demeter bore Kore illegitimately and incestuously to her brother Zeus.[5] When Kore grew up the "all-taking" God of hell (Hades) fell in love with her and with the tacit consent of Zeus, her father, plotted to abduct her. Hades lured Kore with the Narcissus, the flower of hell. When she stretched her hand to pick it Hades sprouted forth from the earth with his chariot and carried off the wailing maiden to Tartarus. Demeter in her grief and anger forbade all plants to flower and fruit. Zeus fearing the extinction of life persuaded Hades to release Kore provided she had not yet eaten from the food of the dead in Tartarus. Kore, however, had tasted a pomegranate which grew in hell and thus could not leave Tartarus. After threats from Demeter and counter threats from Zeus a compromise was reached. Kore should spend three months of the year in the company of Hades as Persephone, queen of hell, and nine months on earth again as the maiden Kore with her mother Demeter, at Eleusis.

The elements of the myth which are relevant to our context are, as follows: the maiden Kore lives chastely with her mother until the separant process of reproduction starts with the seduction by Hades who courts Kore with flowers like so many mortal suitors. However, the Narcissi are the bait flowers of love and of hell — the hell of violent sex which is tantamount to rape. This could have more than one meaning: first, the mythical projection of sex as violence and second, that women were not meant to enjoy sex so that they become, so to speak, martyrs of reproduction. They engage in sex, even though it is painful to them, only because they carry out their duty to reproduce. This conception of sex has an analogy in the Talmudic interpretation of the biblical story of the abduction of Dina, the daughter of Leah, by Shechem the son of Hamor. Said Rabbi Papa to Abagee: "Sexual intercourse in itself is torture (for the woman) because it is written (in the case of Shechem and Dina) that he laid with her and tortured her."[6] It is of interest to our present context that the Talmud regards sex, per se, as painful to women. We prefer, however, to adopt the interpretation of the abduction of Kore as a mythical projection of the violence of sex in the developmental sense. This is feasible because myths have many layers of meanings. One layer may fit one context and a second layer may be appropriate for another context of meanings.

To proceed with the interpretation of the Kore myth: we find the ravished maiden being baited again by the forbidden fruit of Tartarus. We shall substantiate our claim later that both here and in the biblical myth of the original sin, the eating of the forbidden fruit has a connotation of sex. Consequently, Kore's sexual desire transforms her from a pure maiden to Persephone the queen of hell and the spouse of Hades in the same way that Eve's sexual passion caused both her and Adam's fall from grace. We shall deal with this topic in subsequent chapters of this work in conjunction with the child's sex laden relationships with the mother. The complicity of Zeus, Kore's father, in the abduction of his daughter will also be relevant to our exposition of the social phase of separation and the doctrinaire role of the father in socializing his children. Finally, we note that the "pure" participant contrast to the separant reproduction through sexual defilement is the mythical immaculate conception by the Virgin Mary and her mythical equivalents.

Demeter and Kore, the two goddesses of the Eleusinian mysteries, are the feminist dyad of virgin-mother in the original meaning of unwed mother and daughter born out of wedlock. Demeter and Kore seem to be content with their maleless world until the growing Kore is baited by the love and desire for men in the form of the Narcissus flower sprouting from hell. The infernal nature of sexual desire expresses itself in the servitude of the maiden to her spouse, she needs him and depends on him for the fulfilment of her desire and the implementation of her programming to reproduce. There is a complete metamorphosis: the "pure" maiden Kore is transformed into Persephone the queen of hell through her involvement with men, sex and passion. This, no doubt, is a description from the women's point of view depicting the matriarchal rage of Demeter for losing control of her daughter and the chagrin of Kore, the wholesome innocent maiden, being outwardly violated and baited into subjugation to her own passions and desires. The dialectics between the feminine and masculine outlooks on courting and wooing is crucial to our context and we shall devote considerable attention to these dialectics in subsequent chapters.

It is interesting to note that Kerenyi, one of the interpreters of the Demeter-Kore myth, sees the mother-daughter dyad (Demeter-Kore) as signifying life, whereas the girl-husband dyad (Persephone-Hades) symbolizes death.

> Persephone, generally called Kore . . . by the Greeks, differs from Athene in the same way as Artemis. She is a Kore not because she is above all feminine connexions — with her mother or husband — but because she embodies these connexions as two forms of being each carried to extremes and balanced against one another. One of the forms (daughter with mother) is life; the other (young girl with husband) is death. Mother and daughter form a living unity in a border situation — a natural unit which, equally naturally, carries within it the seeds of its own destruction.[7]

Kerenyi bases his interpretation on the Jungian dialectics between opposites, especially Eros and Thanatos. For us, however, the Demeter-Kore, Persephone-Hades myth is a prime illustration of the interplay between the core vectors. The Demeter-Kore relationship stands for unity, identification and hence participation between mother and daughter. In his comment on a Boeotian sculpture depicting Demeter and Kore, Neumann says: "In the unique relief of a feminine cult both enthroned goddesses appear as the twofold aspect of the mother-daughter unity . . . This unity of Demeter and Kore is the central content of the Eleusinian mysteries."[8] It means that the mother-daughter goddess is a single entity based on the relationship between the two.[9] Thus, when this relationship is disrupted the Demeter-Kore unity and hence the goddess is annihilated. The Persephone-Hades dyad signifies, on the other hand, abduction, disruption and a separant subjugation to desire, passion and the reproductive cycles of spatiotemporal existence.

When viewed from the participant mother-maiden unity the baiting of Kore by her own desire (symbolized by her succumbing to the phallus shaped Narcissi) is so outrageously incredible that the lord of hell himself must be held accountable for the rape and abduction (not voluntary desertion) of Kore from her mother. The chaste Kore cannot admit to herself, and even less to her mother, that she was led to disrupt their identity-based unity by her own desire. Kore therefore projects her motive for her separant desertion of her mother for her lover, to the violent coercion by an infernal kidnapper and rapist. Once Kore becomes the bride and bedmate of Hades, eating of the pomegranate, the sex-fruit of hell, she becomes Persphone — literally "she who brings destruction". Sex, passion and desire destroy and disrupt the participant unity between mother and maiden. Contrary to Kerenyi's interpretation, the myth of Kore turning into the separant and disruptive Persephone is an allegory on woman's fate seen from a matriarchal feminist stance. The desire for man baits the pure maiden to leave the identification with her mother and yield to the lures of sex and desire and to her separant programming to reproduce. The crucial point here is that because of Kore's amorous passion for her husband she dies and descends as Persephone to the realm of the dead. The death here is not symbolic, allegorical or representing the life-death cycles of fertility as some interpreters have claimed,[10] but a disruptive death of the Demeter-Kore relational unity caused by the destroying Persephone. Kore is annihilated and transformed into a queen of the dead. This means that both Demeter and Persephone have become two separate entities who long to regain their former relational unity as a single entity. This participant quest is the essence of the Eleusinian mysteries which reenact the Demeter-Kore drama.

The mystai, the participants in the mysteries, were not meant to rejoice or to learn, but to suffer. Yet in the course of the mysteries symbolic copulations were enacted and phallic objects were run up and down the tops of the boots of female mystai who sang obscene songs in iambic meter.[11] These seemingly contradictory functions of the mysteries as rituals of suffering and orgiastic enactments of sexual and fertility rites may be explained for our context as follows: sex is indeed held to be obscene and procreation entails the transformation of the pure Kore into the awful and miserable Persephone. However, sex is a necessary evil and in order to make the fields grow corn and the live-stock multiply one has to bait Persephone by the obscene sex she grew to desire; Kore has to placate her consort Hades by orgiastic rituals. Yet one feels guilty and displays at best an outward appearance of suffering for having to engage in promiscuity. This need to engage in sex in order to be fertile had been ordained by Zeus (chief of the Olympian gods) as he was an accomplice in delivering Kore to Hades. The Greeks knew better than to doubt or disobey their metaphysical programming as displayed by their *Moira*, their lot in life. The Judeo-Christian notions of just desserts for worthy or vile deeds was totally foreign to the Greek conception of man and god.[12] One had to obey the mandate of the gods, however arbitrary they seemed, otherwise one committed the heinous and unpardonable sin of hubris. We shall deal later with the doctrinaire normativeness of fathers towards their sons and daughters in conjunction with the third phase of social separation and the rites of passage from childhood to puberty. At this stage we have the image of the father Zeus conniving to tarnish the purity of his daughter and to disrupt her initial identification with her mother in order to serve the programming of fertility and reproduction.

The mystai experience the passivity of Persephone and her surrender to shameful sex as an inevitable evil, as well as experiencing her inner purpose to reunite with her mother in purity after she has paid her promiscuous dues to hell.[13] This participant longing of Persephone to return to her former purity and partake in her mother's divinity, even when wallowing in the promiscuity and degradation of hell, brings us to the purifying function of the mysteries. The dialectics here are that after Persephone has been subjected to shameful sex and the vicissitudes of procreation, her participant longing for communion with unity will raise her back from hell. She has, however, to undergo some rituals of purification. This was carried out symbolically by the mystai at the Eleusinian mysteries by spending a whole day of purification and atonement in the water and on the seashore at the end of which they became pure and untainted.[14] The purification rites are also necessary to atone for the promiscuous conception of the offspring. The notion here, which has some Gnostic parallels,[15] is that the child has a blessed sacred core which has been profaned by sex and earthly reproduction; because the core is of sacred origin the appropriate rites will reveal its original holiness. This is the meaning of the proclamation at the end of the

Eleusinian Mysteries that "Queen Brino has borne a holy child Brimos", which means that Persephone the terrifying queen has given birth to an awe-inspiring sacred son. The purification rites are necessary in order to neutralize the contamination of the son by the pollution of the mother. This brings us to the extreme participant counterpart to the Demeter-Kore myth and the separant pollution of Persephone relating to her fertility. The ingenious artifact here is to dispense completely with profane sex and retain the unity of mother-child and the purity of birth. The gist of our premise is that full participation is impossible yet the longing for it is ever present. When seen from the Demeter-Kore participant dyad reproduction (represented by the Persephone-Hades dyad of hell) is infernal. The separant stance as represented by myths of creation sees the vector of participation as a hindrance to growth and procreation because it leads to non-being. Sex should be utilized as a participant lure to procreation but not beyond it. The participant outlook is, of course, diametrically opposite: the Gnostics regarded creation, growth and reproduction as evil, and sex as its vile bait. The Christians found a clever compromise for the birth of their saviour: Christ was born in a "pure" birth without the profane mediation of sex.

Immaculate Conception

The goal of participation is the partaking in pre-differentiated wholeness. While this Tantalic goal is impossible by definition, it is precisely this unattainability that lends the aim of participation its enormous strength. The second best in the participant goals of the mother-child dyad is to forgo the separant (and hence derogatory from the participant point of vantage) ordeals of sex. The mother-child participant dyad in unity will not therefore be disrupted by the sex-bound descent to hell of a Persephone. The Immaculate Conception is by the participant Holy Spirit without the intermediary of sex. Virgin birth is also parthenogenetic, for the Virgin Mary was believed to have been born through divine impregnation.[16] This enhances the self-sufficiency of the mother-child dyad and strengthens its quest for participation in unity which in Catholic dogma, at least, has already been achieved.

The virgin birth of Jesus is the most celebrated instance of a divine immaculate conception but there are many other instances of virgin births signifying the widespread incidence of the myth. Danae was impregnated by Zeus who entered through the roof of the tower in which she was guarded, as a stream of gold coins gushing into her lap; Zeus courted Leda in the form of a swan after which she laid an egg from which were hatched Helen, Castor and Polydeuces; Isis conceived her son Horus by the seed of Osiris which she drew into herself after the God's death;[17] Krishna was born to the virgin Jasoda; and Montezuma the Emperor of Mexico at the time of the Spanish conquest was believed to have been born by a virgin birth to his mother who was impregnated by Tlaloc the Aztec, the God of rain. Of special interest is the case of Isaac. The first and second versus of chapter 21 of Genesis state "And the Lord visited Sarah as he had said and the Lord did unto Sarah as he had spoken. For Sarah conceived . . ." This divine visitation of Sarah coupled with the fact that Abraham at that time was a patriarch of a hundred years old, makes the Sarah-Isaac dyad another likely myth of "pure" birth by divine impregnation. This will be of further significance when we deal later on with social separation and the myth of the offering of Isaac. The Sarah-Isaac dyad will be depicted as a relationship of grace and contrasted with the doctrinaire normativeness of Abraham who is prepared to sacrifice his son to the absolute mandate of God as revealed and promulgated by himself.

Mary's purity was absolute because she never had sexual intercourse either before the birth of Christ or after it.[18] Her purity was a function of her abstaining from sex. Mary's chastity was a model preached by the Church fathers. Cyril of Alexandria addressed the women in his congregation as follows:

> Come, O all ye women who desire virginity, emulate the example of Mary, the mother of thy Lord. Consider ye her coarse and meagre food and her sleeping on the ground. She craved for none of the things of this world. The mention of her was always in the mouths of the priests. She never washed herself in a (public) bath. She never adorned herself with face-paint, and eye-paint, and powder. She never decked herself out in brightly coloured raiment, as do all women who love fine clothes. She never tasted wine. She used to sit always with her face turned towards the east, for she was always awaiting the Creator of the world. She never met and talked to any one, except her father, and her mother, and her brethren.[19]

The crucial description here is of Mary rescinding all vestiges of sexual temptation. She waived her feminine attraction in order to be worthy to bear God not through the lures of sinful sex but by a sexless birth. Only a pure virgin can give birth to a pure son of God. Moreover, the child Jesus has been depicted as subduing dragons right after his birth and dragons are an archetypal symbol of sex.[20] We close the cycle of our present premise by linking the sexless mother-child myth to our developmental model. Each one of us is the pure son of the good (holy) mother when fixated at early orality. Untainted by object relationships and not tarnished by our own (as yet non-existent) sexual desire for her, we perpetually strive to reunite with our "pure" objective mother, because in early orality mother and child are still embraced in a pantheistic unity. Object relationships and sexual dialectics with the breast-mother occur at later orality in the course of and after the crystallization of the separate self. Robert Graves intuitively illustrated our present premise when he preached for the return to the grass roots of Christianity by refocusing on the mystical dyad of the virgin born Christ and his great "white" (i.e., pure) mother. This is the aversion of the participant sons of God to the corruption of the flesh.[21] Every early orally fixated child cannot and will not accept the atrocious contention that his divine mother has engaged in lurid sex in order to bring him into the world.

Mary has been likened to the bush that was on fire but not burnt because she conceived a son without being burnt by sex.[22] This means that in giving birth, which is a prime separant dynamic, Mary was not tainted and singed by the obscene and destroying fires of sex. A more radical stance argues that if life is vile and its continuous cycles were initiated by the Demiurge or the devil, then not only sex but procreation itself should be prevented. The Gnostic Saturnius decreed a kind of procreation strike because life on earth and hence marriage and generation are the labors of Satan.[23] The participant longing of the early church fathers and their collective fixation on unity and the nonbeing of early orality might account partially, at least, for their fierce anti-sexuality and their almost Gnostic aversion to procreation. Priests, monks and nuns have emulated the mythical celibacy of Jesus Christ whereas the Church father Origen, prompted by his craving for purity and absolute asceticism, castrated himself and gained thereby the additional fringe benefit of sterility. In a similar vein Mani preached the abstention from marriage, asceticism and refraining from procreation so that the yoke of the evil creator of spatiotemporal existence may be broken.[24] Extreme promiscuity and perversion have also been utilized as a deliberate rebellion against Man's programming to reproduce. This idea has been set out in full in *Salvation Through the Gutters*.[25]

5
Mother Lover

**The sucking of the child at the breast of the mother
is the model of every love relationship**

E. Hitschmann: *Freud's Conception of Love*

In *Salvation Through the Gutters* we posed what seemed to us an insoluble dilemma: "The participation element in sex lands us in a paradox we do not even try to disentangle. The original role of orgasm (very often deplored as a nuisance) is to ejaculate sperm for conception and procreation; yet this very same process is the beginning of another cycle of separation. This dilemma is beyond our reach. It belongs either to the rarified heights of theology and philosophy or to the abyss of cynicism: The human is baited by a moment of bliss to pledge another life to bondage."[1] In the present chapter we shall try to disentangle some knots in this dilemma with the help of new insights gleaned mytho-empirically from the biblical myths of the Original Sin and the Fall as well as from some premise of personality development at early and later orality.

We mentioned earlier that myths have different layers of meanings pertaining to different contexts. The myth of the Fall from grace and the expulsion from paradise may, therefore, have an existential meaning in their separant connotation as ejecting the coagulating self from its Edenic pantheism. This is the meaning we have imputed to the myth of the Original Sin in our previous publications.[2] In the present work we focus on the sexual meaning of the Original Sin and relate it mytho-empirically to the development and differentiation of human sexuality. We shall show that the partaking of the tree of knowledge has a sexual connotation in addition to its cognitive and existential meanings, because the word ידע (*yada*) in Hebrew means both to know and to have sexual intercourse. We shall examine the mytho-empiric symbolism of the serpent as a phallic and as an overall sexual image.

The fruit of the forbidden tree also signifies the nourishing yet sexually arousing breast. The suckling dialectics of infant-mouth/breast-mother has sexual connotations for both infant and mother; and hence has a function in the arousal of incestuous desires at the oral stage of the child's development and the suppression of these desires by the mother. These add a sexual normative dimension to the mouth-breast dialectics in addition to the separant conflictual interaction between the infant mouth ego at early orality and the full nourishing breast-mother, or the empty and hence rejecting breast-mother. The sexual significance of suckling is implicit in Fairbairn's following dictum: "The phallic attitude is thus dependent upon an identification of the object's genital organs with the breast as the original part-object of the oral attitude — an identification which is characteristically accompanied by an identification of the subject's genital organs with the mouth as a libidinal organ."[3] Finally, the differentiation of sexual awareness is also initiated at the oral stage of development by the identification dyad between mother and daughter, and by the mother-son dyad of complementarity.

Ensnaring Lust

Adam before the Fall was perfect; the *Midrash* and the Talmud describe him as "endowed with extraordinary stature. He is frequently said to have filled the world. (He is) physically beautiful, with surpassing wisdom, with a brilliancy which eclipsed that of the sun, with a heavenly light which enabled him to see the whole world."[4] This is the mytho-empirical projection of the omnipresent early-oral self partaking in an Edenic pantheism. Adam is also described as living in perfect angelic bliss and free from concupiscence and sexual lust.[5] This is highly relevant to our present context because the mytho-empirical implication here is that this blissful innocence was transformed into the fallen state of sin through the exposure to sexual lust and the display of concupiscent desire.

The Fall became the prototype of sin because it totally transformed the human being from a unique totality into a vulnerable separatum who had to strive, compete and interact conflictually with his surroundings in order to survive. This transformation from early to later orality which also involves some universal dialectics of sexual awareness, is the second major phase of developmental separation after birth. This might be the mytho-empirical interpretation of St. Paul's dictum that: "It was through one man that sin entered the world, and through sin death, and thus death pervaded the whole human race, inasmuch as all men have sinned."[6] This is the painful (and hence projected later as sinful) transition from the Edenic pantheism of early orality to the conflictual strife of the newly formed self with its surroundings. Indeed, both the Gnostics and the Kabbalists regard the coagulation of a material boundary around the self (the body) as the process and the evidence of Man's fallen state.[7]

The sexual component of the original sin is suggested by some mytho-empirical interpretations of the Fall story. *Genesis Raba* points out the resemblance between the name of Eve (Chava in Hebrew) and the denotation of the word snake in Aramaic (Chevia), and states that the seducer was Eve's snake and Eve was Adam's snake.[8] The *Midrash* here seems to voice the depth-psychologists' imagery of the snakes' sexual significance and hence the implicit sexual connotation of the Fall story. According to the *Apocalypse of Moses* the serpent managed to implant prurient lust in the fruit which he seduced Eve to eat and to offer Adam.[9] The following account of the Fall by the *Apocalypse of Abraham* indicates the sexual nature of the Original Sin:

> And I saw there (in Eden) a man, tall in stature and fearful in breadth, incomparable in appearance, in embrace with a woman, who also resembled the man in appearance and size. And they were standing under one tree of Eden and the fruit of this tree looked like a cluster of the vine; and behind the tree was standing one like a serpent in form, but having hands and feel like a man, and wings at his shoulders, six on his right and six on his left; and they held the cluster of the tree in their hands, and they whom I saw embracing lay with one another. And I said: "Who are these embracing one another, or who is the being betwixt them, or what is this fruit which they are eating, O Mighty, Eternal One?" And he said: "This is the counsel of man, this is Adam, and these are their desires on earth, this is Eve, but he who is between them is the Godless power of their enterprise in ruin, Azazel himself."[10]

The linkage between the pollution by concupiscence of Adam and Eve by the snake, and the reification of Adam's soul by its embedding in a body, is also to be found in the Lurianic Kabbala.[11] The crux of the matter is that the sexual significance of the original sin is linked to its separant existential meaning by the need of a sexual partner. Sexuality necessitates a crystallization of a separate self in order to be able to relate sexually to an alter. A duality or a plurality has to be effected in order for sexuality to achieve its affective and/or physical dyadic intercourse. Our theoretical cycle here seems to be completed by sex being both one of the aims and a major factor in the separant ejection of the nascent self from pantheistic early orality. This gives an apt hue to the words of the *Midrash* which states that when Adan knew his wife (we have already mentioned that knowledge in Hebrew also means sexual intercourse) he knew and realized from what tranquil bliss he was deprived.[12] This is an amazingly appropriate mytho-empirical linkage between the original sin, sex and expulsion of the separate self from the pantheistic omnipresence of early orality.

The order of temptations presented in the story of the Fall begins with the serpent through Eve to Adam. If the serpent is the mytho-empirical archetype of sexual desire, then the cycle of sinful sex is actually initiated by the woman. Indeed, in the *Book of Adam and Eve* the snake is said to have implanted a polluted desire in her and this desire was the root of all sin;[13] Eve then goes on to recount boast-fully how easy it was to seduce Adam;[14] and in chapter seven Adam laments his death to the Edenic bliss because of his seduction by Eve;[15] while in chapter nine Eve admits her role in perpetrating the Original Sin and prays to bear its consequences.[16] What emerges here is an image of an archetypal woman driven by sinful lust and desire which causes her own fall as well as the downfall of the primal Man. The origin of the lust changes from one mytho-empirical source to another. In the scriptures it is the archetypal sexual symbol of the serpent. In the *Apocalypse of Abraham* and the *Slavonic Book of Baruch,* Satanial himself (i.e., the Devil) poured sinful lust on Adam and Eve.[17] In like manner, in the *Book of Adam and Eve,* Adam accuses the adversary (one of the attributes of the evil powers) of seducing Eve who in turn seduced him.[18] Of special interest to our context is the following account by the *Apocalypse of Moses* of the conspiracy between Satan and the snake to drive Man out of the Garden of Eden:

> Satan beheld (to wit) our glory and honour; and having found the serpent, the wisest animal of all which are on the whole earth, he approached him and said unto him (so far in Armenian only: the Greek differs): I desire to reveal unto thee the thought which is in my heart and to unite (with) thee. Thou seest how much worth God has bestowed on man. But we have been dishonoured; let us go and drive him out of the garden, out of which we have been driven because of him. Do thou only become a vessel (tool) unto me, and I will deceive them by they mouth in order to ensare them.[19]

The important phrases here are first the wish of Satan to unite with the serpent which is both a denotation of identity and of sexual union, the snake being a prime phallic image. Second, Satan wishes to deceive man through the verbal enticement of the serpent. Here there is an equivalence and interchangeability between the devil, sexual desire, sin, pollution and the snake. However, as far as Adam is concerned the source of the evil desire is Eve, the archetypal Woman. And this desire is instrumental in ejecting him from the Garden of Eden. We propose the hypothesis, which we shall substantiate more fully in subsequent parts of this work, that sexual desire aroused by the archetypal Woman was instrumental in expelling Adam, the archetypal self, from the togetherness of early orality. But the Woman was also the archetypal mother "because she was the mother of all who live".[20] The result of this sexual seduction by the woman-mother was the "death" of the self to the Edenic pantheism of early orality. (Death as a result of the Original Sin is the expression actually used by the *Book of Adam and Eve*.) This separation of the nascent archetypal self from the omni-presence of early orality was brought about by the eating from the fruit of the tree of knowledge which we shall try to interpret mytho-empiri-cally as the sexual dynamics inherent in the sucking from the mother's breast. This may also be linked to the sexual seduction component in the Fall story.

The fruit of the tree of knowledge (which in Hebrew may be etymo-logically interpreted as the tree of sex) was envisaged as infused with passion and prurience by the snake. (This is the account given by the *Apocalypse of Moses*, the *Apocalypse of Abraham* and the *Slavonic Book of Enoch*.) It was given to Adam by Eve the primal mother. A fruit which nourishes and also has a sexual significance in the mytho-empirical context of early orality can only be the breast. We have already mentioned that at early orality the mouth ego interacts with the breast-mother in a binary manner. If the breast does not give forth milk the mouth ego suffers. Because at this stage the nascent ego is not yet crystallized as a different entity and whatever happens occurs in the neonate's omnipresent self, the pain and "badness" felt by the mouth ego is imputed to himself. The mouth ego lives in a confusing situation where pain, hunger and thirst are perceived by the infants interoceptors as happening in himself, yet the "good" breast-mother does supply milk which is sucked in by the mouth ego, although the source of this food is outside the boundaries of the omnipresence of the neonate.

We shall elaborate later the premise that the child feels sexual excite-ment while sucking his mother's breast and so does his mother. His mother, however, suppresses this sexual excitement which is conceived by her as incestuous when caused by her child's sucking. This suppres-sion of the sexual excitement is transmitted by the mother to the nursing child by intuition, empathy and direct tactile non-verbal com-munication. This creates a severe conflict in the mouth ego. The "good" breast-mother feeds him and makes him very happy because food at this stage is one of the early oral child's few focal concerns. But with the food comes a message of proscription and suppression of what is experienced by him as a very arousing sensation accompanying his food intake. This proscription (i.e., "badness") cannot come from the "good" food itself, nor from the "good" breast-mother who provides it. Hence the mytho-empirical projection imputes the proscribed (and therefore vile) sexual experience which accompanies the sucking of food to an outside vile entity which pollutes the food. However, the "good" breast-mother cannot at the same time be both the provider of food and this vile polluting entity. The mytho-empirical projection solves this dilemma for the simplistic mouth ego by attributing the forbidden sexual sensation to an extraneous "badness" which lured the breast-mother to intake the polluting sexual desire which she then transmits to the mouth ego while at the same time suppressing it herself. The empirical clue to this "interpretation" is the Lurianic Kabbala's description that Adam and Eve sucked the juice of the forbidden fruit which came from the *extraneous* sources denoted as the "side of death".[21] These conflictual sexual dialectics are an additional separant process of early orality which together with the deprivational and conflictual interaction of the neonate with its surroundings, which we have described elsewhere,[22] effect the crystallization of the individual self and its ejection from the pantheistic togetherness of early orality.

One may wonder how our mytho-empirical interpretation may be reconciled with our using Eve as both the archetypal mother and the primal wife. Yet it is precisely this interchangeability between mother and sex mate that is the crux of the matter. The primal mouth-ego is aroused sexually by his mother and at the same time arouses her by sucking her nipples. This is the incestuous sex which brought the Fall from grace (i.e., the ejection from pantheistic early orality). Indeed, in *Genesis Raba* the snake (i.e., prurient sex) is depicted as a voyeur witnessing the intercourse between Adam and Eve.[23] But why should sex be evil in the general context of Genesis when the divine mandate to procreate and multiply is repeated many times in Genesis itself? The answer is that the original sin myth deals with forbidden sex. The mutual sexual arousal of mother and child at early orality is so heinous that it merits the most forceful reaction, namely the Fall from grace, the mytho-empirical equivalent of which is the existential ejection of the separate self from the omnipresence of early orality. The Original Sin myth deals with incestuous sexual arousal, its suppression and its religious, social and ethical consequences. It also provides a mytho-empirical anchor for our contention that the incestuous arousal at early orality and its normative suppression by the mother has important sociopersonal implications which Freud imputed to what he denoted as the Oedipal stage of the development of the personality. This premise, which is only partly shared by the Kleinean oralists, will be developed more extensively in the following chapter. The almost total dependence of the child on his mother for his survival compounded by the devastating approach-avoidance conflict of incestuous sexual arousal and its suppression by the mother (the mytho-empirical essence of the Fall story), lends this myth the formidable stature it occupies in many cultures and mythologies.

One of the implications of the sexual components of the original sin is the shunning of sexual pleasure in many religions, particularly in Judaeo-Christianity. Procreation is not deemed vile as in some dualistic creeds and in Gnosticism, but sex (the extraneous pollution of the Fall story) should not be enjoyed. To this very day (or rather night) some orthodox Jewish communities have their women covered by a bed sheet with a hole in the centre to permit intercourse.

A Serpent in Paradise

We have seen that the snake, the phallic lust of evil prurience, was introduced mytho-empirically in the Fall story through the fruit breast of Eve. This is plastically described as follows by the *Book of Adam and Eve*: "(And the snake) mounted the tree and infused in the fruit which he gave me to eat his pollution; his lust, because lust is the source of all sin."[24] This is the projection of the early oral mouth ego which could not reconcile the "good" mother-breast's nourishing flow of food and warmth with its emphatic proscription of the infant's sexual arousal while sucking the breast. For the breast-mother, however, the vile sexual desire which she feels when being sucked is more direct. In three places the Talmud recounts the myth of the original sin depicting the serpent as having intercourse with her and injecting its polluting poison into her.[25] This second version of the myth, envisaging the direct infusion of sexual desire into the primal mother without the mediation of the fruit, fits the mytho-empirical projection of the breast-mother, the sucking of which arouses incestuous and hence polluted desire. The first version of the myth, depicting the primal mother eating the fruit which has been defiled by the phallic serpent, is the mytho-empirical projection of the mouth ego. The mouth ego is aroused by the breast-mother (i.e., the mythical fruit) and receives the messages of sinful sex from the breast-mother as sensed by her. At early orality the mouth ego cannot but project that the breast-mother is fed the polluted sexual sensations the same way that he is by a fruit-breast. The breast-mother, on the other hand, feels the sexual sensations directly. These sensations are accompanied by her being sucked so that she is aroused by the phallus-snake without the mediation of the forbidden fruit.

It is important to note in this context that the serpent is expressly depicted by the Original Sin myth of Genesis as a talking serpent.[26]

(The strict determinism of mytho-empirical interpretation does not allow any assumptions of superfluousness in myths.) This ability of the snake to communicate verbally with humans makes it a direct partner to their interaction. It also points at the transmutability of sexual messages and sensations between the *dramatis personae* of the Original Sin myth which constitute the mytho-empirical equivalents of the mouth ego and breast-mother dyad of early orality.

The account of the ancient Iranian religions in the *Pahlavi* books describe Azi-Dahaka, the primaeval dragon, as ruling the world by evil cruelty. The dragon drives out Yima the first man from his Edenic abode, cuts him into pieces and marries his two wives.[27] This is a variation on the theme of the biblical Fall story. The dragon-snake is the evil adversary, the vile phallic sexuality which drives out the primal man from his pantheistic early orality. Here the separation is even more radical as the fallen primal man is torn into a plurality of segments. The dragon then avails himself of the primal women.

The sexual symbolism of the snake in many cultures points toward the vast potential of their mytho-empirical significance. Our focus, however, is on a relatively clearly defined aspect of the snake symbolism as applied to the mother-child dyad at early orality. Jung, for instance claims and brings some iconographic support for it, that the serpent in paradise is depicted as female;[28] while Slater brings forth serpentine arguments to support his contention that the snake-phallus symbolism is homosexual.[29] We, on the other hand, attempt to differentiate the gender of the snake symbol depending on the point of vantage of the mouth ego or the breast-mother. For the latter, the snake-phallus is masculine and its masculinity stems from the mother's immediate sexual experience when aroused by her suckling child. Neumann provides support for this premise by mentioning that in Crete and India the snake is an attribute of the female deity but appears to be her male phallic escort.[30]   However, in the story of the Fall, recounted apparently from the point of vantage of the mouth ego, the snake is depicted as female.[31] This stems first of all from the biologically based desire of the female child for the penis, and the male infants awareness of it (the penis) when sucking the breast and being sexually aroused by it. Structurally there is a similarity between the breast and penis; both have rounded domes which spurt liquid and functionally both are sexual objects. Indeed, Karl Abraham,[32] Melanie Klein,[33] and Ronald Fairbairn[34] base a considerable part of their theorizing on these structural, functional and symbolic similarities between the penis and breast.

At early orality there is no differentiation between phallic sensations and the breast. Hence, for the sexually aroused mouth ego the breast he sucks also has a phallic significance. But the breast-mother is female and so is the snake (i.e., the phallic imagery aroused by her). Consequently, for the mouth ego at early orality the breast-mother has a mytho-empirical significance of a female snake-phallus. We may conclude, therefore, that for the mouth ego (both male and female) the breast-mother would be associated with female snake-phalli; whereas for the breast-mother the sexual imagery associated with her arousal while nursing would be of a male snake-phallus. This will have further relevance for us when we deal with gender differentiation at early orality as related to the child-mother dyad.

The separant role of the snake-phallus as representing incestuous sexual arousal may also be implied from the following exposition of the Talmud: " . . . and we observed with the primaeval snake that when it coveted what it should not; what it desired was not given to it and what it had was taken away from it."[35] This mytho-empirical interpretation may mean in our context that the incestuous desire (i.e., the snake-phallus) of the mouth ego for the breast-mother was not and should not have been consummated. Its consummation results in the deprivation of the incestuous mouth ego of what it had at early orality. In other words, it results in the separation from its pantheistic togetherness with its surroundings.

The snake's separant role in the myth of the Fall is also expanded by the Kabbalist Joseph Gikatila: "The primaeval snake in the beginning of its creation . . . had a place in all the worlds . . . without it there would be no life, sowing and growing for any creature under the orbit of the moon . . . but it had to operate outside . . . the Tree of Knowledge. When it took the fruit . . . it introduced the external pollution inside . . . The creations of God when they are in their original (proper) place are good, but when they are out of their place they are bad."[36] This passage asserts the role of the phallus-snake as the universal instrument of sexual reproduction. It reconfirms that according to Judaism, reproduction and sex leading to it is not evil; what is vile is sex related to the forbidden fruit-breast of the mother. Such sex is "out of its place", sinful and disastrous.

The *dramatis personae* of the early oral drama are then the breast-mother and breast-fruit/breast-snake on the mother's side, and the mouth ego and the child/snake-phallus on the child's side. The crucial dynamic, however, is the dialectics of the incestuous desire and the suppression of the snake-phallus of the early oral dyad of mother and suckling child. An addition to the mytho-empirical snake-child imagery is Hesiod's mention of Ceto giving birth to a child: "Half of her is a fair cheeked girl with glancing eyes, but half is a huge and frightening speckled snake."[37] Neumann provides a mytho-empirical anchor for this dyad by describing the primordial snakeheaded goddesses holding children. He notes that "the extreme slenderness (of these goddesses) is presumably connected with the snake nature of these women".[38] *Genesis Raba* supports this dialectic imagery by stating that the snake was the seducer of Eve, and that Eve was the snake-seducer of Adam.[39] This again is a mytho-empirical metaphor of the snake-phallus/sexual desire of the primaeval mother exciting her suckling child by her breast-fruit; and in turn the mouth ego/child-snake exciting the mother sexually by sucking her. This is incestuous and forbidden so that in addition to the expulsion of the mouth ego from its pantheism and the existential separation between the breast-mother and the mouth ego, the serpent-phallus/sexual desire of both mother and son are also suppressed by this early oral dynamic.

The *Book of Adam and Eve* describes this dynamic as follows: "And to the serpent He said with great rage: because thou hast done this and thou hast deceived the righteous of heart thou art cursed above all cattle and above every beast of the field . . . because thou hast ensnared them with your vileness and caused them to be expelled from The Garden of Eden."[40] Incestuous sexual desire and its suppression by the breast-mother seems to be the prime cause of Man's ejection from the Edenic togetherness of early orality.

At early orality the sexual imagery is cathected and exchanged exclusively within the mother-child dyad. The gender of the sexual imagery is focused from the very beginning and not blurred multi-sexually and aroborically as presented by Neumann.[41] For the mother the phallic imagery aroused by the sucking of her breast is masculine and related experientially to her sexual intercourse; whereas for the child the phallic snake is feminine because it stems from the mother. Even if the phallic imagery transmitted over to the child has originated from the father it is perceived as feminine by the child because for the child it comes from the mother.

Sex is conceived as vile and shameful by the child because it brought about the child's ejection from the innocent omnipresence of early orality. Before the separant Fall the primal Man and Woman were not ashamed;[42] whereas the exposure to the fruit-breast and snake-phallus introduced shame to their relationship.[43] This is the shame of leaving the blissful togetherness of the mother-child dyad and of being with each other, to the separant alienation of being vis-a-vis or against each other. Shame is the corollary of the existential loneliness of the crystallization of the separate self. The need to cache our sexual desire stems from the shame of the mother at early orality aroused by her feelings of incestuous sex towards her child and the transmission of these feelings. Guilt is also transmitted by the mother to the child at early orality but by a different mechanism and its implications are more profound. We agree with Melanie Klein that the Oedipal processes take place at the oral phase of development but as we shall try to show in the next chapter, their guilt anchored dynamics are different and their effects more spectacular than she thought.[44]

6
Mouth, Breast, Snake, and Self

Freud's remark that the mother-son relationship
was least "liable to disaster", and provides
"the purest examples of unchanging tenderness,
undisturbed by any egoistic consideration"
is surely the most inaccurate statement
he ever made ...

Philip E. Slater: *The Glory of Hera*

The crucial importance of the oral phase of human development stems
from its being the first exposure of the neonate to its physical and
living environment, and its immediate need to reach a dialectical *modus
vivendi* with it. The initial patterns of adjustment of the organism, its
structured reactions to the impinging culture and the fixations incurred
by its interaction with the mother or mother surrogate, constitute the
raw materials which the core vectors mould into a personality
scaffolding.[1] The oral stage of human development, more than the subsequent ones, is therefore responsible for the initial structuring of the
personality core. The developmental functionality of this seems to be
the very early adaptation of the neonate's organism and psyche to the
environment so that from the very outset the neonate may regulate and
coordinate its dialectical interrelationship between self and surroundings and thus reach a dynamic equilibrium for existence.

Early orality witnesses not only the coagulation of the separate self
and the suppression of incestuous feelings with its wide cultural
implications, but also gender-differentiation through the child's interaction with the mother. When these processes of gender-differentiation
are skewed or traumatized at early orality there may be a predisposition
to gender diffusion and homosexuality as we shall indicate in chapter
seven. The overwhelming developmental importance of the oral phase
does not, of course, exclude the salience of later developmental stages.
For example, the normative indoctrination inherent in the third social
phase of separation effected by the father or his surrogate presiding
over formal and informal rites of passage from childhood to maturity
may have overt and covert sexual components. However, the basic
foundations of both sexual identity and the structure of the personality
core have been laid at the oral stage of development.

The proscription of incest at the oral stage by the mother has wide-spread cultural implications similar in importance to what the Oedipal prohibitions have for the Freudian system of thought. The cardinal difference is that with Freud the originator of the cultural sublimations of incest is the father, whereas with the oralist frame of reference the origin of the proscription of incest and hence of its cultural sublimation, is the mother. The Kleinian system contends that the Oedipal processes take place at the oral phase of human development, yet neither Melanie Klein nor her leading disciples have traced rigorously the cultural implications of their contentions. Ronald Fairbairn, a leading British oralist, states that "in general, Melanie Klein's views seemed to me from the first to represent an important advance in the development of psychoanalytical theory. In due course, however, it occurred to me with increasing conviction that, in certain important respects, she had failed to push her views to their logical conclusions."[2] The sole reliance on clinical analyses by the oralists excluded the use of mytho-empirical and socio-anthropological sources. Melanie Klein states that the superego (i.e., conscience and guilt) are formed by "the Oedipus tendencies (which) are released in consequence of the frustration which the child experiences at weaning and that they make their appearance at the end of the first and the beginning of the second year of life; they receive reinforcement through the anal frustrations undergone during training in cleanliness."[3] She bases her premises on the mouth ego's deprivational interaction with the breast-mother at the weaning period and hence relates her oralist premises essentially to nourishing.

We agree that the infant's deprivational interaction with a feeding/non-feeding breast has a major role in ejecting him from the pantheistic togetherness of early orality. A feeding breast which stops spurting milk into the mouth ego is a disastrously frustrating experience for the early oral infant. Klein also aptly states that "some measure of frustration at the breast is inevitable, even under the most favourable conditions for what the infant actually desires is unlimited gratification".[4] Consequently, the rather harsh food-based dialectics between the mouth ego and breast-mother at weaning and before, contributes to the realization of the early-oral infant that it is not part of mother but confronted against mother. This premise has served us elsewhere as a basis for our linkage between the infant's deprivational interaction with the breast-mother and the formation of its ego boundary and separate self.[5] However, Klein's contention that because the breast does not nourish the male child he turns Oedipally to the father's penis, is both disconnected and farfetched. First, the breast is concretely present in front of the infant's face whereas the father's penis is not. Klein does not explain credibly how the child may be exposed to and be aware of it even symbolically at early orality. Second, Klein bases her theory on the nourishing function of the breast and then shifts bases (so to speak) to the purely sexual function of the penis.[6] The breast spurts food whereas the penis does not. Klein claims that the mouth ego feels Oedipal guilt at its weaning because it imputes the drying out of the breast-mother to its sucking. This is poetically phrased a la Oscar Wilde by Fairbairn that the mouth ego feels that he "kills the thing he loves".[7] To our mind this is a spurious association between cause and effect by unduly imputing to the mouth ego sophisticated inference techniques it cannot have.

We claim that the Oedipal pressures are felt as a sexual arousal by both child and mother while nursing at the breast. This incestuous desire is incidental but different from the food intake and extraneous to it. It is also harshly suppressed by the mother. The child receives a message of guilt for feeling a forbidden sexual desire for his mother by a direct tactile transmission from her as well as by empathy and by non-verbal cues. The Oedipal guilt is transmitted directly and forcefully by the mother or her surrogate so that both the proscription of incest and the guilt for having felt it is ingrained into the child at early orality. An even shallow introspection would reveal that we have a powerful injunction against incest at a much earlier age than Freud claimed, and that it was there as early as we can remember or feel. The crucial point is that the direct proscription of incest and the transmission of guilt by the mother to the child launches the sublimatory processes of culturally accepted avenues at the outset of early orality. Our anchor on the sexual desire of the child and its suppression at early orality and not on food intake as a sublimatory basis for guilty marital bond formations and cultural creativity, is that the sexual drive is so much more pliable than our need for food. Food intake is a binary continuum with one pole of satiety and the other of starvation and death. With sex, however, the variety and combinations are endless. This is why our programming untilizes sex and not food or air intake to spur our separant processes of growth. We are baited by short-lived instances of participant bliss to multiply and procreate, and by a controlled deprivation of sex to create culture.

Our contention of a direct suppression of the incestuous desires of children at early orality by their mothers may also be related to the development of their gender differentiation: this is so because the phallic images are transmitted to the child by the mother in conjunction with her incestuous feelings and their suppression. As we have shown earlier the mytho-empirical sex-based images of breast and snake are interchangeable because they are sexually anchored, whereas the food-based Kleinian image of the breast and the masculine phallus are not so readily interchangeable. Hence our contention that the sex-based dialectics of breast-phallus inherent in the arousal of incestuous desire and its suppression at early orality may also be applied to the differentiation of gender identity at this phase of development. Finally, the continuous sexual desire of the human animal, unlike other life forms, may also be related to the suppression of sexuality at early orality. By suppressing the natural outlet and manifestations of sex at early orality we become sexually traumatized and fixated, and hence sexually sensitized for life.

Another difference between the Kleinian stance and ours is her stressing of the anal-erotic reinforcement by toilet training. We agree with Fairbairn that whilst the breast and the genitals are biologically based sexual objects, faeces are not.[8] Also, Malinowsky has shown that the Trobrianders, who did not make any issue of toilet training, were not concerned at all with the decency or indecency of bowel movements.[9] Consequently, the fact that various symptoms are found in neurotic European bourgeois patients due to an oversevere toilet training are not found in other cultures which are less strenuous in the toilet training of their young, is evidence that there is not a universal anal-erotic phase of human development.

Mother and Child: A Sexy Couple

Slater makes the ingenious observation that in the Oedipus myth the father Laius was a homosexual who refused to take his wife Jocasta to bed. She had to seduce him when he was drunk in order to conceive Oedipus.[10] The main *dramatis personae* of the myth are Jocasta and Oedipus, the mother and son whose forbidden desire for each other is the essence of the tragedy. The sexual dialectics of desire and its proscription within the mother-child dyad is crucial for the child's development. This is because the desire and its proscription occurs at the plastic formative phase of early orality in which the neonate's surroundings impinge on his nascent self with brute force. Second, the desire-proscription dialectic creates an approach-avoidance conflict and a double-bind which in themselves are severe traumatizers.[11] But when the subject of the conflict is sex, which is both the prime mover of procreation and the anchor of our participant quest for love, its effects become cardinal for both personality formation and cultural sublimations.

The link between mother and child is based on a direct non-verbal flow of communication because of the close tactile proximity between them and because at the first year of his life symbolic communication with the child is well nigh impossible. Furthermore, the child is not a passive receptacle of the mother's attitudes and behaviour. The child directs his mother's behaviour towards him by selectively manipulating her by his crying, restlessness or signs of contentedness.[12] The mother-child dyad at early orality is truly symbiotic, and the differential attachment behaviour of mother and child as shown by Bowlby and his associates may be the cues and expression of the differential flow of emotions within the mother-child dyad.[13] Of special importance is the study of breast-feeding carried out by Winter. She concludes that while suckling her child the mother feels very close or "fused" with him. The mother senses a "weakening of the sense of separateness between mother and infant".[14] This sense of closeness allows the mother to better focus her direct flow of non-verbal communication to her infant and imbue it with richer and more subtle nuances. This attachment and proximity may be for both mother and child a manifestation of their participant quest for union. Stated inversely, we may regard the reciprocal participant quest of proximity, attachment and union of mother and child as one of our inbuilt programmes to induce the mother to feed her child and for the child to attach himself to the mother. This quest of union might also be the deeper core reasons for the attachment behaviour of infants observed by Bowlby.

The second "baiting" mechanism which attracts the mother and child to each other for the feeding and the protection of the latter is the sexual pleasure felt by both mother and child while nursing at the breast. This is the separant function of early oral mutual sexual arousal of mother and child to enhance the nurture and survival of the young of the species. The separant function of sex is baited even at early orality by the participant quest of union inherent in sexual desire and attraction. Precisely this primacy of the early oral sexual attraction of mother to child and vice versa makes its suppression so devastatingly traumatic that it was projected mytho-empirically as the original sin and was mainly responsible, as we shall see later, for the sublimatory creation of culture.

Before carrying on our deliberations we have to raise two points of method: first, our theoretical framework is based on breast-feeding but what about bottle-feeding mothers and bottle-fed babies? The studies relating to this topic are contradictory and inconclusive. One representative study states as follows: "Women who do not wholeheartedly desire to breast feed are less likely to be motherly individuals. They are apt to feel that childbirth is hard . . . more apt to feel men have a more satisfying time in life, and are more likely to reject children".[15] Another well designed and controlled study states the diametrically opposite conclusion that mothers who bottle-feed their children were not any more rejecting or cold towards them than mothers who breast-fed their children.[16]

Our possible attitudes to this point of method could be one of the following three: first, we are dealing with a bio-psycho-cultural evolutionary relationship between mother and child which was based on breast-feeding for millions of years so that the relatively recent period in which bottle-feeding was introduced is insignificant. Second, the mother holding the child in her lap, even if bottle-feeding him, has the same or similar sensations to a breast-feeding mother; at the same time the child has similar feelings towards the mother holding him in her lap, for the child is still fed by the natural mother. Third, bottle-feeding mothers and bottle-fed children feel differently towards each other than breast-feeding mothers and breast-fed children. Consequently, our theory holds true only for the latter. We have no way of ascertaining which of these three possibilities is more feasible and until clear-cut empirical evidence is provided each one of the three possibilities is as viable or non-viable as the other. The second point of method relates to a surrogate mother (e.g., nurse, wet nurse, stepmother, adoptive mother etc.). The possibilities here again are either that the surrogate mothers feel and behave towards the child in a similar manner to the natural mother or our conclusions do not apply to surrogate mothers.

Both the mouth and breast are primary erotogenous zones. When the mother suckles her child she is sexually excited by him. Indeed, nursing women describe the nursing experience itself as sexually stimulating.[17] For the mouth ego the sucking of the breast involves sexual excitement because the breast is not only a food source but also or even mainly, a sexual object. The sexual essence of oral sucking has been stressed by Fairbairn[18] and heavily relied on by Abraham[19] who pointed out that the act of sucking in itself has an erotic significance independent of the food intake. This supports our contention that sex is used at the oral phase of development as a participant bait for the separate business of survival. The sucking of food is reinforced by a sexual pleasure incidental to the nourishment. We are, naturally, not able to glean information from the mouth ego as to the nature of his sexual feelings, but Abraham infers the independent erotic significance of sucking from the prolonged thumb and hand sucking of children who seem to derive erotic pleasure out of it not necessarily in conjunction with food.[20] As for the mothers, the participant nature of their erotic pleasure incidental to nursing may be inferred from their statements that their children sucking at their breasts gave them a feeling of weakening of the sense of separateness between them and their infants.[21] It should be stressed that the mutual sexual excitation of mother and child operates by a positive feedback cycle through the arousal of the mother by the infant's sucking which is transmitted back by the mother to her nursing infant thus augmenting his sexual arousal *da capo*. This positive feedback cycle of incestuous arousal is, as we shall see later, severed and stopped by the mother with far reaching psychological and cultural effects.

Although the sexual arousal of the mouth ego is incidental to feeding it may be linked to it by conditioning and by association, so that the feeding itself gains a sexual meaning. This has been noted by Abraham who tried to explain some cases of compulsive eating and obesity as an expression of oral sexuality.[22] The oral-sexual significance of eating was masterfully portrayed in the feast scene from the film *Tom Jones*. It was evident in the Roman orgies as well as in the current practice of going out to dinner as an oral preliminary to lovemaking.

Abraham had the pioneering insight to note the overwhelming importance of oral sexuality.[23] This is even more noteworthy if we bear in mind that Abraham was a member of the inner circle of psycho-analysis presided over by an autocratic master who relatively neglected the theoretical potential of oral sexuality. The overwhelming impor-tance of oral sexuality is evident from the fact that the kiss in many cultures is the prime overt display of eroticism. This should be linked to some infantile phantasies of procreation, analyzed by Abraham, that women become pregnant by being kissed.[24]

Mytho-empirical evidence for the incestuous sexual arousal of the son by the mother is abundant. Uranus was the son of Gaia — Mother Earth. He then married her and fathered Kottos, Gyes and Briareus, the three violent and unspeakably insolent children;[25] Isis is the mother of her husband-brother Osiris and she also bears four sons fathered by her son Horus;[26] when Zeus lustfully threatened to violate his mother Rhea she turned into a serpent overtly intending to ward him off, however the sexually exciting symbol of the snake actually provoked Zeus into copulating with his mother.[27] This shows the Greeks to be masters of the mythological *double entente* where the overt behaviour of the *dramatis personae* is dialectically opposite to their covert meaning. In similar vein Hera, after suckling Heracles, sent two serpents to devour him.[28]

The following quotations of myths collected by Briffault depicts serpents, snakes, lizards and other phallic animals which assault women sexually and suck their breasts.

> In South Australia "the origin of the sexes", we are told, is ascribed to a small lizard, called by the men "ibirri" and by the women "waka". This probably means that the vulva of women is supposed to be opened by the bite of a lizard.

. . . Throughout Polynesia women and girls are supposed to be in danger of being violated by lizards and by eels. In Paumotu, women are careful to avoid sea-eels, and fishermen even make a point of covering them up with leaves if women are present. In Tonga a certain lizard-god was noted for his love of women; he dwelt in a pond, and women who bathed in it became "sick" or pregnant.

Among the Namaquas of southern Africa the serpent is believed to be "very fond of women's milk". A Namaqua "solemnly declared that he had known several instances where it had entered people's dwellings at night, and if it met with a sleeping mother has dexterously abstracted the milk".[29]

Such phallic images stand for sexual desire aroused by women but of special interest are the myths depicting snakes sucking at mothers' breasts. This is direct mytho-empirical evidence for the sexual desire aroused by the mother at early orality. A corroboration of this premise is mentioned by Abraham who notes that in some dialects the words for semen and milk are the same.[30]

Finally, we may point out that female bogies, the main attribute of which is their sexual insatiability, have been related mytho-empirically to the forbidden desire aroused by mothers.[31] By arousing the sexual desire of her child and then forbidding it, the mother raises to archetypal stature the sin, guilt and horror associated with her sex. This is the explanation of the fact that in most cultures an allusion to the mother's genitals is the standard, most widely used curse. Also, the widespread symbolism of the "vagina dentata", the toothed devouring vagina, represents the approach-avoidance horrors of a sexually inviting mother who then harshly forbids her child's sexual arousal and drastically curbs her own.

Good and Bad, Mother, Me and Sex

Melanie Klein, Ronald Fairbairn and to some extent Karl Abraham, have rightly imputed an overwhelming importance to oral eroticism in the structuring of character and personality. Yet their theories and descriptions relating to early and later orality, sucking and biting and "emptying" the breast-mother or being deprived by it, lack clarity and circumspection because they did not provide clear-cut criteria for distinguishing between early and later orality. This we did in *Salvation Through the Gutters*[32] and in the *Myth of Tantalus*[33] by positing the coagulation of the separate self as the dividing line between early and later orality. Before the separation everything happens within the pantheistic, omnipresent mouth ego. However, after the separate mouth ego gains its ego boundary the depriving breast-mother and surrounding objects are identified as such by the nascent ego and treated accordingly. The fixations at early orality may then be clearly related to a pantheistic unity of self, others and objects, whereas the fixations at later orality are anchored on a distinction between self, others and objects.

After the initial separation the dynamics of congruity can then operate by separant inclusion through which the mouth ego aims to "swallow" and incorporate the breast-mother and object; or by participant exclusion by which the mouth ego aims to effect and annihilate himself so that it melts back into the object and fuses with the breast-mother. These dynamics result in the formation of a personality core continuum by the deprivational interaction between mouth ego and breast-mother along the following lines. In figure 5 the mother axis has at one extreme the absent mother, the Genet type foundlings who grow up in institutions with very little care, where the surrogate mother is the fleeting image of the passing nurse. The other extreme is represented by the rejecting mother. This includes a wide range of maternal attitudes: from the openly rejecting mother to the frustrating mother who does not fulfil the infant's needs for nourishment and comfort and is consequently perceived by the child as hating and rejecting. The indifferent mother is the physically or mentally incapacitated mother, or the mother who is overburdened with children and work. She is physically present but emotionally tired and detached. Our mother axis represents, of course, a "skewed" and anomalous continuum of maternal attitudes, because a more or less normal maternal care does not predispose the infant to morbidity.

We shall now recapitulate here the basic structure of our model which we first expounded in chapter two. At one extreme of the child axis is the negative (bad me) ego boundary surrounded by the good object (mother). At the very early oral stage, described by Freud as primary narcissism, by Fairbairn as "mouth ego with a breast" and by us as omnipresent pantheism, the mouth feeds (empties) the breast and is temporarily content. However, disturbances in feeding and other related irritations generate the agony of want and pains of anxiety. Consequently, says Fairbairn, the infant infers that its feeding destroyed the nourishing and comforting breast. This to us is not tenable. At the very early oral stage the mouth entity is not capable of problem solving. Moreover, the me/object dichotomy does not yet exist at this pantheistic stage. Therefore any pain, anxiety and want that occur are in me and only in me because I am omnipresent, and there is nothing except the mouth-anchored me. A fixation at the early oral phase results in the registration of a painful wanting (bad) me where the nourishing (good) something is somewhere in the vague un-

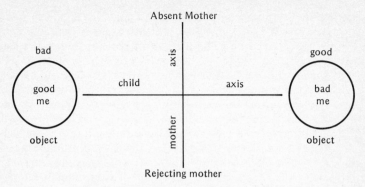

Figure 5 Dialectics Between Self and Mother

chartered outside of me which is, at this stage of awareness, outside of everything. What is present is a painful aching me, and the nourishing and soothing goodness that was previously me is absent out there, hovering out of reach. An early oral fixation is therefore a bad me surrounded by the good (nourishing) object.

At the other extreme of the child axis of our model is the good self surrounded by the bad object (mother). The later oral stage of development is characterized by a partial differentiation of the infant from the mother and the development of ambivalence towards her which is manifested by the biting of the breasts by the child in his moment of aggression. Here again we add our own observation on the nature of later oral fixations. The emerging separation of the self due to the deprivational interaction with mother creates an easily accessible source and a sequential explanation of the frustrations, deprivations and anxieties of the infant. The non-caring, non-feeding mother who is already separate from the suffering (good) me is all-apparent and very often in front of the child's mouth. This location of responsibility is accentuated by the vengeful bite.[34]

The immediate implication of our model to the earlier oralist premises is that unlike Karl Abraham,[35] Klein,[36] and Fairbairn,[37] we hold that the mouth ego's aggression towards the breast-mother and objects occurs only at later orality when both the breast-mother and surrounding objects have been existentially separated from the mouth ego. Also, the aggressive or possessive attitude towards the breast-mother characterizes the later orally fixated separant mouth ego. On the other hand, the early oral fixated participant mouth ego is not aggressively oriented towards the breast-mother but wishes to efface himself and rejoin her in an early-oral communion. Some mytho-empirical anchors for this premise are Jason who displays the typical fear in Greek mythology of mature women. In his special case he is frightened by Hecate who is depicted as surrounded by snakes and underworld hounds.[38] Hecate, the menacing woman, has long been out of the mother-child unison of early orality. She is the depriving mother of later orality with the threatening conflictual hounds and the sexually menacing snakes. Another characteristic later orally fixated conflict with a depriving (step-surrogate) mother is the case of Hippolytus who rejected the forbidden love of Phaedra who avenged herself by slandering him to her husband Theseus who plotted to kill him. This again is a sexually forbidden interaction with a depriving mother who has overtly shown her enticement and subsequent hostility towards her son. Hence it is a depiction of a later orally fixated, post-differentiated conflictual relationship between mother and son.

A mytho-empirical description of early orality may be interpreted from the image of the pre-differentiated Edenic Adam who is endowed with omnipresence and omnipotence in his early-oral paradisal pantheism.[39] The main characteristic of the early oral self once he feels the enticement and proscriptions of the breast-mother, is of a shameful guilt-laden "bad me" because he is not as yet differentiated from his breast-mother and whatever happens occurs within his omnipresent self. We therefore have no need for the oralist dynamics of incorporation and introjection of the breast-mother and objects, because at omnipresent early orality everything is part of the mouth ego. At later orality, however, the breast-mother and objects are cognitively separate from the self, yet the self ever longs to reunite with them. If ego is early orally fixated he would long to efface himself in a participant manner and be incorporated in the object. A later orally fixated ego would aim to swallow and incorporate the object by separant inclusion. As both the "melting back" into the object and its physical incorporation are impossible, the personality core dynamics are a dialectical interplay between surrogate separant mechanism of inclusion and sublimatory participant process of exclusion. Early oral traumas are perceived by the nascent self as happening within its omnipresence. The ontological deprivational interaction with the breast-mother is registered by it as inherent badness and as evidence of a "bad me". Also, the sexual enticement transmitted over to the mouth ego by the breast-mother together with its concomitant proscription are again felt by the mouth ego as emanating from its omnipresent self and hence as the source of shame and guilt. On the other hand, the later orally fixated separate self can and does impute its frustrations and forbidden sexual enticement to a distinctly identifiable "bad" and prurient breast-mother. These dialectics between an early orally fixated "bad me" surrounded by a "good" breast-mother and a later orally fixated "good me" oppressed, tormented and bullied by a "bad" and obscene mother, provides a scaffolding for a personality type continuum and a basis for ethical judgement, of the polarities of pure love and profane dirty sex.

Our model rejects the oralists' basic notion of the internalization or the incorporation of the mother especially as formulated as follows by Melanie Klein:

> Along with the child's relation, first to his mother and soon to his father and other people, go those processes of internalisation on which I have laid so much stress in my work. The baby, having incorporated his parents, feels them to be live people inside his body in the concrete way in which deep unconscious phantasies are experienced — they are, in his mind, "internal" or "inner" objects, as I have termed them. Thus an inner world is being built up in the child's unconscious mind, corresponding to his actual experiences and the impressions he gains from people and the external world, and yet altered by his own phantasies and impulses. If it is a world of people predominantly at peace with each other and with ego, inner harmony, security and integration ensue.[40]

First, the idyllic and harmonious image of the child's unconscious painted by Klein is unwarranted by any shred of evidence or theoretical schemes outside or inside of psychoanalysis. Second, Klein and the other oralists do not explain how and why a parent should be internalized psychically by the child. At most their expositions may account for the identification and complementarity between parent and child, but not for the introjection of the parent by the child.

Our model utilizes the bio-psycho-developmental fact of the infant's feelings of non-differentiated omnipresence at early orality to postulate an initial internalization of the breast-mother. This internalization is later severed and ejected from the circumspect shrinking world of the ego boundaried later oral self. Second, a fixation on early orality with the inherent badness of a depriving mother or a sexually enticing and erotically stifling one, concomitantly introduces a host of petrifying Medusas and snake-coiffured gorgons into the child's troubled psyche because at orality everything happens within the child's undifferentiated self. Third, the alternation between good/bad me and good/bad breast-mother-object cannot be readily explained by the fluctuations in the internalization of parents or the emptying of the breast-mother by the mouth ego.[41] More than these fleeting alternations are needed to crystallize for life an image of a "good/pure" or a "bad/promiscuous" mother. We provide a durable developmental basis for the continua of positive and negative image of self and breast-mother and others, by the transition from a fixation on early to later orality with a lifelong imprint on self-image and the image of parents, other people and objects.

The mytho-empirical evidence for these transitions from the "good" to the "bad" mother abound in profusion. A representative instance can be found in the Egyptian *Book of the Dead*,[42] but the example we cite here is from Greek mythology. The good mother Demeter exists in early oral unison with her nameless ἄρρητος κούρη daughter Kore, meaning that at early orality the daughter is not yet named (i.e., a separate distinguishable entity).[43] The Homeric Black Demeter is described by Kerenyi as follows: The Odyssey furnishes proof that the deadly powers associated with the Homeric Underworld may be regarded as allusions to this Goddess (the historical Demeter Erinys). One such power, the power to terrify, to petrify with fright, to turn to stone, is possessed by the Gorgon's head. Odysseus is thinking of this when he sees the countless host of the dead approaching him: perhaps Persephone has sent the Gorgon's head from Hades! The mass of shades and the frightful apparition are respectively the indefinite and the definite manifestations of the realm of the dead. Though this realm is the domain of Persephone and her husband, the definite form of it points to the original Demeter.

Gorgon-like features are in fact displayed by the Black Demeter, who had a legend in common with Demeter Erinys. The horse-headed goddess was further characterized by having "snakes and other animals growing out of her head". The gorgon's head in conjunction with a horse's body can be seen in an archaic representation of the killing of Medusa.[44]

The later oral characteristics of the terrifying "bad" mother is indicated by Demeter with a head full of snakes. The good/bad Demeter is of special importance here because the child Kore-Persephone is feminine. The early/latter orality transformation of the mother is thus supported mytho-empirically for both male and female children. The differentiation of gender self-concept is also influenced, as we shall see later, by the transition from early to later orality. This transition provides a crucial developmental phase the dynamics of which change, *mutatis mutantis*, with the gender of the child.

Figure 6 presents our initial model as to the sexual dialectics between the mouth ego and breast-mother, and the resultant behaviour patterns as related to early and later oral fixations. We have already presented and described earlier the child's axis of our model. The mother axis is a continuum ranging from the extreme sexually enticing mother to the extreme sexually suppressing mother. The deviant sexual patterns are close to the extremities of the poles whereas the middle-range normal sexual patterns are the dialectical synthesis between the

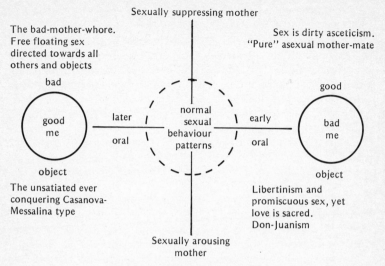

Figure 6 Sexual Behaviour Patterns

more or less equilibriated interaction between the incestuous sexual enticement by the mother and its concomitant suppression. As we are dealing with the extreme (outside the normal range of cases), these deviant sexual patterns would be traumatically fixated at either early or later orality. The ascetic "sex is dirty/sinful" type is early orally fixated by a sex suppressing mother. The resultant participant Tantalic type would result in a "sexually sinful/bad me" combination. The self-effacing participation would be coupled by sexual puritanism and the quest for a pure, sacred love in the image of the asexual, good object/ mother-mate of early orality. Don Juanism is the predisposition of an early fixation by a sexually enticing (arousing) mother. The "bad me" is lured to indulge in bad, (i.e., promiscuous) sex, yet the Tantalic fixation is on a "pure" good-mother object. Hence a Don Juan will jump from one bed to another seeking an eternal "great" love which seems, in a truly Tantalic manner, to be in the next bed but never in the present one.

The later oral fixation by a sexually arousing mother creates the Casanova-Messalina predispositions. The promiscuously oversexed "bad" object-mother has to be overpowered and conquered by the separant self. Yet the Sisyphean Casanova or Messalina have ever to add more sexual conquests to their record. Once a sexual object has been gained another one has to be sought and possessed by the sexually insatiable self. Finally, the later oral fixation by a sexually suppressing mother creates the sexual perversions. The bad-mother-whore and the "bad" sexual expression are denied by the same mother with whom the later oral "good" self is in conflict. The child therefore rejects the mother and with her the accepted modes of sexual outlets. Because the "good" self radiates free floating and un-focused sex all around him in defiance of the proscriptions of the "bad" mother, the sexual desire is predisposed to be cathected to any male, female, beast or inanimate object, the actual selection being made later by socialization and situational factors.

Complementarity, Identity and Sexual Differentiation

The attitude of the parents and especially the behaviour of the mother at early orality is crucial for the formation of gender identity.[45] The empathic relation between mother and child is so strong that many times the mother can predict if and when the child is about to behave in a certain manner (e.g., throw up his food, burst into activity, cry, laugh etc.).[46] This creates a symbiotic cycle of dependencies, identities and complementarities between mother and child. As for the gender identity formation, the normal process at the oral phase of development is the female's identity with the mother like the Demeter-Kore mytho-empirical dyad, and the male's complementarity with his mother in an Isis-Horus manner. (Isis is the mother of her husband-brother Osiris; she also bears four sons fathered by her son Horus.) At the later socionormative phases of development when the father becomes fully conspicuous as a socializing figure the son identifies with his father as a willing victim in the sacrificial rites of passage to the socionormative burdens. These are the identification processes inherent in the social separation phase and projected mytho-empirically by the Abraham-Isaac dyad. The complementarity relationships in the socionormative sacrifice of an Iphigenia and the social separation of a Kore brought about by the connivance of her father Zeus, are instances of the complementarity relationships between father and daughter. Both the identification dynamics of the Isaac Syndrome and the complementarity of father and daughter are dealt with in chapter nine in conjunction with a discussion of the sexual-dynamics of the social phase of separation.

The identification and complementarity dynamics are presented in figure 7. The oral phase of development with its temporal primacy and the dialectics of incestuous arousal and suppression is, of course, more crucial in the crystallization of gender self-concept. Consequently, the image of the father as vicariously presented to the child by the mother

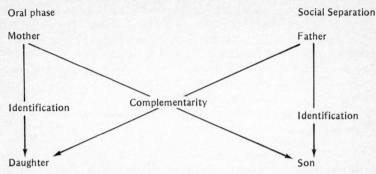

Figure 7 Identity and Complementarity of Parents and Offspring

plays a more important role in the genesis of gender self-concept than the actual father. However, the complementarity and identity with the father at the later social separation is bound to conflict with the initial processes of identification and complementarity with the mother at the child's oral phase of development. Not only is the gender identity bound to undergo some changes at the social phase of separation and at puberty, but also the attraction to and choice of mate is not determined by the simplistic rule of a girl seeking a mate who resembles her father and a boy looking for a wife "like mother". The positive correlation between identification with mother and feminine gender identity may be inferred from the following review of the literature by Fisher: "A large majority of the studies have found that a girl's degree of femininity is positively related to the perception of her mother as warm, nurturant or protective."[47] The mother could not have been perceived as warm and protective without the daughter identifying with her. A mytho-empirical instance of a complementarity between mother and son is between Gaia and Cronos. The Oedipal wish of Cronos to castrate his father Uranus is projected by him on his mother, whereas the incestuous enticement of Cronos by Gaia may be inferred by the collusion of mother and son against father.[48]

The interrelationship between identification and complementarity in the genesis of gender self-concept has not yet been properly documented and studied. According to John Money this is one of the reasons why gender dimorphism is still not properly understood. We hypothesize that the mother encourages the girl to identify with her from the very outset, yet later many conflicts may ensue because of the girl's strong complementary links with her father. Similarly, a mother may encourage strong complementarity with her son, but when the time comes for him to identify with a male figure many problems may occur. One of the most prevalent problems is the relative absence of the male identification model in modern western societies. This leads to what has been denoted by Parsons and Cohen as the Masculine Protest and has been formulated by us elsewhere as follows:

> The female-centered socialization of families would tend to provide ready-made role-models in the family, for girls only. The male in the family, the father, being either physically or emotionally absent, the mother becomes the emotionally significant adult for children of both sexes. As soon as a boy gets to the developmental stage when he needs role-models of his own sex for identification, he must reach out of the family unit into the environment and the mass-communication media for available sources of models. Such models would tend to be either exaggerated, perverted or unrealistic. Moreover, a boy in his latency period or in pre-adolescence, being intolerant of ambiguity or in a state of ego diffusion would tend to adopt models diametrically opposite to those in his feminised socialisation patterns. The *maleness* sought in these models would signify "badness" and aggressivity as opposed to the "kind" and "soft" characteristics inherent in the role-models of his mother, maid, nursery-school teacher and school teacher. With his predisposition for aggressive male role-models, due to his "Masculine Protest", the upper and middle class boy, in his search for such models outside the family unit would tend to associate with peer-groups and age-mates engaged in delinquent, non-conformist, bizarre or rebellious behaviour.[49]

We hypothesize further that the suppression of incestuous sex is more effective at early orality through identification than complementarity. The mother sexually arouses her son much more than she arouses her daughter; the mother's heterosexual excitement while being sucked by a boy would presumably be more intense than the mother's sexual phantasies while being sucked by a girl. Hence the more direct transmission of sexual proscriptions by the mother to her daughter are more effectively internalized by the daughter. The boy has his sexual prohibitions reinforced later by the father with whom he identifies at the phase of social separation. This coincides with the rites of passage phase and the surrogate sacrificial Isaac Syndrome of normative strictness. Thus the incestuous proscriptions towards the mother are sublimated through the identification with the father into absolute normative mandates. The mother, however, is still the symbol of normative forgiveness and, as we shall elaborate later, the image of socially participant grace.

It is important to note that at the oral phase of development and especially at early orality the father is present within the mother-child dyad through the vicarious representation by the mother. Melanie Klein has noted this dynamic in her own model as follows: "The bad qualities

of the breast and his oral-sadistic impulses towards it were largely transferred to his father's penis. In addition, he experienced strong oral-
sadistic impulses towards his father's penis, derived from jealousy and
hatred in the early positive Oedipus situation. His father's genital therefore turned in his phantasy into a dangerous, biting and poisonous
object."[50] In our model we envisage this dynamic differently: at early
orality the "bad me" erotically aroused by the mother is subsequently
exposed to the incest-suppressing (forbidding) messages from the
mother of "bad" sex-phallus images which originate experientially from
her intercourse with her husband and father of her children. These
images are then conceived by the child as the forbidden "bad" father-
phallus. This is forcefully portrayed mytho-empirically by Gaia who
transmitted to her "crooked" (i.e., the early oral "bad me") son Cronos
the evil nature of Uranus, her husband and father of Cronos. This evil
nature was transmitted to Uranus' genitals which were cut-off by
Cronos, by the mandate of his mother, as a symbolic suppression of his
own incestuous desires.[51] The Hesiodic myth is especially pertinent
in this context because at early orality the "badness" of the child's
incestuous arousal, as symbolized by the father's "evil" genitals, is projected by the mother and transmitted over to the child as indeed recounted by the myth of the castration of Uranus by the collusion of
Gaia and her son Cronos. The castration of the father is actually the
symbolic ejection of the (forbidden) father's penis from the mother-
son dyad in which it was initially introduced by the vicarious phallic
imagery of the mother.

The suppression of the father's sexuality as represented by the
phallic images transmitted within the mother-daughter dyad also
operate on a basis of identification. As a result the incestuous proscriptions are directed towards all the males present in the immediate
vicinity of the girl. These males naturally belong to the nuclear family.
Other rules of extended forbidden mating outside the nuclear family
are learned by socialization and are as basic as those relating to the
nuclear family which were ingrained at the oral phase of development.
The males of the family present at this oral stage are included in the
basic proscriptions of incest. But at the later stages of development
when the maturing girl is exposed to other males who were not previously present, and hence not forbidden by the post oral proscription
of incest, she would be sexually attracted by them. In like manner the
complementary relationships of the mother and son will effect a proscription of an incestuous desire towards all females present physically
or symbolically within the family at the oral and post oral phases of
development. But when the boy matures and is exposed to other
females outside his family the oral and post oral proscription does not

apply to them and they become legitimate objects of his sexual desire.

The close mother-child relationship at orality, the culturally ordained different attitudes of parents towards their neonate boys and girls, and the mother's encouraging of her daughter to identify with her and her son to complement her, make for effective dynamics of gender self-concept formation at the oral phase of the infant's development. It has also been noted that mothers display a softer, more feminine attitude towards daughters whereas from about seven weeks after birth mothers display a harsher and more masculine attitude towards boys, expecting them to be more independent.[52] The chances are therefore greater that the boy would be traumatized and hence fixated at early orality. The girl, on the other hand, would be more likely to be traumatized by the contrast between the soft feminine attitude of the mother and her identification with her at early orality, and the harsh weaning processes of later orality. Also, the girl at post orality would be likedly to be exposed to the complementary conflicts with her father whereas the boy at post orality would be attuned to the less conflictual identification with his father. The harsher and stricter suppression of the boy's sexual arousal by the mother at early orality makes for a greater likelihood of the boy's early oral traumatization.

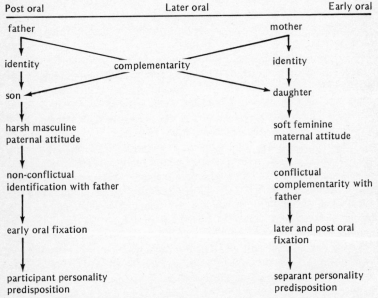

Figure 8 Parent/Offspring Relationship and Gender Identity

Because of this the girl is more likely to be later orally fixated and hence predisposed towards a separant personality core; whereas the boy fixated at early orality is more likely to be of a participant predisposition. The implications of this initial dimorphism are wide and far reaching both for personality development and for the attitudes and behaviour related to gender identity. This development dynamic as related to sexual dimorphism and the personality core is set out in figure 8. Finally, we note that we did not find any psycho-biological or mytho-empirical evidence for the so-called penis envy which Freud and some of his disciples stressed as the main source of the woman's sexual identity. Nor did we find any need for this alleged dynamic for the explanation of the dimorphism of gender identity.

The Slaying of the Incestuous Dragons

The proscription of incest impregnated by the mother into her children at their oral phase of development manifests itself with the boy as a fear of castration and with the girl as fear of penetration. The enormity of this proscription which is demonstrated mytho-empirically in the original sin is also manifest in its being contrary to the biological primary functions of the male and female genitalia. The quest of the male's penis to penetrate and be absorbed is a participant quest, while the female's vagina is structured to separantly absorb. The primary identification of daughter with mother makes for a more effective internalization of the fear of penetration. This, together with the biological barrier of the hymen, made virginity in many cultures the most prized asset of a girl to be bartered at puberty with the biological fulfillment of raising children, the social status of marriage, the security of a family and the protection of a husband. The fear of castration of the boy is more complicated because it is ingrained not by identification with the mother but through the vicarious and more elaborate complementarity with her. This fear is strong enough to curb incestuous desires throughout a man's life and to generate lifelong feelings of guilt and shame for having had them. Moreover, this proscription of incest has sexualized the life of Homo sapiens. Unlike all other fauna and flora the human being is sexually sensitized and impassioned throughout life. We shall try to show later that this proscription of incest at the oral phase of human development is largely responsible for sex being the main anchor for man's participant quests, for the formation of the family and its sublimation into creativity, revelation and hence into culture.

The foremost mytho-empirical anchor to our contention as to the harsh proscription by the mother of the incestuous feelings of her son is the Hesiodic myth of the castration of Uranus. Of special importance is that the wicked image of Uranus and his "shameful" behaviour is conveyed to Cronos by his mother Gaia, who says "We shall repay your father's wicked crime. For it was he who first began devising shameful acts".[53] This is the image of the father's "bad" phallus formed at early orality by the sexual arousal of sucking at the mother's breast. The vile incestuous phallus is radically suppressed by its castration. The crucial point here is that the act of emasculation is carried out by the son through the urging of the mother. This means in our context that the son, by his suppression of his incestuous desire towards his mother, deracinates the father's phallus from the mother-son dyad at early orality. The Hesiodic myth also depicts the emasculation as occurring during Uranus' intercourse with Gaia. This is also in line with our model that the mother envisages her husband's phallus through her arousal by her son at early orality analogous to the arousal by her husband in actual intercourse. The suppression of the son's incestuous arousal of his mother thus involves the symbolic removal of the father's penis from the mother-son relationship. This thereby makes the relationship proper and normatively acceptable. Our interpretation of such castration is that it is the maternal based legitimization of procreation and culture. Only when the incestuous desires of sons towards their mothers are drastically curbed (castrated) can the libidinal energy be re-channelled towards normatively sanctioned procreation and culturally approved creativity.

The slaying of snakes or dragons as a mytho-empirical symbol of the suppression of the incestuous desires towards the mother and the asexualization of the sexually enticing mother are so widespread that it is sufficient to mention just one representative instance. Serpents sent by Hera to kill Heracles were strangled by him. Although Hera was not the biological mother of Heracles, she nursed him at her breast.[54] This makes Hera the surrogate mother of Heracles and as far as early orality is concerned it fits our model of the mother or its surrogate and child dyad. The sending of the snakes to kill Heracles are the obvious phallic-symbols of the incestuous and hence fatal desire aroused by Hera; the killing of the snakes by Heracles stand for the suppression of this incestuous desire. This and other mytho-empirical sources (some apocryphal Christian sources tell of the infant Jesus leaving his mother's breast and subduing a cavefull of dragons) point at the suppression of the incestuous desires not only as a means of legitimizing the mother-child dyad but also as a condition precedent for the normative acceptance sanctioned by transcendence and social approval of both mother and child.

Erich Neumann mentions some neolithic fertility rites and later myths in which mothers or their surrogates arouse the sexual desire of their sons and then castrate them.[55] Neumann, however, failed to realize the mytho-empirical significance of these rites as the purging of the mother-son dyad of forbidden incestuous sex so that the libido of the child can be redirected towards approved objects. The deep primary importance of the suppression of the early oral incestuous desires of children towards their mothers as a condition precedent for their normative legitimization within the family and outside it may be inferred from the universality of curses, defamation and swearing which derogate the mother's genitalia.

An interim summary of our present premise points to the socio-normative importance of the suppression of incest within the oral mother-child dyad not only for the regulation of familial relationships, but also for the creation of a basis for socialization and acculturation.

The implication of this conclusion is so vast and relates to so many frames of references and areas of knowledge that it transcends the limits of the present work. We shall, however, point out some attributes of these implications which have an overview relevance to our present context. The Freudian conception of the formation of the human family and for that matter the sustenance of human culture as masterfully expounded in *Totem and Taboo* and Freud's other writings, is related to the suppression of the incestuous attraction towards the mother and the normative resolution of the Oedipal conflict with the father.[56] This primal renunciation by the son of his instinctual drives and their sublimation into normatively accepted channels is ordained and carried out under the terms set out by the father and his abstraction (i.e., the law and the normative system). A wild and at this stage rather vague conjecture as to how this male chauvinist Freudian system would be affected by our model, which posits the mother and not the father as the main suppressor of incest at the oral stage of human development, is that the mother is the prime initiator of human culture. It would be presumptuous to develop this theme more extensively in the present context. However, an intriguing mytho-empirical exposition in the direction of this focal concern has been attempted by Robert Graves in his *White Goddess* where he traces the early myths of the Hebrews, Greeks and Celts to the primary mother-son dyad.[57] Graves reviews some manifestations of the dominant mother-goddesses and reveals links between the suppression of sexual desire towards the great mother-goddesses and their realms of dominion. For example, Demeter the goddess of fertility and Danae the goddess of agriculture support our conjecture regarding the mother as the prime initiator of human culture. The arousal of incestuous desires and their suppression being related to fertility and agriculture were the central concerns of the ancient Greek culture.

Another classic attempt to trace the matriarchal origins of culture was carried out by Bachofen. The following quotation demonstrates to what extent one may attribute to woman the creation of culture:

> The elevation of the human race and the progress of ethics are closely linked up with the rule of woman. In like manner the introduction of regularity and the cultivation of the religious sense. The enjoyment of every higher pleasure must be closely associated with the matriarchy. The longing for a purification of life arises earlier in woman than in man, and she also possesses to a higher degree the natural faculty of effecting it. The entire ethic code that follows upon barbarism is the work of woman. Her contribution to society is not only the power to give life, but also the ability to bestow all that which makes life beautiful. Hers is the earliest knowledge of the forces of nature, hers is also the presentiment and the hope that conquers the pain of death. Viewed from this angle, the gynaeco-cracy appears as a testimony to the progress of civilization. It is the source and guarantee of its benefits, as well as a necessary educational period in the history of man. It is therefore in itself the realization of natural law whose patterns must be observed by entire races as well as by individual beings.[58]

It should be stressed that our model is meant to be universal, it applies to both matriarchal and patriarchal societies. Our exposition relates to the initial sublimation of the blocked incestuous desire towards the mother at early orality and its rechannelling into culturally approved creativity. The patrilineal and matrilineal taxonomy of societies in the anthropological sense relates more to the source and promulgation of normative authority. In our model this converges with the social separation phase of human development in which the father presides over the normative rites of passage and the social indoctrination and placement within the group. The doctrinaire normativeness of the father inherent in his suppressing and sacrificing role, which we have expounded in the Isaac Syndrome,[59] is still a male role in matrilineal societies and is performed by the maternal uncle. This has been noted by Ernst Jones and conceded by Malinowsky as a "decomposition of the primal father (in matrilineal societies) into a kind and lenient actual father on the one hand a stern and moral uncle on the other".[60]

The most solid mytho-empirical support for our model is provided by the myth of the original sin itself. The snake, the phallic symbol of incestuous desire, is to be ever suppressed by divine commandment. God decrees to the serpent that He "will put enmity between you and the woman, between your brood and hers. They shall strike at your head, and you shall strike at their heel."[61] Of special interest here is that the scriptures mention only the mother-child dyad in relation to the suppression of incestuous sexual desire. At the oral phase of human development the scene is exclusively dominated by the mother-child dyad, the father being absent from the *dramatis personae* at this time. The primal mother is instructed by the myth of Genesis that after the suppression of her own incestuous arousal she should direct her desire to her husband within the normatively institutionalized boundaries of the family.[62] The directives of Genesis which are most salient to our present context are decreed to the primaeval son as follows: "With labour you shall win your food from it all the days of your life. It will grow thorns and thistles for you, none but wild plants for you to eat. You shall gain your bread by the sweat of your brow."[63] The meaning of this is that after the suppression of the incestuous involvement with the primal mother at orality the libidinal potential is directed towards the strenuous manipulation of the environment by the primal son and his conflictual Sisyphean grappling with the object to create agriculture which was apparently the most striking cultural innovation in the times of the chronicles of Genesis. We may even hypothesize, without trying to substantiate the hypothesis at this stage, that the transition from the Edenic gatherers and hunters' societies to the agricultural toilers of the land societies was related to the crystallization of the human family by, among other things, the suppression of the incestuous desires within the mother-child dyad at orality. This provides a socio-anthropological dimension to the original sin myth and its application to the genesis of culture in addition to its mytho-empirical significance for the formation of the personality core and the dimorphic gender self-concept.

In conclusion we may note that our programmer, be it chance, God, the Devil or whatever, has chosen sex or rather its suppression as a means for the genesis of culture because of its infinitely wider malleability than the other basic drives. If one is deprived of food one dies but the deprivation or blockage of some sexual manifestations create culture. This, of course, has been expounded by Freud. Our innovation is that human culture has been initiated by the proscriptions of incest by the mother. This makes the mother-woman the prime mover of human culture. She is the one who inplants in her children the first seeds of the achievement motive.

We have noted earlier that women tend to be more later orally fixated and hence more separant. This again is developmentally appropriate: in the first year of its life the main problems of the infant relate to its need to learn to adjust to his objective environment and to reach a *modus vivendi* with it. The early separant directives of the mother and her instructions for acculturation are geared to the infant's needs. Later on, at the social phase of normative placement, the father introduces his more abstract and more normatively participant acculturation mandates. The mother deals with the small matters of culture such as the way the children should be fed, dressed and sheltered; whereas the nature of God, the essence of morality and whether man is endowed with free will or is spurred by strict determinism, are left to the husband to decide.

7
Inclusion, Exclusion, Sacred, and Profane Love

The burden of sexual performance is on the man,
the burden of trying to guess when she's interested,
what she wants, how she wants it, and so on.
What we have established is that the male
will have to give up his position as sex expert
and the one with the greater sexual facility —
which he doesn't have.

W. Masters and W. Johnson: *Homosexuality in Perspective*

The Separant and Participant Bases of Gender Dimorphism

In the previous chapter we mentioned that the male tends to be more participant biologically because he is programmed to enter the female and cause his genetic heritage to be absorbed by the female ovum, which biologically "swallows" the sperm in a separant manner. We also pointed out the greater likelihood of the boy being early orally fixated and for this reason more participant than the girl, who is more likely to be later orally fixated and therefore more separant in her personality core structure. However, we are dealing here with probabilities and continua so that the biological participant predisposition might be changed in form and intensity or even set off entirely by a later oral fixation and a separant Sisyphean cultural imprint. For instance, the separant predisposition of a girl may be changed by a participant early oral fixation and a Tantalic, that is participant cultural imprint.[1]

Some biological facts and processes linked to gender dimorphism are related to the predisposing base line of separation and participation. First of all males of most animals take the initiative in courting and the whole process of sexual reproduction entails the movement of the sperm towards the relatively stationary ovum which absorbs it.[2] The sperm's goal to be absorbed by the ovum is biologically participant whereas the ovum's quest to absorb and "swallow" the sperm is biologically separant. Erikson has stated this premise figuratively as follows: "Sex differences . . . seem to parallel the morphology of genital differentiation itself; in the male, an external organ, erectible and intrusive in character, serving the channelization of mobile sperm cells; internal organs in the female with vestibular access, leading to statically expectant ova."[3]

Cultural studies of dreams of tribal societies as well as some projective investigations and semantic differential analyses of groups in occidental societies have revealed that the self concepts of males and females are related to the functional attributes of their genitalia. Males saw themselves as moving and penetrating spaces, which in our context would mean that they projected their participant aim of entering and being enclosed or absorbed;[4] whereas females saw themselves as stationary and open to absorb very much in line with the separant "swallowing" nature of the vagina and ovum.[5] The basic separant nature of women has also emerged from studies summarized by Fisher according to which they tend to feel that they are "left by love objects who go off 'there' and leave her 'here'. The love object has motility and leaves but she has to stay where she is and therefore finds herself alone."[6] The separant elements here are that the women saw themselves as stationary in relation to the moving objects and that their anxiety was centred on objects leaving them, contrary to their Sisyphean aim to incorporate and control the unruly objects.

Findings by Fisher and others show that girls and women seem to be less anxious of their bodies than boys and men.[7] This not only disclaims any support for the "penis envy" which Freud and some of his disciples imputed to women, but also sustains our contention that woman has a clearer and stronger body image than man because of her later oral separant fixation. The finding that women experience their bodies as more clearly differentiated and their body boundaries as more definite and secure than men,[8] makes for a more realistic and more pragmatic conception by the woman of objects, people, flora and fauna, than the early oral fixated more participant man. Women were also found to have significant positive correlations between the feelings of the definiteness or substantiality of body boundaries and the strength of body awareness.[9] While Fisher gives some plausible explanations for his findings, our model provides the core basis for these observations.

We have explained elsewhere that a strong ego boundary is related to a later oral fixation whereas an amorphic and weak ego boundary is linked to an early oral fixation.[10] We have also related an early oral fixation to the more Tantalic participant type whereas the later oral fixation is more characteristic of the participant Sisyphean object manipulator.[11] The greater likelihood of boys being early orally fixated has been explained by us in a previous chapter of this work as related to the harsher more manly treatment and expectations of the mother from her infant son. The male child is therefore more likely to be traumatized at early orality. The mother will identify more with her infant daughter and hence will allow her more attachment and proximity with a lesser likelihood of a fixation at early orality. The likelihood of a later oral fixation of the infant daughter is greater because the transition from the close identification with the mother to the harsh disengagement of weaning is more traumatizing. These facts link the basic biological pre-disposition towards separation and participation to the developmental fixations at early and later orality. Simply put the more separant woman is more aware of her body than man. Fisher describes the body orientation of women as follows:

> From an early age the girl is encouraged to decorate herself, to experiment with different kinds of clothing, and to be aware of the impression her body is making upon others. Also, she is continually challenged to learn to adapt to the cyclic changes in her body pro-duced by menstruation. But even further, as she matures she receives the implicit or explicit message that her principal life role will revolve about having a body sufficiently attractive to interest a man in marrying her and ultimately to fulfill a child-bearing role with her body.[12]

It is our contention that woman's body orientation is not initiated by the female-role socialization but begins with the bio-psychological core dynamics which predispose a girl to be more separantly anchored on her ego boundary, and hence both on her body and on the object. She is programmed by these core dynamics to be more aware and recep-tive to the female bodily roles to bait the male to love her, marry her, impregnate her and provide her and her children with subsistence, pro-tection, social status and security.

The mytho-empirical anchor for the biological separant predisposi-tion of the woman is provided first of all by the female vessel symbolism mentioned earlier. In many cultures female goddesses are depicted as vessels and urns. Such depiction represents the containment and bearing of offspring.[13] This vessel symbolism and the separant "swallowing" nature of woman is also present in the mytho-empirical portrayal of the "bad" mother-woman. Neumann states that:

> Hell and the underworld as vessels of death are forms of the negative death-bringing belly vessel, corresponding exactly to its life-bringing side. The opening of the vessel of doom is the womb, the gate, the gullet, which actively swallows, devours, rends and kills. Its sucking power is mythologically symbolized by its lure and attraction for man, for life and consciousness and the individual male, who can evade it only if he is a hero, and even then not always.[14]

In similar vein the earth and fertility goddesses in many cultures and mythologies stress their separant nature by being fecundated and then containing and absorbing the participant male impregnation in order to sprout forth with fertility and growth.[15] In the imagery of the early Kabbala *Malchut* the archetypal mother is described as receiving and absorbing the flow of abundance from *Yessod,* the male element in the Kabbalist "spheres".[16]

The second biological premise which contributes to greater object manipulating separatism of the female of the species are her pregnancies, childbirth and the immediate need to control, arrange and organize her and her offspring's proximate environment to ensure shelter, protection and nourishment to her neonates. This basic biological difference between woman and man, which has the widest psychological and social implications, forfeits any claim for the equality between the social roles of the sexes by whomever it is made — be it feminists, communists, or the Israeli kibbutz movement. The following is an apt reaction of a Czech woman parachutist when asked about the equality of sex roles in her country. "Our parachutes are the same as theirs, we jump from the same planes, we've got guts, and our performance isn't much different from the men's, but that's where emancipation ends. I'm married, I'm employed, and I have a daughter. And a granny. If I couldn't say: 'Granny keep an eye on her', my sporting career would be at an end."[17] A cross cultural survey of sex roles in the United States, China and in the Soviet Union revealed that most of the housework and child care is still mainly in the domain of the feminine role. The males do not as a rule participate in the rearing of children and in the routine domestic chores. They are also not expected to do so by the prevailing normative system.[18] In the Israeli kibbutzim the trend is to return to the practice of full-time care of children by the mother within the nuclear family and to narrow the scope of the communal child care. The main reason for this is that "kibbutz women aren't interested in equality, they are interested in children".[19] This should be evaluated by the fact that equality was and is the basic tenet of the kibbutz movements' ideology.

The childbearing function of the female is also related to the cyclicality of some of her hormonal secretions with whatever bio-psychological effects this might have on her behaviour. The interim summary of our present premise points to the initially more marked bio-psychological separant potential of the female. She is more attuned to the pragmatic manipulation of her objective environment linked to her childbearing and rearing functions. The male, on the other hand, is more biologically participant. He seeks to enter, be ungulfed and to be absorbed. Psychologically the male would also be more Tantalic, that is more anchored on abstractions of totality, the non-corporeality of ideas and the transcendence of non-being. We also have John Money's assertion that testosterone and other androgenes enhance the abstract thinking of males.[20] Thus, while woman is programmed to manipulate her sex to achieve the goals of childbearing, rearing and family formation, the male is predisposed to be lured by these baits of sex and love to achieve the aims of such programming. The dynamics of sex are the ideal means to our programmings' ends because they may be sublimated into almost any bio-psychological dynamic and social role linked to our core vectors. This makes for an effective control of the sublimated bio-psycho-social processes by the underlying sexual dynamics, and the adjustment of these sublimations to an indefinite number of contexts and situations in which man and woman may find themselves. This extreme multiformity of sex enables man and woman to structure a common denominator, form-wise, between their mutual expectations. In this way they may create a common enclosure for their relationships although the contents of their expectations may be light years apart.

The bio-psychological predisposition to gender identity is reinforced and finalized by socialization and especially by the interaction of the children with their parents. This has been aptly phrased by Diamond as follows:

> Sexual behaviour of an individual, and thus gender role, are not neutral and without initial direction at birth. Nevertheless, sexual predisposition is only a potentiality setting limits to a pattern that is greatly modifiable by ontogenetic experiences. Life experiences most likely act to differentiate and direct a flexible sexual disposition and to mold the prenatal organization until an environmentally, socially and culturally acceptable gender role is formulated and established.[21]

The parents wait for nine months to ascertain the sex of the child and right after the moment of birth, with the announcement "It's a boy, it's a girl" (as vividly described by Money),[22] a whole chain of sexually dimorphic reactions is set into motion: names, dresses, celebrations and the attitudes of parents and relevant others are differentiated by the sex of the neonate. As mentioned earlier the non-verbal empathy and cues by the mother transmitted to the child, and the selective reactions of the latter to the mother's cues, constitute a major dynamic for the determination of the child's gender identity. The sex of rearing is, therefore, the finalizing constitutive determinant of gender identity whereas the biological sex is only a predisposing basis for it. This is evident from the studies of hermaphrodites and illustrated by a macabre case of two identical twin boys. The penis of one of the boys was accidentally totally burnt by a cauterizing circumcision. The injured boy was subsequently raised as a girl and her gender identity became female.[23] Studies by Hampson and Hampson were fairly conclusive in their results that the sex of assignment and rearing, and not the predisposing biological sex, is the major cause for the determination of gender roles and identity.[24]

The central role which the mother plays during orality in the determination of the gender identity of her offspring is hence evident. The mother deploys this role by her direct, tactile and immediate non-verbal messages to her child, and by the reinforcement of the infant daughter's identity and the infant son's complementarity with her. Lewis et al. found a link between the mother-infant relationship and gender dimorphism. Their findings allow an inference of gender identity feed-back effects at orality within the mother-child dyad.[25]

Kohlberg points out that once a girl has labelled herself as feminine she will try to emulate her mother and selectively absorb from her environment those cues that will reinforce her feminine gender identity.[26] Consequently, girls, because of their identification with their mother (a readily available gender model), reach an earlier and better defined gender identity than boys. The male infant lacks a gender model at orality and this complicates and confuses his gender identity formation. This finding emerged from a study by Katcher who stated that:

> Girls erred less than boys because mothers are the principal adult models during early childhood and they usually see their mothers dress, bathe and toilet; they thus receive considerable experience with female characteristics. Boys neither have this opportunity nor experience comparable relationships with their fathers. They are therefore more confused about sex differences. After all, children only need to know one of the sexes in order to differentiate accurately on the basis of experience.[27]

Of similar importance to our present context is the finding by Goldberg and Lewis that mothers tend to maintain greater physical proximity to their six month old daughters than to male infants of the same age. "This differential treatment of female and male infants by their mother as related to their 'staying close' (more for girls) and 'moving off out there' (more for boys) seems to be fostered very early."[28] These findings support our claim for the greater likelihood of the boy being fixated at early orality. The complications and confusions in his gender identity formation because of a lack of a proximal gender model are compounded by the treatment by his mother "befitting a man". This raises the probabilities of an early traumatizing fixation of the boy at early orality, with a resultant greater likelihood for a participant Tantalic core disposition. The girl, on the other hand, has a closer and smoother dyadic relationship with her mother in early orality. She also has a close and directly reinforcing gender model to identify with from the very first day of her life. The chances of her being traumatized and fixated at early orality are, therefore, much lower. Conversely, her chances of being traumatized at later orality are much higher because the transition from closer proximity and identification with the mother to the vicissitudes of weaning and role complementarity with her father would be much harder, and hence more traumatizing than for the later and post oral boy. Here again we have an empirical support for the greater likelihood of a later oral fixation of the girl with a consequent higher probability for a separant object oriented and environment manipulating disposition.

Women are physically less aggressive than men,[29] yet psychologically more aggressive.[30] This is in line with our conception of the more separantly manipulative woman and the more participantly striving man, whose physical aggression is a display dynamic to enhance his acceptance by the woman. Most of the male/female dimorphisms of core personality parameters may be traced, to our mind, to the female more separant and male more participant core personality traits. This may also be inferred from the following summary of male and female personality traits by Kagan:

> In sum, females are supposed to inhibit aggression and open display of sexual urges, to be passive with men, to be nurturant to others, to cultivate attractiveness, and to maintain an effective, socially poised, and friendly posture with others. Males are urged to be aggressive in face of attack, independent in problem situations, sexually aggressive, in control of regressive urges, and suppressive of strong emotion, especially anxiety.[31]

Women have also been found to be more suggestible, passive and yielding than men.[32] This again is in line with the more separantly enticing role of women.

Mothers are usually culturally conditioned to treat their female infants more softly than their male infants. This presumably anticipates the manly role of the male in society. The males are trained earlier to distal behaviour, that is to less proximal attachment to the mother; whereas the infant daughters' more proximal attachment to mother is tolerated and often encouraged until the phase of weaning.[33] This again helps to explain not only the greater likelihood of the male infant to be early orally fixated but also the male's subsequent participant hardship to cope with his objective and human environment. As a result the male is bound to be more irritable, frustrated and hence more aggressive towards his environment.[34] The female infant, on the other hand, has an immediate and direct identification with the female role. This empathy based socialization into the female role is, of course, nurtured by the mother who is likely to be more separant herself.

This initial oral socialization of the daughter by the mother through a dyadic bond of empathy and identification is likely, even at this early stage, to provide the girl with an initial separant predisposition. Moreover, after weaning and the post oral complementarity conflicts with the father the girl is more likely to experience an object bound fixation which augments her separant predisposition. This makes for the girl's more Sisyphean anchor on her environment, and her ability to manipulate it to provide the basic needs of shelter and subsistence for herself and for her offspring. Women are thus more attuned to object relationships to other people, and are "more finely tuned to make adjustments to stimulus changes".[35]

The greater Tantalic predisposition of the male to seek abstractions, ideas and transcendence through his inner self can be traced to his early oral complementarity based conflicts with his mother and the fixation related to his traumatic treatment by her both in her assignment of more manly roles for him, and her harsher suppression of his oral incestuous desires. This Tantalic predisposition makes for a more restless seeking of aims and ideals to subjugate himself to. This could be linked to the males greater achievement orientation as well as his greater adventurousness. Seeking new adventures, new innovations and unknown gambles have participant Tantalic attributes since they involve the quest of the unknown and the unfathomable pre-differentiation of non-being.

Of special importance are the findings, replicated by many researchers, that women are more "field dependent", that is object dependent in their spatiotemporal orientations; whereas men are more "field independent", that is not dependent so much on their objective surroundings for their orientations and decision making. This has been paraphrased by McClelland as follows: "Women are concerned with the context, men are forever trying to ignore it for the sake of something they can abstract from it."[36] This basic premise is linked to other findings according to which women are more gregarious and more interested in their objective environment and in other people.[37] Women also display a higher verbal proficiency than men,[38] and we ourselves have shown elsewhere that language is more of a separant than a participant means of communication.[39] Men, on the other hand, have been found to be less concrete, more abstract and also less adjustable to their environment.[40] It is of special interest to note that we have recently verified empirically that field dependence is linked to the separant Sisyphean predisposition, whereas field independence is one of the characteristics of participant Tantalic types.[41] This provides another empirical anchor to our linkage of gender dimorphism to the separant participant core continuum. We may sum up our present premise by recapitulating that woman is predisposed to be more separant (Sisyphean) and man more participant (Tantalic) on all the three focal levels of biology, personality core and cultural imprints. However these are only predispositions and probabilities. There might well be and indeed there are many women who have been early orally fixated and later imprinted by participant cultural norms so that they became Tantalically oriented towards love and life in spite of their biological separant predisposition. On the other hand, the male participant biological predisposition would be overpowered and all but subdued by a subsequent later oral fixation and Sisyphean cultural imprints.

A person's final disposition as Sisyphean or Tantalic will determine his basic aims and attitudes towards his partners in love and sex. The separant Sisyphean would ever aim to control, subjugate and objectify his partner, whereas the Tantalic participant wishes to be controlled, subjugated and absorbed by his partner. We have specified in the introduction that the core Sisyphean and Tantalic personality components may be arranged on a continuum between the two poles of the extreme ideal types. We shall continue our exposition, after an interlude on homosexuality, by describing the attitudes of these polar types towards their partners in an affective dyad bearing in mind that in reality each human being has a different combination of Sisyphean and Tantalic components in his or her personality core, depending on the specific bio-psycho-cultural developmental configuration.

The Homosexuals

We believe that homosexuality is related to some parent-child dynamics at the oral phase of human development, and linked to the core dynamics of participation and separation. Our study on "Personality Core Dynamics and Predisposition Towards Homosexuality",[42] is an empirical illustration of the application of the major premises presented in this chapter. Limitations of space unfortunately prevent us from presenting the study in full. We do however explain our basic approach vis-a-vis other approaches to homosexuality, and present the major conclusions of our study.

The focus of our study is on the dichotomy between an early oral and a later oral fixation as related to both gender identity and the separant-participant continuum. We use gender identity not in the meaning attributed to it by John Money and the Hampsons, but in the sense of identification with the female or male role.[43] Our premise is that the passive homosexual would be more related to an early oral fixation, whereas the active homosexual would presumably be linked to a later oral fixation on the object. This, of course, runs contrary to the accepted Freudian premises that the differentiations of sexual identity occur in the genital-Oedipal phases of human development, which take place much later than at the oral phase. It must also be stressed that our premise goes further than the current premises of the oralists because we claim that the crucial developmental stage is the differentiation between the pantheistic holistic existence of early orality in contradistinction to the phase of self-crystallization in later orality, when object relationships become possible.[44] In our theoretical model this is the crucial developmental phase, both existentially and as regards the organism. Omnipresence ceases with the crystallization of the separate self vis-a-vis the rest of the surrounding objects: this dethrones the ego and makes him a rather insignificant and vulnerable separatum which has to fight his way in order to secure a continuing existence.

Differentiation, which is linked to separation, becomes crucial in the crystallization of the self concept vis-a-vis relevant objects and others. Whatever happens at this stage of development is bound to be carried on throughout one's life. The magnitude and force of existential experience at the oral stage of development is far greater than in later phases and this is why we can claim that the potent processes at this phase predispose a person towards certain types of personality and behaviour patterns which have their decisive influence later on in life.

The coagulation of the self marks the cutting-off point for the most basic developmental dichotomy: from birth and early orality to the phase where the ego boundary is formed around the emerging individual separatum, and from later orality through the formation of the ego identity onwards. In the first phase any fixation that might happen and imprint thereby some character traits on the developing personality, is not registered by a separate self capable of discerning between the objects which are the source of the fixation-causing trauma and himself as its recipient. The experiencing entity is a non-differentiated pantheistic totality. On the other hand, if the traumatizing fixation occurs at the later oral phase after the objects have expelled the self from their togetherness by a depriving interaction with him, the self may well be in a position to attribute the cause of pain and deprivation to its proper source, that is to the objects.

In this context we partially follow Fairbairn's conviction that in the oral phase fairly stable patterns of behaviour develop which, though potential and rudimentary at such an early stage of human development, are predisposing.[45] We must stress that by linking our differentiation of the types of homosexual behaviour to the polarity of fixations at the oral stage we provide only a descriptive scaffolding for the understanding of the variants of such behaviour. By studying the bifurcation towards different types of homosexual behaviour we do not present the complete causative chain of how and why homosexuality rather than heterosexuality has taken place. We just point out some predisposing pressures, yet leave out additional conditions.

The pioneering work of Kinsey has already established a continuum between heterosexuality and homosexuality.[46] Kinsey himself hypothesized a seven-grade transition from heterosexuality, at one end of which the fantasies at intercourse or any other sexual excitation are completely homosexual, even if the other partner is of the opposite sex. The typology of homosexuals themselves has been more problematic. One of the more recent ones has been constructed by Ovesey and Person along the following lines.[47] The pressures towards the development of both types of male homosexuals occur in the pre-Oedipal stage after the age of three. The cause in both cases is separation anxiety leading to an unresolved Oedipus complex. Yet the causes of this separation anxiety differ and thus produce the two types. The mother of the feminine type is intimate, seductive and domineering and, therefore, very frightening; the father distant, hostile or rejecting. The mother of the masculine type is less frightening and the father definitely threatening. Consequently the aim of the sexual act is satisfaction of dependency and incorporation of the mother in the feminine type, and humiliation of the partner and assertion of his own masculinity in the masculine type. The feminine type accepts his homosexual identity since sexual relations with a woman are identified with suffocation and annihilation; while the masculine type does not accept it and wishes to become heterosexual.

We agree with Ovesey and Person that the predisposition to homosexuality develops prior to the age of three but are more specific in relating it to the oral stage and to our wider personality theory.[48] The passive type of homosexual conveys characteristics of our Tantalic personality type, whereas the active homosexual would not be an extreme separant Sisyphean type but would be significantly more separant than the passive homosexual. Our study is a more radical departure from the psychoanalytic explanation of male homosexuality than that presented by Ovesey and Person. We place the aetiological process at the oral stage and then relate the two types of homosexuals to fixations at the early and later oral stage. This affords a more specific explanation for the existence of two types of homosexuals than the separation-anxiety syndrome offered by Ovesey and Person. Moreover the latter provide no explanation for the occurrence of this separation anxiety, which is a direct derivative of our more comprehensive personality theory.

We postulate that an early oral fixation is linked to the participant Tantalic type of personality which has not coalesced into a proper ego boundary, and is therefore not anxious to separate itself from the object (i.e., the mother). Furthermore he is incapable of doing so effectively. When the fixation occurs at the later oral stage some measure of separation has already taken place, accounting for the differences in family matrix perceptions of the two types of homosexuals. Our differentiation between early and later oral fixation attempts to account for these too. It is not so much the parents themselves who differ in the two types of homosexuals, but the two types of homosexuals who differ in the perception of their parents. (It must be emphasized that the characteristics of the parents were in both our and other researches based on reports of the subjects and not of the parents themselves.) The inability to separate from the mother of the early oral fixated passive type makes him perceive her as engulfing and stifling him, while his love object is male. Therefore the relationship with the mother is conflictual and ambivalent. The later oral fixation of the more active type has partially separated him from the object, his mother, who is perceived as "bad" (i.e., despotic, wilful and sexually attached to him).

Our research differs from most others in that our population was not composed of psychiatric patients so that our findings were obtained after controlling somewhat for other mental disturbances. Of course our population is a very small one and is not normally distributed on any pertinent variable. But then no random sample of homosexuals would have been possible to obtain anyway, and we are careful to point out the very tentative nature of our findings and conclusions.

The hypotheses derived from our theory were largely verified. The passive type of homosexual was found to seek oral gratification much more excessively than the active type, to have an aversion to his body and a strong wish to be engulfed by his love object. He was found to be excessively promiscuous just because he could not attain this total fusion, blaming his successive partners for this inevitable frustration. His aversion to his own body, which is perceived as ugly, coupled with the impossibility of finding a satisfying permanent partner, explain the finding that he is much more fearful of old age than the active type, though both types of homosexuals have no legalized family ties to fall back upon in old age. The more active homosexual, on the other hand, was not found to have any excessive oral activity and to have a tendency to preen his body rather than to hate it. This is in line with his conception of his ego as good and beautiful due to his later oral fixation. He was found to seek fusion with his love object just as much as the passive type but the fusion is of the opposite nature. He wishes to engulf the "bad" object and incorporate it in his "good me" rather than the reverse. He was also found to be promiscuous but less excessively so and rather for punitive reasons – the object is "bad" and requires punishment, and thus subjugation. Betrayal is one such means of punishment. Being more active and more satisfied with himself he is less fearful of old age. He believes in his ability to continue finding partners both because he takes the initiative and because his looks will not forsake him.

This study is only a scaffolding for the core characteristics of predisposition to homosexuality. A scaffolding, naturally, cuts through many levels of analysis and this is precisely what we have done. We have to point out that the research and theorizing of early orality is full of pitfalls, but we have no doubts that whatever happens in this very early stage of development, and especially the relationship between the neonate and his mother, are largely responsible for the predisposition and bifurcation towards heterosexuality or homosexuality.

By Love Possessing

The separant way of loving is to include, incorporate and "swallow" the other into oneself. The implementation of this Sisyphean aim is impossible by definition so that the surrogate inclusionary techniques of the separate lover is to subjugate, manipulate, tyrannize, oppress and patronize his objects of love and sex. The following quote from Henry Miller's *Sexus* is an apt portrayal of the separant sexual bully who treats his partner in sex as a lifeless objectified chattel:

> "You never wear any undies do you? You're a slut, do you know it?" I pulled her dress up and made her sit that way while I finished my coffee. "Play with it a bit while I finish this".
> "You're filthy," she said, but she did as I told her.
> "Take your two fingers and open it up. I like the color of it".
> . . . With this I reached for a candle on the dresser at my side and I handed it to her.
> "Let's see if you can get it in all the way . . . "
> "You can make me do anything, you dirty devil".
> "You like it, don't you?"[49]

Norman Mailer in his *An American Dream* envisages an even more far reaching inclusion: Mr Rojack, the novel's hero, projects on Ruta his sexual object, a total compliance with his separant aim to incorporate her within himself. Rojack proclaims that Ruta "was becoming mine as no woman ever had, she wanted to be part of my will".[50] The Sisy-phean, as we shall demonstrate with a case study of Casanova in the following chapter, ever looks for new sexual objects to conquer. How-ever, once the object has been conquered a new target is sought for inclusionary subjugation. The Sisyphean may also focus not on the whole person but be enamoured by the eyes, be infatuated by the lips or be mesmerized by the breasts of the love object. This stems from the nature of the Sisyphean's emotional attachment to a person or parts thereof, as targets for absorption, manipulation and overmastering, and not as partners of a mutually satisfactory emotional and physical encounter.

The sadomasochistic dyad of the passionate torturer and the volup-tuously tortured is also Sisyphean in essence. The infliction of mental and physical pain has always been a prime mode of subjugation, mani-pulation and control. The sadistic ego may devise subtle and sophisti-cated modes of painfully manipulating alter so that the latter may see no choice but to willingly submit to his/her artful tormentor. Pure and courageous heroes and heroines who always manage to outwit and vanquish their sadistic tormentors are in the exclusive domain of pulp magazines. In real life and especially within the confines of monogamy, man and woman may devise such ingenious devices of mutual torment compared to which the repetitive spanking and gory cruelties of the Divine Marquis would seem crude and heavy-handed. Moreover the masochist is bound also to manipulate the sadist into providing the type of torment suitable to his specific gourmet palate for esoteric pain. Even if the partner in a passion dyad is not a masochist, he or she is very quick to realize that their sadistic partner needs them much more than they need him. Once they realize that they have this trump card they can and they do manipulate him into a Sisyphean interdepen-dence. The sadomasochistic dyad is, therefore, an extreme Sisyphean interrelationship in which one party objectifies the other and manoeu-vres him to cater for his own separant whims and aims. The Sisy-pheanism of the sadomasochistic dyad is also apparent from its cyclic conflictual nature: the masochist creates conflicts so that he may be abused and tormented whereas the sadist provokes conflicts in order to be able to inflict pain and torment. This may eventually lead to a self-defeating deadlock: we can envisage Leopold von Sacher-Masoch kneeling in front of the Marquis de Sade begging to be whipped, while the Divine Marquis, although brandishing his whip, says No with a sadistic smirk on his face.

The ultimate in Sisyphean possessiveness is to kill for love. This is what Oscar Wilde meant in his *Ballad of Reading Gaol* when he lamen-ted that "each man kills the thing he loves". The master of this genre of amatory Sisyphean possessiveness is Jean Genet, the self-confessed murderer who writes from his experience of the ecstasy and elation of killing a man: " . . . I would like to kill a handsome blond boy, so that, already united by the verbal link that joins the murderer and the murdered (each existing thanks to the other), I may be visited, during days and nights of hopeless melancholy, by a handsome ghost of which I would be the haunted castle . . . "[51] This is the ultimate possession of the murdered by the murderer. The irreversible acquisition of the beloved victim by his passionate executioner.

In his book *The Romantic Agony,* Mario Praz comments on the various works by Pushkin and Gautier based on the account of the *Liber de Viris Illustribus* that Cleopatra used to kill her lovers after having sex with them:

> Cleopatra, like the praying mantis, kills the male whom she loves. These are elements which were destined to become permanent characteristics of the type of Fatal Woman of whom we are speaking. In accordance with this conception of the Fatal Woman, the lover is usually a youth, and maintains a passive attitude; he is obscure, and inferior either in condition or in physical exuberance to the woman, who stands in the same relation to him as to the female spider, the praying mantis, etc., to their respective males: sexual cannibalism is her monopoly. Towards the end of the century the perfect incarnation of this type of woman is Herodias. But she is not the only one: the Helen of Moreau, of Samain, of Pascoli (Anticlo) closely resembles her. The ancient myths, such as that of the Sphinx, of Venus and Adonis, of Diana and Endymion, were called in to illustrate this type of relationship, which was to be so insistently repeated in the second half of the century. The following point must be emphasized: the function of the flame which attracts and burns is exercised, in the first half of the century, by the Fatal Man (the Byronic hero), in the second half by the Fatal Woman; the moth destined for sacrifice is in the first case the woman, in the second the man . . . [52]

Without engaging into Praz's argument as to the alternations between the male and female passionate murderer, his comments and descriptions aptly illustrate our premise. The extreme Sisyphean lovers, both *femme* and *homme fatale,* prey on their paramour as an act of exclusive possession. Their dominance of their miserable partner in the amorous dyad must be so complete that no-one else must be allowed to share the passionate favours of their lovers after they have shared their fatal bed. The possessive lover/killer is not content with a mere subjugation of the soul or body of his beloved, only the immolation of his paramour on the altar of his passions will do.

On a philosophical level the Sisyphean possessiveness begins once the lover objectifies his partner. In Buber's terminology the Sisyphean manipulation of the paramour by the lover is an objectified "I-it" relationship because of the possessive attitude toward the lover. Possessiveness is also the main ingredient of sexual jealousy. Descartes defined jealousy as "a kind of fear related to a desire to preserve a possession".[53] The Sisyphean jealousy is more than a fear, it is a claim of exclusiveness on the beloved as an object, as a piece of property. The separant lover preaches chastity to his beloved and encases him/her in moral physical matrimonial or punitive chastity belts because he regards them as his sole and exclusive personal belonging — an engulfed extension of his person. Consequently the actual or imaginary seducer of ego's paramour is not just a trespasser but aims to cut-off the extended self of the possessive lover as projected by him on his partner.

By Love Possessed

Robert Graves' "real woman" in search of the "real man" is the Tantalic woman looking for the ideal superman by whom she may be possessed, and whom she may worship and acknowledge as her master.[54] This participant longing to be absorbed by an all embracing omnipotence is a surrogate quest to revert back to the totality of pantheistic early orality and to be fused with the omnipresence of non-being. An extreme but not infrequent instance of this is the case of Lou Andreas Salomé who moved from one luminary to another including Nietzsche, Rilke and Freud in search of the ever elusive perfect master-lover. Frau Lou expressed the polar participant stance that love is a "yearning for reunification of all our faculties and utter fusion with our loved one".[55] The Tantalic quest of participation through love may be projected onto metaphysics like the Kabbalist *tikkun*, the mending of the cosmic catastrophe of the breaking of the vessels, which is the process of salvation envisaged as the constant mating of the male part of divinity with the female divine presence (the Shechina). The participant conception of sex is also apparent in, of all places, the quietist Hasidic directives on the proper modes of prayer and the learning of the *Torah*. "One should pray and study the Torah", instructed the Maggid of Mezhirech, "as if one is about to ejaculate a drop of semen from one's whole body when one's whole strength is present in that drop."[56]

The paradox in the participant quest for unification by love and sex is that these are probably the only human activities in which a partner is needed. This makes love and sex the prime basis for our programming to interact and to relate to a plurality. The implications of these basic dynamics are enormous because from this need to relate to a sexual partner and its sublimatory suppression, both reproduction and culture are initiated. Yet these basic separant mechanisms are generated in many instances by the bait of a participant longing for union and fusion with the object of love. We have already mentioned in the introduction the "baiting" nature of sex. Here, however, we note that even if an amorous quest is participant, in the last analysis it serves the aims of our separant programming to reproduce.

The participant desire to annihilate oneself in order to fuse with the beloved may be linked to self-destructive tendencies which are instrumental to ego's Tantalic goal of self-effacement and of being absorbed by his or her lover. It is not physical death or suicide that is the aim of the Tantalic lover but the continuous and rather strenuous (depending on the intensity of his love) efforts to be debased and humiliated. This stripping of the infatuated ego's self-esteem and hence the obliteration of his ego identity, facilitates the obliteration of his separate self and its being engulfed by the lover. It should be stressed that this is the description of the amorous self-destructive infatuations of the polar Tantalic participant type. As this course of his emotional involvement was mostly determined by an early oral fixation and other core personality dynamics, ego's amorous behaviour would largely be motivated unconsciously. As his self-debasement would be unlikely to be reciprocated by the coveted emotional acceptance by the beloved alter, such self-destructive Tantalic binges are not very likely to be terminated by nervous breakdowns or suicide. Usually the Tantalic lover is jolted out from his "bad trip" by a traumatic abuse from his paramour. He or she would then emerge from their nightmare, as seen retrospectively, and recuperate for a while; but not for long, because they are destined by their core-personality dynamics to ever look for the "great consuming love" of their Tantalic dreams.

The subjugation of the Tantalic lover is the most consummate. He yearns for the total submission of body and soul to his lover while desiring passionately that his wilful sacrifice is graciously accepted. Oscar Wilde in *De Profundis*, which was written in the form of a letter to Lord Alfred Douglas, writes about his carnivorous separant paramour: "Having made your most of my genius, my will power and my fortune, you required in the blindness of an inexhaustible greed, my entire existence. You took it."[57] Wilde was well aware of his Tantalic subjugation to his greedy lover yet the self-annihilating thrust of his love was so overpowering that he could not help but plunge headlong to his perdition. He then recounts that he knew that to apply for the arrest of the Marquis of Queensberry, Lord Douglas' allegedly libelous father, was a fatal error. But Wilde found himself coerced by the futies of his consuming love and hence unable to resist the disastrous demands of his lover. Wilde, down and under in Reading Gaol describes how he totally sacrificed his dignity, will power and freedom not to Douglas but to his love for Douglas. Wilde's professed abject slavery was not to a person but to a Tantalic infatuation. Douglas sponged shamelessly on Wilde and ultimately made him a bankrupt. The most fantastic revelation by Frank Harris, Wilde's controversial biographer, but corroborated by G. B. Shaw, was that they both tried to dissuade Wilde from suing Queensberry. Wilde was convinced but then Bosie (Lord Alfred's nickname) Douglas came in.

> At Oscar's request I repeated my argument and to my astonishment Douglas got up at once, and cried with his little white, venomous, distorted face:
> "Such advice shows you are no friend of Oscar's."
> "What do you mean?" I asked in wonderment; but he turned and left the room on the spot. To my astonishment Oscar also got up.
> "It is not friendly of you, Frank," he said weakly, "it really is not friendly."
> I stared at him; he was parroting Douglas' idiotic words. "Don't be absurd," I said; but he repeated:
> "No, Frank, it is not friendly," and went to the door and disappeared.
> Like a flash I saw part at least of the truth. It was not Oscar who had ever misled Douglas, but Lord Alfred Douglas, who was driving Oscar whither he would.[58]

Wilde, knowingly serving as a tool of Douglas' rabid vendetta against his own father, could nevertheless not resist being sacrificed to the Moloch of his paramour's parricidal hatred. Wilde succumbed to the fatal demands of his lover although he recognized them at the outset to be absurd and insane.

We have here the sacrifice of dignity and the forfeiture of the sense of choice which are the dual skeletons on which an ontological self-concept may support itself. By sacrificing these Oscar Wilde sacrificed his self. The question whether Bosie (Lord Alfred Douglas) was worthy of this ultimate sacrifice is superfluous because the essence of the Tantalic total submission is that it becomes a goal in itself, ordained more by the lover's core dynamics than by the identity and characteristics of the paramour. When ego is in the grip of a Tantalic carousal of self-sacrifice to an idol the lover discards normal recognition of time and reality, and rushes after his glittering projections on his beloved. This self-sufficiency of the Tantalic involvement in a self-destructive love is portrayed by Truffaut's cinematic story of Adele H., Victor Hugo's love-crazed daughter. Adele falls in love with Pinson, a British Lieutenant who is consistently indifferent to her. She follows him to

Nova Scotia, Halifax and Barbados. Among other things she paid his debts, feigned pregnancy and procured a whore for him as proof of her love. Her self-sufficient and self-regenerative Tantalic love craze is portrayed by her chasing her amorous *fata morgana*. When she finally catches up with Pinson she looks through him as if he was so much hot air and carries on chasing the projected inner vision of her romantic will-o'-the-wisp.

Another case of Tantalic total submission emerges from the diaries of Cosima Wagner. She is full of self-debasement and self-denial towards R. (Richard Wagner). She is willing to sacrifice herself for him and live only through and for him. When he plays his music she is overcome with exaltation and adoration for him. She is even willing to give up her children if by this she can better serve R. Cosima writes in the entry of 1 February 1869: "I took a walk in the garden and once more pondered in my soul what I have already pondered so often: the meaning of life and of our mission in it: I know for certain that self-denial, self-sacrifice, is the only thing that gives our life value and meaning, and gladly will I flee from every happiness and every pleasure . . . Even in the hours of greatest trial I have never seriously considered separating myself from R., because I know no one who loves him as I love him."[59]

These three representative cases differ widely in their setting and context, yet their relevance for us is similar. Oscar Wilde literally annihilated himself by his self-negating amorous infatuation. Adele H. followed her phantasmagoric delusion of an ever-escaping perfect love into the total self-sufficiency of madness. Cosima Wagner enclosed her world into the egomaniacal person of R. and was totally absorbed and depersonalized by her self-effacing love.

Amour Sacre; Amour Profane

We hypothesize that the quest of a person for a "pure" sacred love is related to his/her participant early oral fixation and an exclusionary longing to partake in their "good" mother object. Per contra, the separant quest to control the object is linked to a wish to objectify and manipulate the partner in the sexual dyad. This profane love is related to a later oral fixation on the "bad" object-mother and the inclusionary aim to dominate. We present our hypothesis schematically in figure 9. Our continuum envisages a predisposition of the early orally fixated male to seek a madonna-like immaculate love. If in addition to his fixation the male's incestuous oral sexuality has been harshly suppressed he might find a combination of large breasts (an over inflated reminiscence of his early oral fixation) and restrained

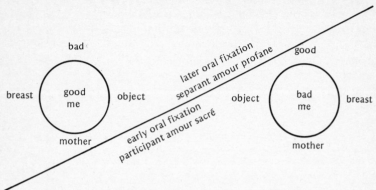

Figure 9. Personality Types Related to Sacred and Profane Love

demeanour quite irresistable. This might have been one of the main reasons for the popularity of the girl-next-door-idol with the accentuated bust of the 1940s created by Hollywood to cater for the mother-longing and home-sick soldiers of the Second World War.

Early orally fixated girls are bound to dream about the proverbial virtuous knight on the white horse, many times to the detriment of her — and especially her parents' — matrimonial plans. A later orally fixated girl would pursue sex in a truly Sisyphean manner. She would aim to subjugate her sexual partner and use him for the satisfaction of her hedonistic passions and tastes. Both love and sex are conceived by her as conflictual — an ever recurring battle of wits, stamina and sexual potency. Her amatory exploits recognize only victories or defeats — nothing in between. Mutually satisfying encounters and intersubjective rapport are outside her range of emotions and conceptual contexts. The Sisyphean woman is also bound to use sex and love as a means to achieve personal, matrimonial and social ends. In such cases a strict suppression of incest by the mother might have brought about a bipolar predisposition towards sex and love. The strict Catholic upbringing of a Fellini, for instance, contributed to the cinematic creation of an extreme bi-modality of the ascetic saint and the whore — the fragile and sexless mother-woman-lover and the vulgar and sinful female sex object.

The bipolarity of *amour sacre* and *amour profane* was alluded to by Freud who said that "The erotic life of such people remains dissociated, divided between two channels, the same two that are personified in art as heavenly and earthly (or animal) love. Where such men love they have no desire and when they desire they cannot love."[60] Melanie Klein's bipolarity of oral, breast-mother and post oral genital-mother can also be related to our context: the early oral fixated Tantalic Don Juan seeks the love of the good object-breast mother and the post oral genital-mother who he gains by his amatory exploits, but who does not satisfy him. The Sisyphean Casanova, on the other hand, chases the genital-mother in order to dominate her, but following each new orgasm Casanova realizes that after a momentary feeling of omnipotence he is back to square one so he resumes his chase after another and then another with the delusive hope, alas, that "this time it is going to be different". But "this time" always proves to be just like any other time. We shall elaborate on this theme in the following chapter where we present an illustrative case study of Don Juan and Casanova.

Regarding sex as "dirty" is a cultural and linguistic conditioning which is related more to socialization than to early or post oral fixations which only predispose a child to a polar attitude towards love and sex. John Money recounts the following hilarious usage of "dirty" sex words which illustrate this premise:

> The cultural relativism of dirty versus clean sexual terminology is well illustrated by the complete reversal of the categories in English usage in Nigeria. In the history of acculturation, the moral taboos of sex were taught by missionaries and administrators who used only clean words. These were the words that became taboo. The dirty words, used as part of the vernacular of sailors, traders and the like, became part of Nigerian vernacular English, with no taboo attached. In consequence, today it is as forbidden to say sexual intercourse, penis and vagina on Nigerian television as it is to say fuck, cock and cunt on BBC television. In Nigeria, the latter terms are considered normal and respectable. In individual conversation, the same holds true. To say that a young woman has a vagina or that she has sexual intercourse is an affront to modesty that is not tolerated. The correct and expected reference is to her cunt and to fucking.[61]

F. Scott Fitzgerald had a strict Catholic upbringing and the mentor of his youth was Monsignor Cyril Fay. This might very likely be linked to the polarity of his women heroines. *This Side of Paradise* depicted the *amour profane* seductresses, while headings in other stories depict *amour sacre* madonna-like fair ladies. The hero of *This Side of Paradise* describes his first kiss: "He had never kissed a girl before, and he tasted his lips curiously, as if he had munched some new fruit." This is the tell-tale oral exposure to the forbidden fruit followed by "sudden revulsion . . . disgust and loathing".[62] Self-detestation and repugnance are the immediate wages of sinful "dirty" sexual passions.

The beauty of ugliness is the affective and many times sexual attraction to the maimed, the crippled, the deformed, the hideous, the repulsive and the unclean, all of which is just a more extreme form of an attraction to the "dirtiness" of sex. This may range from para-philiacs who are sexually aroused mostly or solely by cripples, to a Genet for whom the more ugly and disfigured a person, the more magnificant he was.[63] The most ardent troubadour of the beauty of ugliness was perhaps Baudelaire who sang the praises of beggar maids, the seductiveness of hags, and the loveliness of brothels and skeleton-like beauties.[64]

A mytho-empirical support for the nature of "dirty" sexual passion is the evil Circe who turns the men who desire her into swine (i.e., "dirty" sex befits the pigs which wallow in their own refuse in the pig-sty). Moreover, Circe, the bad-mother-woman sends Odysseus to Perse-phone who, as we have shown earlier, is the mytho-empirical post oral, sexually-defiled transformation of the early-oral "pure" maiden Kore.[65]

8
Casanova and Don Juan:
The Impossibility of Love

When love enters in, both parties are usually dupes.
Giacomo Casanova: *History of my Life*

You possessed every woman — and therefore none.
Edmond Rostand: *The Last Night of Don Juan*

The myth of Don Juan and the less than credible memoirs of Casanova present two archetypal woman chasers who are spurred by diametrically opposite motives. Casanova aims to conquer womanhood in toto; for him each woman is an insignificant link in an endless chain. He is after sex, the *amour profane* that treats woman as a chattel or as an object. The goal of Don Juan, on the other hand, is to be immersed into universal womanhood; to be absorbed by the eternal feminine. Nothing short of complete grace can satisfy him so that his amatory exploits are bound to disappoint him. Don Juan longs for an *amour sacre,* for an ethereal "Eternal Woman, delicate and pale . . . Eternal Woman master-piece of the male".[1]

Casanova is baited by his current paramour to seek the ideal sex goddess, whereas Don Juan is baited by each one of his temporary loves to seek the pure graces of the great-mother-woman. This is why Don Juan is obsessed with transcendence. He longs for communion with divinity through the graceful mediation of woman. In an opposite manner Casanova pays lip service to God because it is expedient to be religious in a theocratic society in the same way that it is good for business to be a member of the Rotary club in Middletown USA. Being an extreme Sisyphean manipulator of his environment and dabbling in magic in keeping with the fashion of his times, Casanova also prays to God, an activity he considers to be a rather inexpensive method of having one's wishes granted.[2]

Don Juan and Casanova present the two polar archetypes of emotional involvement: Casanova is a separant object-oriented achiever who sublimates his desire to "swallow" his objective surroundings on his passion to overpower and enslave the archetypal sexual woman. Don Juan is a participant pursuer of pantheistic grace who in order to

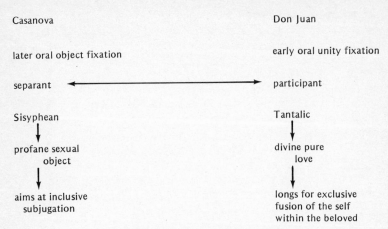

Figure 10. Casanova – Don Juan Continuum

achieve it is every ready to be annihilated, even at the price of the fire and brimstone of hell. Hence both Casanova and Don Juan are failures. The Sisyphean Casanova always chases the perfect carnal woman who invariably evades him in the particular woman with whom he happens to have sex; whereas the Tantalic Don Juan longs to be enslaved to the perfect idea of womanhood but this ever eludes him in his shifty love affairs. The main characteristics of the Casanova-Don Juan continuum are outlined in figure 10.

Casanova wishes to possess whereas Don Juan longs to be possessed. We differ, therefore, from another comparison between Casanova and Don Juan which imputes to the former the seeking of hedonistic pleasure whereas the latter, according to that interpretation, is spurred by a desire to conquer.[3] We envisage Casanova and Don Juan as occupying the extreme poles of a continuum in between which each one of us could be placed. It should be pointed out that whoever may be tempted to accuse us of male chauvinism because we employ the two masculine archetypes may be reassured that we use them for illustrative purposes only in order to highlight some of our main theses in the present volume. The figures of Don Juan and Casanova have been chosen because of the abundance of available material on the myth and on the man. Those who are so inclined and able may well choose a feminine continuum having at its Sisyphean pole a Messalina, devouring men as sexual conquests; and on the Tantalic extreme a Lou Andreas Salomé ever chasing the genius of supermen in order to be subjugated by them.

A Don Juan would be early orally fixated longing to be united with the pantheistic, good-pure-graceful mother-woman. He would, there-fore, be baited by a sacred bodyless love. Casanova, fixated presumably at later orality, would conceive his mother-woman as antagonistic and vile, an object to be won over and possessed by lewd sex.

Casanova moves from one conquest to another like a hunter marking his kill on the butt of his gun. He assures us that in the darkness "when the lamp is taken away, all woman are alike",[4] and what he expects from a woman is to relieve his sexual tension.[5] Both Don Juan and Casanova are sex maniacs. Yet for Casanova his sexual exploits are proof of his competitive choice, whereas for Don Juan his loves are signposts on his endless pilgrimage to assert his uniqueness vis-a-vis his divine love. Casanova jumps an obstacle course from one body to the other whereas Don Juan runs from heart to heart.

The Man and the Myth

Giacomo Casanova was born in Venice on 2 April 1725 to his actor father and his seventeen year old mother, a cobbler's daughter whom his father had seduced. When he was one year old he was entrusted to the care of his maternal grandmother who raised him. His mother became an actress and neither she nor his father had much time for him. After his father's death when he was about nine years old, he was handed over by his mother to be raised by a foster family. This familial rejection predisposed the young Casanova to a later oral fixation and a separant anchor on the object.[6] His lifelong quest to regain the lost object was cathected onto his preoccupation with eating (swallowing the object), his craving for sensuous pleasures and his obsession on women, particularly on women and mostly on women. Casanova him-self linked his preoccupation with objects, food and sex as follows: "Cultivating the pleasures of the senses has always been my main con-cern and I have never had a more important one. Feeling that I was born for the fair sex, I have always loved women and done my best to make them love me. I have also been passionately fond of good food, and I have always been fascinated by objects which have aroused my curiosity."[7]

Casanova was ever smitten by each girl he encountered and through his irresistible passion to overmaster this endless row of women, he became their slave. His extreme separant Sisyphean orientation mani-fested itself in his burning ambition to achieve wealth, social status and fame. This achievement orientation was most likely the result of a maternal prodding, about which there is some evidence in his memoirs.[8] When Casanova lost his sexual potency he started to write his memoirs.

These, alas, he executed mechanically and repetitively (very much like his sexual acts) and without a literary talent. Apart from his being an *arriviste* he reveals himself to be a shameless snob ever preoccupied with his own and his friends' genealogical trees.[9] He is a name-dropper with even the headings of the chapters of his memoirs being mostly a list of the important people he has met and, of course, the women he has bedded. Casanova's memoirs are twelve volumes of boring gossip on celebrities, flat descriptions of the author's sexual triumphs, humorless social repartee and recordings of financial manipulations, banquets, meals and self-aggrandizing escapades.

Casanova's memoirs reveal a shallow personality without any depth or dimension of introspection. He spent all his life scanning with his snob's antennae any gathering or celebration in which he could take part in order to further his social climbing, seek new women to seduce and above all, to alleviate the understandable boredom he felt in the company of himself. When nobody invited him any more to social occasions sex became a mere memory and he was stuck with his dull self. He then began to write about his drab and stale memories. I should be beatified as a martyr for having struggled through all the twelve volumes. Their value, however, lies in their portrayal, despite some transparent attempts at primping and prettifying, of a monster. Casanova is a total and complete egotist. Others are important to him only when and insofar as they may serve his financial and sexual endeavours. He has a psychopath's need for excitement. He considers it to be his due that all others should stimulate and entertain him. Whenever something is amiss others are to blame but rarely himself. He was also an imposter of the kind who believed his own lies.[10]

Casanova seems to have been incapable of having deep and sincere feelings towards anybody. He was a shameless liar,[11] a kleptomaniac,[12] and an informer for the Inquisition on, of all things, girls who danced in the nude. He believed that the world was his apple and he would exploit everything and everyone around him in order to achieve his aims. His ideal was the chameleon because of its ability to adjust instantaneously to changing surroundings and colours.[13] A large part of his memoirs is devoted to monotonous accounts of his financial exploits. These included the stealing of money from his benefactor, a pious bishop; the squandering from his mother the heritage of his brothers[14] and the extortion from his grandmother of all she possessed during her lifetime.[15]

The value of the memoirs however, lies in the presentation of how Casanova saw himself and the way he wished to be remembered.

In contrast to the unknown truthfulness of the Casanova memoirs, Don Juan is a true myth. There is a mytho-empirical value in the various plays based on the Don Juan myth because they utilize the basic scaffolding of archaic realities *in illo tempore*. The lover who is infatuated with the unattainable ideal of feminine perfection cannot be satisfied with artless flesh and blood imitations. In the chasing of the woman of his dreams Don Juan kills and destroys everyone and everything which stands in his way. And in the end he destroys himself. This myth is simple, strong and real because while it has occurred endless times in real life with many variations on the basic theme, the core of the myth remains constant. The various playwrights who have utilized the Don Juan myth might have changed settings and subplots, but the core myth is still at the basis of the drama to serve as an anchor to their own archetypal and mytho-empirical projections. For our present purposes we have disregarded plays and other literary works such as Byron's *Don Juan* and Pushkin's *Kamenyi Gost*, whose utilization of the basic Don Juan myth was scant or lacking. The myth of Don Juan is archaic and universal because it represents the archetypal unquenchable thirst for a participant love. A recent survey of the Don Juan literature and related works of art has counted no less than 500 plays, novels, critical works, operas and films.[16] These have been classified, analyzed and taxonomized by scholars into periods and styles. For example, the classic *commedia dell'arte*, the romantic and the modern Don Juans.[17]

As we have pointed out earlier, myths have many layers which are superimposed on the archaic core. These layers might be variations on the theme of the core myth as projected on it by its various dramatic, literary and artistic interpretators. However these variations do not interfere with our purposes so long as the core ingredients of the myth are present in a given interpretation. These, as recorded in the first version of the play in the first half of the seventeenth century by the Spanish monk, Gabriel Tellez, alias Tirso de Molina, are more or less as follows: Don Juan impersonates the fiance of a duchess in a king's palace in order to seduce her. He is caught but manages to escape. During his escapade he is shipwrecked and is saved by fisher girls. He promises marriage to the most beautiful of them, seduces her but after one night escapes again. When he reaches his home town he seduces the daughter of an illustrious commander on the eve of her marriage. Don Juan is caught and the commander comes to avenge the honour of his daughter but is killed by Don Juan. On his way to exile he manages to seduce another bride and stays with her his customary one night. When he returns to his hometown he enters a church in which he finds the statue and tomb of the murdered commander. He tweaks the beard of the statue and invites it to dine with him. The statue accepts the invitation for dinner in the course of which he flings Don Juan to hell.

This is a Christian myth of love, sin and damnation. Love may be both the longing for purity (for the sacred archetypal mother-woman) yet when it alternates with vile sex it leads to hell. Nevertheless, the romantic agony of longing for an unattainable love makes the quest of love by itself the saving grace. Indeed in some versions of the myth the unreachable beloved is instrumental in transferring the sinning Don Juan from hell to heaven. We have here a myth in which damnation and salvation alternate and sometimes intermingle. The damning component of the myth is overt — the libertine Don Juan is hurled to hell; the saving layer of the myth is more clandestine — the unachievable love effects a saving grace because the unquenchable longing lends the love a Tantalic permanence.

Don Juan is a chivalric knight attracted by his early oral fixation on the pure and sacred great-mother-woman who is left dissatisfied and nauseated by his frequent carnal encounters with an endless assortment of women. The plot of the myth is no doubt simplistic. Goldoni wrote about it that "never had so much applause, for so many years, been bestowed as for this play; the very actors marvelled and some, slyly or innocently, used to say that a pact with the devil kept up the concourse to this foolish comedy".[18] Many share the criticism imputed to Einstein, that Da Ponte's libretto to Mozart's *Don Giovanni* is a rather poor adaptation of a *commedia dell'arte* version of the Don Juan play. But all these critics should realize that an archaic myth is not usually very direct nor overt. Only at various covert levels of mytho-empirical interpretation may the features of the myth be profoundly elaborate. Also the happy ending of Tirso de Molina's version, in which the villain is hurled to perdition and the duchess marries the duke (and they live happily ever after), catered to the imperatives of the church and the public taste. This is not unlike the modern television series of *Kojak*, *Columbo* and *Charlie's Angels* in which justice always prevails.

Don Juan had a servant who changed names in almost every dramatic version of the myth. This servant represents the worldly separant to Don Juan's dreamy participation. He was pragmatic whenever Don Juan was romantic. He was lucrative and bourgeois whenever Don Juan was spiritually idealistic. He was a Sisyphean Sancho Panza to Don Juan's Tantalic Don Quixote.

To be in Love with Love

Don Juan longs to be united with the absolute woman by an eternal embrace so that every brief amorous encounter with the women he chases or happens to meet leaves him more frustrated and bitterly dissatisfied. Hoffman describes this Don Juanic hunger for the perfect love as follows:

> There is, indeed, nothing here on earth more exalting for the inner nature of man than love. It is love that, so secretly and powerfully effective, disturbs and transfigures the innermost aspects of existence. Small wonder, then, that Don Juan hoped to still, in love, the longing that burned in his heart. And it was here that the Devil slipped the noose around his neck! Through the cunning of man's hereditary enemy, the thought was planted in Don Juan's soul that through love, through the pleasure of the flesh, there could be achieved on earth that which exists in our hearts as a heavenly promise only, and which amounts to just that longing for infinity which weds us to heaven. Fleeing restlessly from one more beautiful woman to another, drinking his fill of their charms from burning passion to the point of drunken and exhausted satiety; believing himself always deceived in his choice, hoping always to realize the ideal of ultimate satisfaction.[19]

If we disregard Hoffman's pious references to heaven and the devil, his statement is very much in line with our conception of a Tantalic Don Juan who longs for the graces of the ideal woman which his drinking from the charms of the far from perfect temporary paramours fails to satisfy. In similar vein Grabbe, who produced the most ambitious, elaborate and profound Don Juan play, has his black knight assure Faust, Don Juan's alter ego, that: "Everything possible has been done. But you love the impossible — the infinite."[20] Don Juan's love is infinite, boundless and timeless, and thus unreal and out of reach.

"Love is the only creative omnipotence", declares Don Juan. Tantalic love is a quest to revert back to early orality when the self and the graces of mother-woman were still united in omnipresence and omnipotence. Tantalic love is impossible because it concentrates exclusively on a projected perfection of woman. The transcendental nature of this projection reduces all mortal imitations to insignificance. The Don Juanic dilemma is either to make do with an endless succession of surrogates for the feminine ideal, each of which he rejects, or annihilate himself in a crescendo of a *Götterdämmerung* which hopefully would reunite him with the absolute and with perfect womanhood, a course to which he ultimately succumbs.

Don Juan defies death because his Tantalic love makes him seek the annihilation of his temporal existence in order to reunite with the absolute which contains in its engulfing unity his perfect beloved. In most of the versions of the play Don Juan displays a suicidal courage as if he actually courts death. In the play by Tirso de Molina, Don Juan gives his hand to the commander's statue and assures it that he is not afraid, he expects challenges and even if it were hell itself he would give him his hand.[21]

In many versions of the play Don Juan's longing for his perfect love is linked or even equated with his quest to partake in the grace of God. In the version by Zorrilla, Don Juan Tenorio declares: "I worship Dona Ines (Donna Anna). I'm convinced that Heaven has granted her to me to turn my steps in the paths of righteousness. I didn't love her beauty nor did I worship her charms. Don Gonzalo, what I adore in Dona Ines is her goodness. That which judges and bishops could not bring me to with threats of jail and sermons was accomplished by her purity. Her love has transformed me into a new man; it has renewed my whole being. She can make an angel of one who was a devil."[22] To long for Donna Anna is to seek participation in the totality of God. What makes the sacred love of Don Juan a romantic agony is that his approach to his beloved is barred by the impossible. The Don Juan portrayed by Flaubert laments the "impossibility of perfect communion, however adhesive the kiss. Something hinders and makes a wall of itself".[23] This barrier between himself and his perfect beloved is sealed tight and cannot be passed. All Don Juan can do in this temporal existence is to move from one woman to another while fixing his gaze upwards to his sacred love, or else aim to unite with his pure love in the immaculate infinity of the ever after through perdition.

Yet it is not woman that is loved but love that is loved. It is the longing for the absolute, the wish to solve existential riddles, and the escape from ontological loneliness which his programming has directed him to anchor on a particular beloved mortal knowing only too well that she is no match for this awesome burden. Don Juan's participant longing for a woman is unattainable; the archetypal mother-woman who bears for him the sole hope for the graces of partaking in unity is beyond his grasp. The paradox and tragedy of Don Juan is that his Tantalic self craves to partake in unity through his love for an unreachable and pure *amour sacre*, while the amorous encounters that are within his reach quickly become distasteful. Don Juan would prefer a pure love, even though it was unrealizable, to the heaps of profane female bodies which are his for the taking.

On a core personality level of analysis the Tantalic Don Juan aims to revert back to the bliss of pantheism and the ultimate graces of the tranquillity of non-being. However amorous and sexual relations epitomize the interaction between two human beings who are likely to differ biologically, psychologically and socially from each other. Consequently the Tantalic quest to partake in unity and the amorous relationship between man and woman are bound to conflict from the very beginning. The dynamics of the Don Juan myth clearly demonstrate this.

The Tantalic Don Juan does not take temporal existence seriously for he makes a joke of everything.[24] He "finds all earthly life dull and shallow" for which he feels a deep contempt.[25] What elates him is his yearning for his eternal love.

> Three thousand lovely names! Three thousand women's names!
> Not one you did not stammer tearfully!
> And not one of these three thousand loves
> Drowned the fire of love that ate your soul,
> The fire which rose, the day you died, out of your blood
> Into the sky, like a forgotten angel![26]

Don Juan seeks his way back to a lost God through the love of a woman, the one and only all-consuming infatuation which will serve him as a vehicle to revert back to his early oral omnipresence. When he embraces his great lady he will fuse with her in "silent bliss"[27] and, thereby, ultimately "share God's Throne".[28] In the same vein the impossible love for Donna Anna is a prototype of a Madonna — a spiritual and rather sexless yet all-embracing love reminiscent of Robert Graves' White Goddess, the Judaic Shechina and the Gnostic Sophia. This archetypal good mother-woman is the harbinger of Tantalic grace and the forgiveness inherent in the partaking in unity. Indeed Donna Anna chose to stay in purgatory and wait for Don Juan in order to allow him a chance for salvation.[29] After the statue of the commander stretches its stone hand to hurl Don Juan to hell the spirit of Donna Anna stretches her hand and offers the dying Don Juan a forgiving ascent to heaven proclaiming that "love saved Don Juan".[30] This love was not profane nor sexual, but innocent and devoid of all sensual passion. This sacharinic happy end was, of course, aimed at the church and the simple tastes of the common people.

On a deeper level of examination this offer of salvation has a mytho-empirical significance.[31] Don Juan, the Christian knight, is saved by the immaculate, spiritual and sexless love of the pure mother-woman, in this way proclaiming the worthlessness of the vile and profane sex in which he wallowed all his temporal life. The beautification of the innocent and spiritual love implies the condemnation by Don Juan himself of the vileness of carnal sex.

Don Juan's passion is not to possess the women's bodies which he has in abundance, but to be possessed by the one love which he cannot acquire. What worsens his agony is that when he embraces each of the women he seduces, he really wishes to love them and ardently hopes that "this" one will be a match for his burning, amorous ardor. When he declares his impassioned love he truly means it but when the inevitable disenchantment sets in because the woman that happens to share his bed is light years away from the woman of his dreams, he becomes dejected, morose and desperate. His craving to be loved by the ideal woman and to be subjugated by her, which is the focal passion in Don Juan's life, is not to be realized during his temporal existence. This participant inaccessible love pierces Don Juan's soul and torments him continuously.[32] This romantic agony without solace has been acknowledged by Rostand who describes his Don Juan as being "nothing but an agony . . . only agony . . . which cries for loving arms".[33]

For the present context Don Juan's agony may be interpreted in terms of the projection of his participant core longing for non-being on the love for an ethereal ideal woman. Yet at the same time he strenuously tries to quench this spiritual longing by a succession of female bodies. He thus attempts to achieve his Tantalic amorous goals by Sisyphean means. This basic Don Juanic dynamic is not only self-defeating but is wrought with unbearable suffering and misery. The daredevil Don Juan seems to be almost relieved by his temporal death − he actually stretches out his hand freely to his stony executioner. In some versions of the drama the play ends by demonstrating that only after being relieved of his temporal miseries does Don Juan have any chance of being saved by the forgiving mediation of his wholesome perfect love which was excluded and out of reach in the here-and-now. Don Juan's is a mytho-empirical *mourir d'amour* − a self-annihilation for love.

Short of destroying himself in order to immerse himself into the boundless graces of his spiritual love, Don Juan makes a clear dichotomy in his temporal pursuit of women between body and souls. He derogates the former and cherishes the latter. In the play by Shadwell Don Juan offers his body, which he belittles to the bickering ladies who quarrel over him.[34] Lenau points out that "Don Juan would like to be pure, to be a virgin adolescent".[35] The Don Juan portrayed by Rostand "pressed naked souls against himself", not bodies.[36] He courts ecstasy which is literally the exit of the soul from the body. He "handled only flesh that smelled of soul".[37] Bodies were aplenty but the real bait were the souls, the sparks of Divinity chipped off from their origin and embedded in profane flesh. Don Juan was their self-appointed collector to bring them as an offering to his sacred love in order to gain entry into her boundless grace.

Don Juan's way out from his dilemma, without recourse to the radical solution of self-annihilation, is to be infatuated with his longing to stay in love with his love irrespective of the possibility of its attainment. This is the archetypal solution of the Tantalic participant: to disregard the goals and to raise the striving to achieve them to the stature of aims in themselves. In this vein the Don Juan depicted by

Musset seeks a love for an ideal beauty, for "an impossible being who did not exist", yet the search itself provides him with *raison d'être*.[38] The clearest expression of this premise is voiced in the play by Rostand:

> *Devil*: Then you had in mind a dream you didn't even want to find?
> *Don Juan*: It's possible. If I had found what I sought I might have died of boredom. I wanted naught, only the joy of searching – for myself, alone.[39]

The search for the ideal love and not its finding makes it eternal. A fulfilled love kills the longing for it. For the amorous yearning to be a goal in itself and hence independent of its realization, the love should remain impossible. This is in line with the decision by Kierkegaard to renounce his love for Regina Olsen and award, thereby, his loving longing for her absolute permanence. In like manner Beckett's play has it that Godot should not appear so that the waiting for him gains boundless timelessness; Dostoevsky's Grand Inquisitor pleads before Christ that His appearance weakens the ardour of the people's yearning for the Second Coming; and in Judaism it is argued that the zeal for a Messiah who has not yet come is infinitely more intense than for one who has already been proclaimed.

Finally, we raise the question of why Don Juan keeps trying to seek love by an ever changing succession of women when he knows that they are not the ideal woman he is after, and he also knows from past experience that casual encounters were dissatisfying because he was craving for a spiritual communion which they could not help him come to? The answer to this query lies in the essence of Tantalism: Don Juan is baited by his participant core vector and early oral fixation to strive to reach the perfect mother-woman irrespective of the remote or total lack of resemblance of the actual amorous encounters with the ideal. The Tantalic craving is a dynamic strain: the longing is continuous so that if one object is reached and proves to be disappointing the strain process is immediately directed towards another one which has not yet been reached and is, therefore, not yet a disappointment.

Seduce, Conquer, Possess

The separant maxim guiding the life of Casanova is that the mind obeys the body.[40] The primary entity is the spatiotemporal existence of Man whereas the soul, if it exists (of which Casanova is not so sure), is secondary and many times subservient to the body. It follows that love, the spiritual precursor and companion of sex, does not figure very prominently in Casanova's attitude towards women. Love for him is the orgasm, especially the orgasm and mostly the orgasm. For Casanova, love equals sex. When a woman asks him if he loves her and he replies in the affirmative, what he really means is that he desires to have sex with her. The epitome of Casanovite love expresses itself in the reaching of orgasm together. Love beyond the tactile friction of bodies is almost inconceivable for Casanova. His love expresses itself almost exclusively in the craving of his flesh for female flesh. His immediate falling in love is related to the time it takes him to have an erection when observing a new sexual object. Casanova's equation between sexual desire and love is apparent from his following statement, which he deemed to be so crucial and profound that he accentuated it by italics: "Love kisses the face only to thank it for the desires it inspires and since its desires have a different goal, love becomes irritated if that is not attained."[41]

If love equals the passionate manipulation of the body and the senses, and Casanova seems to have anchored his separant core vector almost completely on love (i.e. sex), then the pursuit of hedonistic pleasures is the main if not the sole preoccupation of the Sisyphean Casanova. This philosophy of the supremacy of sensuous pleasure was expounded by Casanova as follows: "Pleasure is immediate sensual enjoyment; it is a complete satisfaction which we grant to our senses in all that they desire, and when, exhausted or wearied, our senses want rest, whether to catch breath or to revive, pleasure becomes imagination; imagination takes pleasure in reflecting on the happiness which its tranquillity procures it. The Philosopher is he who refuses no pleasure which does not produce greater pains and who knows how to create pleasures."[42] In consequence morals, guilt and inhibitions have no place in sex. For if sex equals love everything which heightens the pleasures of the senses is permitted and commendable. Casanova describes the pleasures of onanism, voyeurism, exhibitionism, male and all kinds of female prostitution, and also having sex while watching an execution. This last act epitomizing, presumably, the encounter between the crescendos of love (which equals sex) and death.

Casanova is very nearly a textbook psychopath. He was completely "present oriented", whatever he craved for he had to have immediately. He was unable to postpone the satisfaction of his pleasures.[43] He despised most men and exploited everyone around him. His powers of intrigue and ingenuity of manipulation reached Byzantine magnitudes when he schemed a strategy to bed a woman. Casanova may well fit a psychiatric pigeonhole, but for our purposes he signifies the extreme Sisyphean sexual manipulator who has to possess a woman in order to prove his separant competitive choice. Like his mythological counterpart burdened with his rock Casanova was condemned to always chase women. After he succeeded in bedding a woman he lost interest

in her and ran after another. The separant Sisyphean, completely
attuned to the object (in this case a woman), can only function through
the dialectics of a strain process with the object. Unlike the Tantalic
type, who is not lonely in his solitude, the Sisyphean cannot bear to be
by himself. He needs always to interact with objects and, in Casanova's
case, to chase women.

Casanova's separant need to overpower the object and his core
vector Sisyphean achievement orientation was almost exclusively
focused on the seduction and the sexual possession of women. His life
was characterized by a constant need to be engaged in erotic seductions.
Countesses and prostitutes, young and old, fair and ugly, all were suitable objects for Casanova's insatiable craving for sexual possession.
Indeed possession is an apt description of his amorous goals. Nothing
less than total submission of his current sexual target satisfied him but
once the erotic object had been achieved he lost interest because the
competitive striving to possess a woman fired his sexual desire, whereas
her actual procurement dulled it. For Casanova the subjugation of
women represents the separant "swallowing" and overpowering of his
objective surroundings because women to him were reified chattels,
impersonal objects to be acquired and owned.

Casanova divided human beings into those who command and those
who obey, those who subjugate and those who are enslaved, with
nothing in between. He is at pains to assure us that he has never lost his
freedom to a woman, implying thereby that invariably he was the
master of women without ever being subdued by them.[44] The doubtful
veracity of this statement is irrelevant. What is pertinent is that
Casanova presents himself as the ultimate male chauvinist with all
women being his for the taking, while he is to be taken by none. It is
typical of the separant Casanova that, in one instance, in order to ward
off competitors away from his new erotic prey, he warns her about the
"snares by those whose only occupation in Paris was to deceive girls
and to put no trust in the gilded words which a man full of ardor will
address to you to obtain your favors; believe him when deeds will have
preceded words, for after enjoyment the fire goes out, and you will find
that you were betrayed."[45] At the same time he was scheming and
searching for the quickest way to bed the girl himself. Casanova's single-
mindedness concerning the sexual possession of women made it crucial
for him to succeed in each of his erotic campaigns. A failure in one of
his schemes of seduction was conceived by him as a major catastrophe,
a disaster which filled him with outrage and a sense of worthlessness,
which indeed it should have because the conquest of women by
seduction was Casanova's profession and vocation in life.

Casanova regarded his seductions as battles waged, combats staged and wars to be won. This is in line with his separant need to "devour" (i.e., include within himself) and win his sexual objects on a competitive basis. Casanova describes one of his sexual conquests, actually a *ménage à trois,* with two girls as follows: "It was now my part to invite my fair enemy to begin a battle whose tactics could be known only to love, a combat which, enchanting all our senses could have no fault but that of ending too soon; but I excelled in the art of prolonging it. I clasped her frenziedly, at the same time reveling in the ecstasy I saw on the face of Angelica, who was witnessing so splendid a combat for the first time."[46]

Lovemaking is a combat. The bedding of a girl should be planned like a military operation, and the girl herself is the enemy. As everything is fair in love and war, and for Casanova love (sex) is war, he would do anything and everything irrespective of morals, common decency or the law, to win his sexual combat. This is in line with our conception of the separant personality type of which Casanova is an extreme instance. His later oral fixation makes him see himself as the "good self", an egocentric *crème de la crème* confronted by a bad mother-woman-object who has to be fought, attacked and if possible subjugated. Casanova despised women. His only aim was to possess them sexually which to him was tantamount to triumphing over and vanquishing them as a trophy of victory. This is why he was not so particular about the appearance of a woman, her age, or whether she lived in a castle or in a brothel. The goal was to have a woman sexually. This having (i.e., taking and possessing) was the essence of the sexual act for Casanova. His utopian dream was to bed, and hence conquer and subjugate, all womankind. The only unforgivable sin of this Ghenghis Khan of the boudoir was to refrain from laying a girl when he had the opportunity to do so.[47]

The Sisyphean Casanova was spurred mostly by the dynamics of seduction. He aimed to prolong the time it took to procure his prey because once he had his share of orgasms with a woman he lost interest in her. This might also be the reason why Casanova was very much attracted by modesty. The more shy and chaste a girl was the more he was drawn to her.[48] This is because the process of her seduction would be more elaborate and more serpentine, and therefore more rewarding. Also innocence should be seduced all the way until it reaches and enjoys dirty and profane sex. Casanova aimed to overpower the profane mother-woman by her own weapons, that is by vile sex. If she had some Tantalic spiritual innocence in her so much the better, the triumphal profanation would be sweeter. Casanova enjoyed "dirty" sex and scatology. He was especially aroused by the clothes of a nun.[49] In his case this is not so much fetishism as a symbol of a Sisyphean rebellion against his own religious indoctrination and its Tantalic adulation of the sacred love for the pure mother-of-God woman symbolized by the gown of a nun. His copulation with the nun had more than a tinge of a profane ritual: it was a defiant sacrificial demonstration to the immaculate mother-woman up there and above, that in the here-and-now the only sacred service man and woman can perform for each other is to quench their raging desires by eruptions of sex and by loads of orgasms.

The Losers

We have already pointed out that both Don Juan and Casanova are failures. The former seeks immersion in the graces of archetypal womanhood, but is left with a succession of brief, amorous liaisons which fail to satisfy him. The latter craves to "swallow" and possess all womanhood in order to assert his oral omnipotence, but all he achieves is an endless array of copulations, each of which give him a pitifully short illusion of omnipotence. Don Juan is baited by love to achieve the goals of his participant core vector to partake in unity; Casanova is baited by sex to realize the craving of his separant core vector to overpower his objective and human surroundings. Don Juan is a Tantalic failure whereas Casanova is a Sisyphean failure.

Our programming has cleverly baited all of us, each with a particular lure to fit our personality types and core vectors, to carry on its design which is unknown to us but which necessitates a continuous chain of reproductive cycles. What is fascinating in these dynamics is that both Casanova and Don Juan seem to be aware of their programmed baits yet they are unable to resist them. In this they follow their mythological counterparts. Sisyphus who keeps pushing his rock upwards although he knows that it is bound to roll down the hill again, and Tantalus who keeps reaching out towards the visions which give hope to quench his thirst and promise to sate his hunger, although he knows that they never fulfill their visual pledges.

Yet both Casanova and Don Juan found a way out of their baited impasse. Casanova immersed himself in sex as if it was not a baited means to our programming ends to reproduce, but an end in itself. He raised each seduction and each orgasm to the stature of creative art. Fellini understood this premise when he made his Casanova retort to praise of his sexual performance that he is an inventor, a creator of wonderful inventions. By absorbing himself totally into the intricacy of sexual intercourse Casanova halted its drudgery and turned it into an act of creation. Sex, like any other separant object-relationship, may be imbued with different meanings and given different significations by different people. An anarchist Sade aimed to annihilate society by attacking the normative system with his total libertinism, and then stifling sex itself by repetition; whereas Casanova aimed to utilize the medium of sex to express his creative ingenuity. In this manner he also attempted a Camusean rebellion. If one is baited by one's programming to engage in repetitive sex one might as well invest in it one's creative ingenuity and thus make the best of this baited bondage. We can imagine our Casanovite Sisyphus carving out of his rock the facades of the erotic sculptures on the Khajurāho temple in India. Don Juan's way out from his Tantalic impasse is more radical. His ultimate grace, which he seeks through love, is the spiritual *amour sacre* which is time-less and boundless, and not to be found in spatiotemporality. He there-fore brings about a spectacular *ex-stasis* (i.e., an extrusion from the here-and-now) through the good services of the stone commander in order to reach non-being and with it, hopefully, a partaking in the time-less bosom of the pantheistic early-oral mother-woman.

Both Don Juan and Casanova were also failures in another sense. For all their apparent supremacy over women and their disdain of them, both, in the last analysis, were controlled and dominated. Don Juan seeks communion with the archetype of the ideal woman yet he is baited by a simple smile to believe that the actual woman he encoun-ters possesses at least some of the grace he is after. This gives the specific woman in the company of Don Juan a trump card. While he is with her he hopes that she might be the harbinger of the grace for which he yearns. When he realizes that she cannot grant him the time-less bliss he longs for he turns to the next woman and the one after *da capo* — forever having the same expectations from each link on his endless chain of paramours. In the play by Tirso, Tisbea realizes this dynamic by declaring that: "Of all the girls whose rosy feet the waves kiss on these shores, I alone am not ruled by love. I sail in my little boat with my companions. I like to catch the little fish lashed by the waves. I wander free from the prisons which love fills with fools. My only pleasure is to give the fish my baited line. Others suffer and mourn, but I spend my youth without a care. I let the silly fish leap into my net and I alone do not fall into the snares of love."[50] The implication of this passage is that in the amorous encounters between man and woman the latter does the baiting — it is man that is "hooked", not woman.

Moliere recognizes Don Juan's dependence on his itinerant loves. "I must tell you that a Beauty sticks in my heart, and that attracted by her charms I have followed her quite to this city."[51] Rostand presents his Don Juan as saving the "Eternal Woman" but meanwhile being taken advantage of by the women of flesh and blood whom he chases:

> The Delilahs and their kind were made by Man
> And every clever woman knows the plan.
> At the hour when Desire steals his wit
> She returns to Man his little counterfeit:
> Eternal Woman, delicate and pale . . .
> Eternal Woman . . . masterpiece of the male![52]

When Don Juan attaches himself to a woman with the idea that she presents perfect and eternal womanhood, she manipulates him like a pawn to gain some mundane benefits.[53] Don Juan is under the impression that it is he who seduces but in fact it is the other way round. The women have chosen Don Juan by consenting to be seduced by him. The devil mocks Don Juan by the following vivid metaphor: "Oh how I seduce, says the iron to the magnet."[54] Women may seem to be seduced but "Woman enjoys Don Juan as man does his courtesan".[55] Finally, even in hell, purgatory and heaven, the Don Juan of some versions of the play is dependent on the forgiveness of his dead paramours to guide his soul to partake in the feminine graces of unity.

Casanova also proved to be a slave of his desires and hence of the women who aroused them. His sexual encounters many times cost him dearly as his chance erotic encounters were quite often with greedy women, conniving courtesans and thieving common prostitutes. They exploited him materially and involved him in their power skirmishes and intrigues which landed him in prison and exposed him to the danger of dying in the torture chambers of the Inquisition. Like all "other oriented" separants it was important for him to win the affection of others. In fact he declared it to be his sole aim.[56] He also yearned to be loved by his sexual partners although he did not wish or rather was incapable of loving them himself.[57] This indeed is the epitome of dependence of one human being on another.

Both Don Juan and Casanova were plagued by the vicissitudes of the least interest principle, although may times they also utilized it to achieve their own manipulative ends. In the play by Tirso de Molina, Tisbea proclaims the most concise formulation of this principle. "This is the game of love: to love those who hate you and to despise those who adore you."[58] Indeed in those versions of the play in which Don Juan's love was carried over to hell, purgatory or heaven it was for those women who rejected rather than accepted him.

Casanova also recognized the viciousness of the least interest principle as becomes apparent from the following passage of his memoirs: "We complain of women who though they love us and are sure that they are loved, refuse us their favors; and they are wrong. If they love us they must fear to lose us and hence must do all that they can to keep alive our desire to attain possession of them. If we attain it nothing is sure than that we will no longer desire them, for one does not desire what one possesses, so women are right in refusing to yield to our desires."[59] This displays a rare fairness to women and an acknowledgement of their right to defend their interests. Although Casanova was a master manipulator of the least interest principle he was also many times its victim. Being an extreme separant he always took it very hard when he was rejected by a woman. His rejection was usually replete with depression, self-pity and temper tantrums. Sexual conquests were his life's focal concern so that every rejection irrevocably tarnished his sense of choice and worth, and could not be blotted out by subsequent sexual triumphs.

Cad About Town

Casanova was the almost perfect separant object-manipulator. It is appropriate, therefore, to examine how he treated his objective surroundings which included, of course, human beings. He tended to manipulate people and exploit them for his own ends without recourse to his conscience which remained rather clean because he rarely used it. He was an artful liar and even proud of hies lies especially if he could get away with them. He was not particularly fond of keeping his promises and although he did not beatify betrayal à la Jean Genet, he practised it regularly and betrayed almost everyone around him as a matter of course. His practical jokes smack of moral Daltonism. He recounts some of them as follows:

> We would often spend entire nights roaming through the different quarters of the city inventing and carrying out all sorts of impudent pranks. One of our favorite pastimes was to untie gondolas and let them drift down the canal, enjoying the owners' curses in advance. We would wake up midwives and tell them to hurry to the house of some lady who was not even pregnant. We did the same thing with doctors, making them run half-dressed to the house of some great nobleman who was in perfect health. The priests also had their turn: we would send them to some husband who was sleeping peacefully beside his wife and had very little interest in their extreme unction. If we saw an open door we would creep into the house and suddenly terrify the sleepers by shouting that the door of their house was open. We were overjoyed whenever we could enter a belfry, for we would then alarm the entire parish by sounding the tocsin, as though some terrible fire had broken out. We would then cut the bell ropes,

so that the churchwardens would be unable to summon the faithful to mass the next morning.[60]

One of his practical jokes actually killed a man but he was determined to deny it.[61] He calls the raping of a woman by a group of eight thugs, of which he was one, a "noble exploit".[62] Where sexual seduction is concerned all deceit is permitted and every snare commendable. He recounts at length in his memoirs how he assured a young girl that he could never seduce her, only subsequently to deflower her after performing a fake marriage with her.[63] During the time he was still a man of God and the church he never felt any contradiction between his divine vocation and his lechery. Being so completely separant and hence tyrannically possessive this master fornicator demanded total fidelity from the women he seduced.[64]

Casanova the archetypal separant object-manipulator believed that one either manipulated one's environment or was manipulated by it, and by this criterion he measured success and failure. Similarly he believed that power reigns supreme and as the powerful are also just, therefore the weak and the powerless must be unjust. Casanova was passionately involved in the intrigues of most of the royal courts in Europe and of the Holy See. He would virtually prostrate himself with abject flattery before anyone whom he suspected of having any vestige of power. He was a snob and a name-dropper who used any pretext to be seen in the company of important people. One of the main characteristics of the separant object-manipulator and *arriviste* is to be the camp follower of the high and mighty. In other words he was "other directed", always trying to ascertain what others expected of him and complying with their expectations if it suited his goals. The following is a typical excerpt from the social credo and value system of Casanova: "I saw that to accomplish anything I must bring all my physical and moral faculties into play, make the acquaintance of the great and the powerful, exercise strict self-control, and play the chameleon to all those whom I should see it was my interest to please."[65]

An Ayn Randist egoist would seem to have the altruism of a Franciscan Friar when compared to Casanova. Everything he covets should be his for the asking. When he was openly wooing an advocate's wife and the husband showed his resentment, Casanova was flabbergasted: "I was amazed at the advocate for he could not fail to know that he owed me his wife."[66] Plain and simple, the husband *owed* Casanova his wife. When Casanova failed to get what he wanted it is mostly others who were to blame, rarely himself. He accused everybody in sight for his frustrations and blamed them with a resentful self-pity for having betrayed him. His need to assert his separant worth and choice on a competitive basis made it necessary that his feminine escorts should be deemed more beautiful than others because it raised his worth and esteem. This again is utilizing women as reified objects to achieve one's separant ends. In Casanova's world of power, money and sex, everything is interchangeable with everything else. Power with money, power with sex and of course, sex with money. Deflowering a virgin, for instance, cost 25 gold louis.[67] Casanova's separant core vector, including his motivation to achieve power and money, was anchored on sex. He would go to any length and expend any amount of power manipulation and money to gain entry to his ad hoc sexual target. Thus his sexual adventures become simplistic, repetitive and predictable: another false declaration of love, another threat, another disguise as a fake officer in the army or another false promise of marriage — all to get the lady in bed, even if just once, and the devil take the consequences.

Moira and Rebellion

Casanova believed in his *Moira,* in his lot in life and in his predestination. He accepted the world and human society as they were. He did not aim to change them. All he wished was to exploit them to his advantage. Many times his compulsive lechery ran him foul of the law and of the Inquisition, but he became so expert in the double-talk of the church and the hypocrisy of the nobility that he invariably extricated himself from quandaries in which his philandering and debauchery landed him. In fact Casanova had much of the Greek separant spirit in him. He relied on his predestined *Moira* lacking any notions of guilt or culpability, and meanwhile fornicated like a satyr. It was inconceivable to Casanova that God wanted man to renounce the pleasures of enjoyment which have been implated in man by God himself. Casanova could not imagine that the Great Being could enjoy the griefs, the sufferings and the abstinences offered to Him in sacrifices by fanatics and ascetics. "They are madmen," says Casanova, "God can demand of his creatures only that they practise the virtues whose seed he has sown in their souls."[68]

Fellini grasped this characteristic of Casanova by portraying him as mounting one woman after another and sighing like a Sisyphus that he is carrying out his duty. Casanova did not believe in the ever after but tried to accept life as it was. He had no rebellious inclinations and was careful not to transgress his fate and destiny because this would constitute hubris dreaded by all believers of *Moira* from the times of the Homeric Hymns to the present day.

Don Juan, on the other hand, is a rebel. His rebellion is first of all directed against a repressive and cynical creator "playing a cruel game with the pitiful creatures created out of his mocking moods".[69] Don Juan hurls his defiance against a metaphysical providence which baits him by love to other mortals for ends unknown to him. In the play by Grabbe, Faust, Don Juan's alter ego defies the ambivalences and ambiguities of the Bible as follows: "You Great Book, you Bible-Rock of Faith, they say — burdened with variants and double meanings, full of wisdom and strange aphorisms: your leaves offer no refuge in this raging storm, parched and withered, they fall like foliage in autumn; for, if I do not feel it within myself, not a thousand Bibles, not a thousand Paradises, not all the Eternities can lead me to salvation!"[70] Don Juan thus shares the basic philosophical stance of the Existentialists who deplore the "thrownness" of Man into this world and the silence of God vis-a-vis the human predicament.

Don Juan's second target of rebellion is bourgeois values. Unlike Casanova who seemed to enjoy the duplicity, the rituals and the stylized hypocrisy, Don Juan mocks his rival suitors with acrid sarcasm: "How long will it go on? How long until the Señor speaks of cloak and beret, of money and dowry, of procreation, child-rearing, and education?"[71]

Most versions of the play depict Don Juan as a non-repentant metaphysical rebel who sticks to his defiance even on the brink of hell. For our context Don Juan's rebellion is relevant on two counts. First, his insistence on seeking the spiritually impossible even if there cannot be any chance of its realization. This often involves grave danger but then "only in danger does life take on any meaning".[72] Don Juan thus preceded Nietzsche in his mandate to Man to imbue meaning into his life by living dangerously. Second, even if man is small and insignificant in spatiotemporality, his soul is timeless and infinite. "My dear Knight," says Faust, "you have shown me the universe, high and low — yet, believe me, small as man may be, he is far greater than the world. He is infinite; strong enough not to bother with taming the devil, but also strong enough to hope that he may one day share God's throne, even if he has to fight for it."[73]

The myth of Don Juan has a message for Man: in his rebellion Man can become a junior partner in Creation. He may be small, weak and miserable but his defiant spirit has to be reckoned with and cannot be ignored even by a silent God.

9
The Sacrificial Bondage

When Isaac again saw Abraham's face it was changed,
his glance was wild, his form was horror.
He seized Isaac by the throat, threw him to the ground
and said, "Stupid boy, dost thou then suppose that I
am thy father? I am an idolator.
Dost thou suppose that this is God's bidding?
No, it is my desire."

S. Kierkegaard: *Fear and Trembling*

The third phase of separation is the socionormative indoctrination marked by the imposition of social responsibilities and the rites of passage from the forgiveness of childhood to the burdens of adulthood. In most cultures the father or his surrogate is the doctrinaire figure who is instrumental in imposing on both his sons and daughters the many norms and duties, in this way preparing them for their social roles. The imposition by the father of the duties of the normative system of society on his son has been described by us elsewhere as the Isaac Syndrome[1] and will be adapted to fit the present context. The mytho-empirical model for the consecration of the daughter to the harsh exigencies of the normative system of the group might be the offering of Iphigenia by her father Agamemnon as dramatized by Euripides.

Whereas the first victimization of the child at orality is maternal, blocking the free expression of the child's incestuous desires, the second is paternal as it coerces the child and harnesses him into the normative system of society of which the father is deemed to be the agent within the family. Usually this coercive and normative victimization is backed by the absolute authority of God, the fatherland or the secular deity of materialist dialectics. As in the mytho-empirical model of the offering of Isaac there is usually a symbiotic relationship between the stern doctrinaire father and a metaphysical source of absolute authority. It is important to note that this continuing victimization of the child by his parents from early orality onwards is an integral part of the separant processes of development and socialization. The maternal victimizations leads to the Sisyphean sublimation towards cultural creativity, and the paternal victimization leads to the separant insertion of the pubescent individual within a normative pigeonhole sanctioned by society.

The mother is the symbol of grace. She stands for the carefree participant longing for the forgiveness and irresponsibility of children within the family fold prior to their being harnessed within the normative burdens of society through the doctrinaire authority of the father. In some tribes the rites of passage from childhood to puberty are presided over by the elders while the mothers join in the wailing of the circumcised, aching and suffering sons.[2] A mytho-empirical corroboration for the mother being the image of grace for the pubescent son is the angel who orders Abraham not to slaughter Isaac. The angel is invariably depicted by the iconography of the offering of Isaac as female.[3] It would not be far-fetched, therefore, to regard the female angel as representing the mother Sarah.

The Offering

On a previous occasion we presented the Isaac Syndrome as the paternal normative aggression against children countering the Oedipal pressures of children against their father.[4] The main thrust of the mytho-empirical offering of Isaac, however, is the sacrificial enmeshing of the young into the disciplinarian boundaries of the normative system of society. All normative breaking-in involves varying measures of sacrificial curbings of the well-being and freedom of the pubescent young to the "welfare" of the group. These sacrificial indoctrinations are performed by the father acting as intermediary between the young and the social rules which are sustained through his authority by secular or divine transcendence.

Some time ago the martially effective but heavy mouthed Chief of Staff of the Israeli Army thanked the parents of cadets in an officers' training course "for donating their sons to the service of the Jews in Israel". The macabre paradox inherent in the Isaac Syndrome is that for the individual bereaved parent the loss of a son in war for the glory of the fatherland is the sacrifice of everything for nothing. Yet this offering of the young to the martial Moloch has been going on from time immemorial, it is going strong today and gives no signs of subsiding until the end of days.

Literature abounds with the sacrificial coercion of children to the carnivorous exigencies of the normative system. Kafka's letters to his father reek with the agonies of a son being abused by his father in the name of bourgeois morality. Kafka's relationship with his father is, no doubt, related to his description in *Metamorphosis* of Mr Samsa, the petit bourgeois father, who degrades his misfit son out of shame and fear of the social norms. Frank Wedekind in his play *The Awaking of*

Spring portrays a father who justifies the commitment of his son to a notorious institution for juvenile delinquents (because the son made love to a girl) by his conviction that the institution stresses and enhances Christian thought and logic. The boy's mother, like her archetypal image in the iconography of Isaac's offering, prays for grace and forgiveness. The mother laments that their son who is basically a good boy is bound to become a hardened criminal in the institution. But paternal stern judgement prevails and the boy, Melchior, is confined in an institution for delinquents for the heinous crime of having had sex with a girl. Wedekind's play focuses the sacrificial coercion of parents onto our context, namely the suppression of sexual manifestations in the name of social propriety, morals and religion.

Paternal sanction and raging admonition bursts forth from Francis Bacon's portrait of "The Screaming Pope".[5] In this painting Bacon uses Velázquez's serene portrayal of Pope Innocent X seated with full regalia on his throne and covers it with a transparent projection of a frozen scream. The pope's mouth is wide open and it seems to emit shrieks of horror, howling curses and yells of damnation. These might have been the howls of Bacon's own authoritarian father when he found out that his adolescent son was a transvestite.

By free association we mention the recent televized interviews with Pope John Paul II whose benign face of a good natured Polish peasant became hard and stern whenever he reconfirmed the church's proscriptions against married priests, abortion and homosexuality. Indeed sex remains one of the normative fortes of the church as if it realizes that sexual roles are Divinity's choice media through which it may manifest its programming of humanity. The persistent proscription against the free manifestations of sexuality, and especially paraphilias between consenting adults, has induced John Money to label the official secular and religious authorities as sexual dictatorships hunting sexual heretics.[6] This indeed is the extension of the Isaac Syndrome to the social and group levels where the authoritarian figure of Abraham permeates the power structures of society and religion.

The Oblation of the Daughter

Mothers usually warn their children when they are naughty: "You wait when Daddy comes back home and I tell him all about your behaviour today." The mother implies that she herself does not wield the normative rod but that it is the role of the authoritarian figure in the family (i.e., the father) to mete out sanctions to whomever they are due. The doctrinaire role of the father is equally directed towards the son and the daughter. The contents of the social norms imposed by paternal authority vary, however, with gender. The son is coerced to undertake the burdens of social responsibility whereas the daughter is harnessed into her feminine roles of marriage, household duties and childbearing.

A partial mytho-empirical feminine counterpart to the sacrificial rites of passage inherent in the Isaac Syndrome may be inferred from the Demeter-Kore myth. Zeus, Kore's father, was instrumental in ejecting his daughter from the family fold and the protection of her mother and her delivery to his hellish brother Hades.[7] The implication here is that Kore was taken away from the protective care of her mother by the collusionary devices of her father and exposed to the trials of matrimonial servitude to her husband, an experience registered by the pubescent Kore as coercive and infernal. Yet this is the social essence of a daughter's betrothal who is given in marriage to the appropriate husband as determined mostly by the political calculations, social expectations and economic needs of the father of the bride.

The most striking feminine parallel to the Isaac Syndrome, replete with the gory sacrificial details and the enormity of its socionormative implications, is the sacrifice of Iphigenia to the exigencies of socio-religious commands through the authoritarian agency of her father Agamemnon. Iphigenia is sacrificed to the glory of the group and to patriotic honour, which is the extension of the glory and honour of Agememnon himself, in the same way that the normative authority of Abraham was the extension of Divinity. Unlike Abraham, who never doubted the commands of God, Agamemnon waivers and rages against the need to sacrifice his daughter for the glory of the army and the honour of the mob. This stems from the differences of the Judaic and Greek conceptions of divine authority. For Abraham, God's commands were the epitome of justice which could not be doubted and should not be questioned, whereas the anthropomorphic Greek Gods made no pretence of being just.

In the care of Iphigenia the Greeks knew that the Gods were the pronouncers of $\alpha\nu\alpha\gamma\kappa\eta$ (necessity) and $\mu o\iota\rho\alpha$ (fate), which were the prime movers of Greek religion and the Greek normative system. The outcome, however, was the same: both Isaac and Iphigenia were sacrificed to the divine projections of socionormative mandates. According to the *Midrash*, Abraham ran joyfully to the altar and bound himself on it.[8] Iphigenia, however, was not so willing a victim. In one of the most shattering monologues in world drama she pleads with Agamemnon:

> Had I the voice of Orpheus, O my father,
> If I could sing so that the rocks would move,
> If I had words to win the hearts of all,

> I would have used them. I have only tears.
> See, I have brought them! They are all my power.
> I clasp your knees, I am your suppliant now,
> I, your own child; my mother bore me to you.
> O, kill me not untimely! The sun is sweet!
> Why will you send me into the dark grave?
> I was the first to sit upon your knee,
> The first to call you father, . . . [9]

At the end however, she accepts her fate and goes to the altar with the patriotic announcement of "Bid my father come and touch the altar. I will bring this day victory and salvation unto Greece".[10] Like Sarah in the offering of Isaac myth, Clytemnestra, Iphigenia's mother, is the figure of grace condemning the paternal cruelty as expressed by the divine mandate to sacrifice her daughter for the glory of Greece.

To sum up our present premise we avail ourselves of a model we have presented previously (figure 7) and add to it some new components to form figure 11. The implications of this model are that whereas the oral maternal inducement to creativity is mainly in the realm of a separant organization of one's environment and its instrumental manipulation, the paternal socializing prodding is more towards socionormativeness and its transcendental and ideological bases.

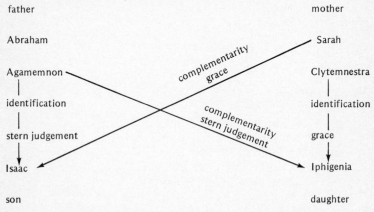

Figure 11. Child/Parent Relationship: Authority and Grace

Mother's Grace

The vicissitudes of social separation, the cruel rites of passage from childhood to puberty, the harsh coercion into the delimiting social norms and the sacrificial horrors of the Isaac and Iphigenia syndromes are all presided over by the father. They induce both male and female children to long for the cushioned forgiveness and lenient protection of mother. For a homosexual Proust this longing became so intense that he closed himself in a padded womb-like room and wrote volume after volume idolizing his beloved mother. For the fiercely heterosexual Camus his great love for his mother may have turned into a generalized longing for the grace of womanhood, rather than for a specific woman. Hence Camus had "a lifelong quest for the tender friendship of women."[11]

It might well be that the chivalrous adoration of ladies and the troubadours' odes to the graces of women, stemming from the crusades in the Middle Ages, were spurred by the insane trials of the hordes of cross-bearing warriors sacrificed to fight impossible wars by a stern absolutist God. The graceful tender mother-woman was the vision of everything adorable and merciful back home, in stark contrast to the squalor and death ordained by a graceless, unforgiving and uncompromising father God.

It is rather relevant that in the original Hebrew of the Bible,[12] as well as in Aramaic and Syriac, the word Grace is *Hessed* which also means incestuous and sinful. This shows, etymologically at least, that the graceful longing of the son for his mother seems to have sexual and incestuous undertones. This, of course, is a corollary of the suppressed, incestuous desire of the son for his mother at orality and its relegation to his subconscious. *Prima facie* this might explain the attraction of boys to girls who remind them directly or symbolically of their mothers, since their amatory and sexual longing for their mothers is blocked by the deeply internalized prohibition of their very early incestuous desires. The parallel attraction of daughters to men resembling their fathers in some relevant or vicarious characteristics might also be related to the dynamics of complementarity. The pubescent daughter, through identification with her mother, would be attracted to a complementary authoritarian figure linked to the normativeness of the father. Of course these relationships vary in actual families where the role of the father is soft and benign and where the mother is harsh and authoritarian. The various combinations of identifications and permutations of complementarities between parents and children of equal and different gender are virtually endless and the tracing of their effects on choice of lovers, sexual partners and males must remain outside the realm of the present work.

The Superfluous Parents

We have specified earlier that after the reproductive functions of parents have been consummated they experience a post-fulfillment decline. This is apparent in the menopausal woman and in aging men whose prostrate glands have degenerated. On the other hand most of the generative power and all the possible protection seems to be provided in abundance for the young of the species — the neonate and the foetus. It is well known that the malnutrition of the mother hardly affects the foetus because it draws whatever it needs without any regard to the welfare of its mother. Our programming seems to have placed reproduction at the top of its priorities. We claim that one of Freud's most spectacular errors was his statement that "Broad vistas open up for us when we bear in mind the fact that man's sexual instinct is not at all primarily meant to serve purposes of reproduction but is intended to furnish certain forms of gratification."[13] The *raison d'être* of sexuality is to bring about reproduction but as our programming has scaffolded all life on the dialectics between the participant and separant core vectors, sex had also to be integrated in their dynamics. Hence sex is used by our programming as a participant bait to serve the purpose of reproduction utilizing the rather transient pleasures of sex as a bait to effect fertilization.

In times of stress and danger the organism rushes to reproduce in order to fulfil its *raison d'être*. This is probably the reason for Margaret Drabble's observation that "whenever war breaks out, everybody leaps into bed with everybody. To keep the human race going, destroy and procreate".[14] This primal need of the parents to reproduce makes the offspring infinitely more important to the parents than the parents to the offspring. The parents' needs to care for their young are far more intense than the children's wish to be cared for. As the saying goes, "The cow craves to feed the calf more than the calf wishes to be fed". Consequently the parents' expectation for thanks and appreciation from their children and a reciprocation of care from them when parents reach old age is many times sadly lacking. Our programming makes it quite clear that it is the children that are all important. Once the parents have fulfilled their procreative functions they are all but superfluous.

Parents who are not otherwise creative often regard their children as their sole creation. This might bring about a Sisyphean clinging to children as objects which in extreme cases manifests itself in a Medusan petrification of children by their subjugating parents. Moreover when parents possessively regard their children as objectified chattels they cannot bear the children's efforts to liberate themselves from the stifling parental yoke by trying to establish an intersubjective liaison with a lover or a mate. Worse still parents may try to rescuscitate their own amatory longings and phantasies by involving themselves vicariously in the love affairs of their children, often with disastrous results for both young and old. Parents many times emotionally black-mail their children for love and attention and on a more sophisticated level they may prod their children to achieve creative goals which the parents themselves could not or did not have the opportunity to accomplish. Indeed we claim that the maternal Sisyphean socialization of her children at orality is very much linked to their achievement orientation whereas the later paternal normative indoctrination is supposed to mold the young into the accepted socio-transcendental cast as conceived by the mediating authority of the father.

J. H. Brenner, one of the early morbid Existentialist Israeli authors, called one of his books *Bereavement and Failure.* For many years the liaison of this title was incomprehensible to me until it dawned on me that the loss of an offspring for a parent is the ultimate failure. Parents are programmed metaphysically and biologically, conditioned psychologically and indoctrinated culturally to reproduce and rear offspring so that their loss is tantamount to the destruction of their ontological reason for being. The loss of a parent to an adult offspring is many times painful but is ultimately accepted as the natural course of life. The loss of a young child to a parent, on the other hand, is inevitably experienced as a catastrophic blow which usually results in a permanent emotional handicap and in many cases in a crippling mental incapacitation. The death of a child for most parents causes a traumatic change of their *Weltanschauung* and in some cases a radical change in their order of priorities, meanings and even the course of their lives. There is no armistice for bereaved mothers and the patriotic glee of victories in wars are hardly ever shared by bereaved parents whose sons were killed fighting. They feel cheated and a red hot rage at themselves for having either actively or tacitly participated in the sacrifice to the mirage of patriotism and abstract notions of glories, ideologies and creeds reinforced by the waving of coloured rags. The shouting of slogans by be-medalled marionettes and the self-important verbosity of hypocritical politicians is no compensation for the searing pain which can never be communicated to anybody who has not experienced the same loss. Such pain cannot even be dulled by sharing it with their partner in bereavement.

The Parental Investment

Parental investment is defined by Trivers as:

> . . . any investment by the parent in an individual offspring that increases the offspring's chance of surviving (and hence reproductive success) at the cost of the parent's ability to invest in other offspring. So defined, parental investment includes the metabolic investment in the primary sex cells and refers to any investment (such as feeding or guarding the young) that benefits the young. It does not include effort expended in finding a member of the opposite sex or in subduing members of one's own sex in order to mate with a member of the opposite sex, since such effort (except in special cases) does not affect the survival chances of the resulting offspring and is therefore not '*parental* investment'.[15]

In most species, including Man, the parental investment of females from the size and number of their sex cells to their subsequent caring for the young far exceeds the investment of the male. However in some species males may build nests, brood eggs and help feed and protect the young. In these species the customary more striking display features of the male and its more active courting behaviour is invested in the female.[16] The general rule is that the gender that invests less actively courts and "runs after" the gender that invests more in its parenthood. The latter, however, holds the prerogative of choosing a mate from the competing individuals of the opposite sex.[17] Consequently in most species, including Man, males compete for females who choose their suitable mate by various overt or covert techniques. Trivers does not try to explain the deeper dynamics for parental investment and choice of mate. We, however, attempt to link the parental investment premise with our core vector dynamics of separation and participation. Trivers points out that the pattern of relative parental investment is strongly linked to the differentiation of mobile sex cells fertilizing the immobile ones.[18] It is precisely this differentiation that is linked to the polar dynamics of our core vectors. The more mobile and participant male sperm court and seek the immobile ovum to be absorbed by it. Analogously the less investing and more mobile participant male competes with other males for selection by the less mobile and more investing separant female. We thus provide a core-programming dimension to the sociobiological premise of parental investment.

The male is so wasteful in his enormous number of spermatozoa as compared to the limited number of the females' ova that this in itself makes the less investing participant male actively seek the more investing separant female. The male seeks the adventures of courting, the competition with his peers over the females' favours and the pleasures of mating; whereas the female is more interested in the attention, care and protection which her potential mate can provide her and her off-spring. This is the common model but in cases where males have a larger role in nest building and offspring care the roles may be reversed, with females competing for the sexual favours of males.[19] The interesting point is that the male, having invested less in his amatory relationship, is ever tempted to leave the female he has just copulated with and seek a new adventure. The females, however, women included, tend to be less promiscuous because they look for a more lasting relationship. In some societies copulation, especially the first one, is so preciously special that the worst sin a virgin can commit is to have pre-marital sex. In such cases she forfeits her social position, her marital future and many times her life. Consequently females favour monogamy more than males who are only reluctant monogamists. This sociobiological premise may be interpreted by us that the more separant woman is programmed to seek a more steady relationship with a man on whom she can ever rely for support and protection for her and her children. Man, on the other hand, is programmed to seek the archetypal mother-woman. Yet this goal is never achieved so that after one love affair and after one orgasm males continue to seek, in a true Tantalic manner, more love affairs and different orgasms. Women, whatever the feminists claim to the contrary, are content to have a family cared for by one husband whereas the basic tendency of man is for polygamy.

The participant males are more mobile so that they may court the more stationary females with greater vigor, consequently the males' metabolism is quicker.[20] Females are not only less mobile but also less spontaneous in their choice of mates. For the less investing male the encounter might be just another passing amorous or sexual episode, but for the more investing female the socioeconomic welfare of herself and her children is at stake. Of special relevance is the phenomenon of female mice aborting when exposed to the smell of a new male,[21] meaning that a new and more vigorous master of the house has arrived who has chased away the previous one so that the female mouse is ready to be impregnated by the new and obviously more successful mate. Separant expediency, pragmatism and quick adaptability is always advantageous for the female of the species whenever the welfare of her family is concerned.

The separant choice of the female is based on her need for a strong and vigorous (i.e., genetically healthy) male who is willing and able to care for her and her offspring. The female uses many manipulative devices to test her potential mate's suitability for his roles as familial protector and provider. She develops studied coyness and shyness which induces the male to court more vigorously and persistently to prove his serious intentions.[22] Not to be promiscuous for a woman is to safeguard her greater parental investment so that "she does not give it away" without the appropriate sociobiological renumeration in offspring, family and social status. The male, on the other hand, tends to be more promiscuous because of his greater participant mobility and lesser parental investment. This premise might also help explain the fact that most prostitutes are women. Their higher parental investment and their greater separant interest in the establishment of a family and the rearing of children renders them more reluctant to be promiscuous. Hence they have to be induced by money and other renumerations to sell their sexual services. This might also be the reason for the stigma attached to prostitution because women debase, thereby, their parental investment and act contrary to their separant core vector which programmes them for motherhood and family formation. In like manner rape is condemned and abhored because it violates the possibility of the choice of a mate by the proper sociobiological criteria.

10
Homo Sexualis:
The Sex-Anchored Animal

Clearly the naked Ape is the sexiest primate alive
Desmond Morris: *The Naked Ape*

Biologists usually insist that Man is just another mammal "except for", and then they go on and ennumerate the many differences. With sex, however, the differences between human beings and other animals are not only numerous but also formidable. Some of the most conspicuous differences are first of all that man, except for some short periods at the beginning and the end of his life, is almost constantly sexually alert and passionate, whereas most other animals are sexually receptive only during their periods of estrus. Most animals have breeding cycles which are related to the weather and the seasons of the year. Man, however, may breed throughout the year and around the clock. It is interesting to note in this context that the more domesticated an animal is the less distinct are its sexual cycles.[1] Hence with other animals too, culture (i.e., artificial and artifactual changes of environment) blurs the original patterns and reproductive cycles of sex.

The separation between the pleasures of sex and its reproductive function is a unique human feature. Man is probably the only species which tends to impute to it romanticism, shame and many times guilt. Man uses contraceptives and sophisticated stimulating devices aiming to derive maximum pleasure of the sexual act which becomes an aim in itself. The numerous paraphilias and rape are almost exclusively within the domain of the sexual behaviour of the human animal. All this is the corollary of human's sublimatory anchor on sex and its derivations of lust and love as a surrogate means to fulfil both the Sisyphean and Tantalic quests of the individual human beings. Hence sex is everywhere: in the lure of advertisements, in downtown smut shops, in airports and on news-stands. It thickens the air of cinemas, shrouds television screens, hovers over the lawns of colleges, coffee houses and resort shows. It is on the minds of vacationers, convention-goers and scientists who scan the participants at the opening session of scientific conferences for possible mates for the night. It is projected by ayatollahs prescribing *chadors* for Iranian woman, by rabbis preaching the purity of the family and by popes condemning abortions.

Many theorists relate this human obsession with sex to the unique development of pair bonding of man and woman. The human hunting societies favoured the evolution of the loss of estrus and a sexually ever-willing woman who is continuously receptive to her sexually ever-able mate who unexpectedly comes back from a hunt after a long absence. The many times long and unexpected hunting trips of the male and the continuous sexual receptivity of his female (apart from his own uninterrupted lust) made him both jealous and quite often sexually deprived.[2] His jealousy and anxiety were somewhat relieved by creating stable bonding with his mate back home, while his constant sexual craving was sublimated into song, cave painting and other modes of creativity. We may ask, however, why is modern society even more dominated by sex than its hunting and gathering predecessors? Also, what were the personality core dynamics which accompanied the evolution of the constant sexual eagerness and receptivity of our hunter-ancestors?

The answer to these queries could well be provided by our present premises. These postulate that the initial suppression of the free expression of sex was effected by the maternal proscription of incest which sublimated the libidinal potential and channelled it into separant cultural creativities of which the hunting tools and weapons may have been some of its manifestations. Consequently the loss of estrus and the development of pair bonding could have been the evolutionary and concommitant social manifestations of the maternal incest taboos. These in turn were reinforced by paternal, normative and religious indoctrination. The blocking of the free expression of sex by the maternal proscriptions of incest and the normative-sacrificial paternal doctrines of an ever-sexually aroused human being has a double effect. First, it is sublimated into the maternal Sisyphean culture of the environment and the paternal religious and Tantalic ideologies. Second, sex becomes an anchor of unfilfilled aims and cravings, both separant-Sisyphean and participant-Tantalic. Therefore the more Sisyphean a society is the more it provides opportunities for achievement-based failure experiences. Hence in modern fiercely Sisyphean societies, sex reigns supreme both as a symbol and as an alternative outlet to frustrated achievement goals. The most conspicuous image flowing from the communication media through advertising and entertainment is the female body luring and baiting the sexually obsessed male. In participant traditional societies the norms and religious mandates are also sex related:

marriage, adultery, female attire and behaviour are the focal concerns of theocracies such as Saudi Arabia and Khomeini's Iran. It is also characteristic that the legendary founder of the Hasidic movement, the Besht, said that: "Prayer is an intercourse with the Divine Presence. Like in intercourse, one should gain entry by moving and wriggling, but later one can be still and be glued to the Shechina (the Divine Presence) with the utmost attachment."[3]

Only human beings have sexual problems even if physically fit. This is because their culture-based aims and quests, both Sisyphean and Tantalic, are imbued with sexual manifestations and linked with sexual alternatives. Consequently when personality dynamics and cultural quests are impeded, distorted or blocked, corresponding disturbances of the sexual functions may occur.

Sisyphean Shame and Tantalic Guilt

A separant personality in a Sisyphean society is very much dominated by the "generalized other". The shame of "what will they say" (i.e., the anxiety about the imminent disapproval of the generalized other) is the main normative control of the separant bourgeoisie. In our model this stems from the maternal proscription of incest sublimated into separant patterns of culture regulated by Sisyphean normative controls. A polarized double standard has evolved in the moral *Weltanschauung* of the bourgeois and the society which breeds him. One can engage in promiscuity, adultery and fornication so long as the neighbours or, God forbid, the press are not aware of it. Discretion is the pass word in the sexual exploits of the bourgeoisie and scandal is anathema. Such double-decked sexual mores have been described by Stephen Zweig in his autobiographical account of *Fin de Siècle* Vienna,[4] and by Max Nordau's *The Accepted Lies of Human Culture* in which he exposes the moral hypocrisy of nineteenth-century Europe including its sexual habits. Nordau relates that: " . . . a debutante who blushes with shame (when sex is mentioned), may readily climb into the wedding bed of a moneyed tycoon in order to fulfil her passion for parties and fancy health resorts."[5] Nineteenth-century European bourgeoisie seems to have outwardly ignored the sheer existence of sexual desire, frequented a vast number of venereal disease infested whorehouses, patronized hordes of streetwalkers, and supported innumerable courtesans and mistresses.

Of special interest is the report by the dissident Soviet sexologist Mikhail Stern that official Soviet policy regards sex as non-existent. Sex in the USSR is ruled by normative repression and prudishness.

Stern says that: "Sadomasochism and drink often rule the male-female relationship. Violence, alcoholism and sex form an explosive cocktail." Stern believes that 45 per cent of Soviet women are frigid. He cites a 1974 Soviet sex guide which recommends mineral water douches and vacations in warm climates as cures for female frigidity. Stern continues: "To Soviet men, holding back an ejaculation to satisfy the woman is considered an immoral act with grave physical and psychological consequences. As a result orgasm is an almost exclusively masculine privilege . . . unaware that the woman possesses any erogenous zones, the man usually imagines that as soon as his penis penetrates her vagina, the woman will be overcome with joy."[6] Prostitution is rife despite official efforts to wipe it out. If Stern is to be believed sexual mores in the fiercely separant Soviet Union are not dissimilar to the sex life of the bourgeoisie of nineteenth-century Europe.

A quick glance at some representative instances will convince us that these double-standards of sexual attitudes dominated not only the power structures and normative systems of nineteenth-century bourgeois Europe but also the Middle Ages and back to antiquity. Auguste Comte, that cornerstone of positivism who initiated an intellectual revolution in nineteenth-century Europe, was living for quite a long time on the earnings of his prostitute wife. This did not harm his eminent status among philosophers, statesmen, theologicans and businessmen.

As a sweeping generalization we can state that those nearer to the law makers and rule setters feel freer to infringe upon these laws and rules without being stigmatized or regarding themselves as deviant. "What the Rabbi permits himself to do, should be forbidden to an ordinary Jew." Ranulf and Aristophanes informs us that the Athenian aristocrats revered the traditional morality in public but never took it seriously in private. In *Ion* Euripides eulogizes the rape of Kreusa as a young girl by the God Apollo who apparently had a taste for minors. Kreusa laments and accuses: "You, son of Leto, who dispenses your oracles to all without distinction, you, the lawgiver, you allow yourself at the same time to ravish maidens and desert them to beget children and not care if they die." The Greek deities with their human frailties, not unlike the mortal elites, felt themselves free to infringe upon laws that they themselves had made. The proximity of the lawgivers to the law seems to make them lax in compliance. Agostino Chiqi had one mistress buried in the chapel of St Gregorio and had his son by another mistress baptized in the presence of the Pope and fourteen cardinals.[7]

The separant shameful concealment of sex is a hangover from the proscription of incest. It is symbolized mytho-empirically by the cladding of Adam and Eve after their sex-linked fall from grace. Yet only sex is shameful; reproduction is dutifully acclaimed and cherished as the *raison d'être* of life. The participant based components of the original sin as well as the later paternal indoctrination on the purity of daughters and the religion-based chastity of wives, reinforces the guilt aspect of sex. In traditional Tantalic societies the guilt element of sex is so marked that a considerable part of the religious norms and rituals revolve around the concealment and disguise of all sexually arousing parts of the human body, replete with the covering of the whole woman's body including her face with a shapeless piece of dark cloth and the shearing of her hair. This struggle with the external vestiges of sex is basically a fight with one's own projections of sexual desire. The strictness of the puritan's suppression of sex is a measure of the fierce internal battle aroused by the guilt-laden suppression of his own sexual desire. In some oriental societies this guilt-based strictness of sexual mores is so formidable that an infringement of them by females incurs a sanction of death executed by members of the offenders own nuclear family. This extreme guilt-based restraint of sexual expression makes for a displacement of the guilt-ridden sex onto the whole of culture. Thus we encounter the erotically sad songs of the Arab Bedouins; the guilt-obsessed Iranian Shi'ite Moslems flagellating one another and the Greek Orthodox Liturgy wailing the sadness of crushed love, punctuated periodically by the lewd winks of a Zorba.

The Lure

In the introduction to the present work we stated our basic hypothesis that sex is programmed to serve as a partial reinforcement to our core personality vectors, both separant and participant. In the present section we propose to elaborate further this baiting function of sex and love.

Sex has been shown by us to be mainly a separant mechanism of procreation. Sexual desire and love serve as a partial participant reinforcement to induce male and female to engage in an otherwise mechanical, repetitive and many times uncomfortable copulation. The boundless plasticity and elasticity of the lure of sexual desire makes it an ideal medium for the reinforcement of goals which are very different or even diametrically opposed to each other. This malleability of sexual desire allows each individual to realize through it, partially and for a limited time span alas, his or her core vector aims. A woman may reinforce through sex her basic bio-psychological separant quests by sexual phantasies at the time of orgasm, of including and incorporating the male within her. The participantly skewed male may seek (through sex) to be "swallowed" and incorporated by the woman. If a man or a woman are fixated at the oral stage of development contrary to their basic biological predisposition, the manna-like sexual desire will mould itself into phantasies to reinforce the specific core quests on the participation-separation continuum of the sexual partners.

As sexual desire has been sublimated into culture by maternal suppression of incest and paternal sacrificial normative indoctrination, it may serve also as motivational fuel to Sisyphean creativity and Tantalic revelation. Yet when sublimation fails man and woman may turn to sex and love as an alternative to frustrated ambitions and disenchanting creeds. Love and sex then become temporary solaces for the drudgeries of life and the ontological meaninglessness of existence. Stanton Peele has recently compared the addicting manifestations of sex and love which are not unlike the addiction symptoms of the opiates.[8] Love and sex are a conspicuous lure to reproduce designed by our programmer. Because sexual desire has evolved with humans into an ever-present force it has been sublimated into cultural creativity and revelation which provide an outlet of authenticity to an otherwise painful, absurd and meaningless "thrownness" into this world. Love itself may afford some limited solaces to the dire vicissitudes and drudgery of human existence.

The bait of sex seems to be continuous throughout human growth: just after birth the mouth ego rushes to suckle food and is reinforced by the sexual excitation effected by the sucking of the nipple. Later on sex is sublimated into creativity by the maternal proscription of incest and by the paternal normative prohibitions. The lure to court the other sex is motivated by love and the actual process of procreation is finally baited by sexual intercourse and orgasm. Indeed some species mate in a complex, uncomfortable and many times brutally painful manner, so that we may assume that they would never have mated without the pleasant or ecstatic decoy inherent in sexual intercourse. The *Peripatus* male fish, for instance, has his reproductive duct within a sharp spine which in intercourse drives through the female body and ejaculates its sperm in a cavity within her body.[9] Insects also have a vastly complicated and many times absurd manner of sexual intercourse: "In the majority of cases the male penis points backward and the whole organ has to be inverted before it can enter the female's genital opening. This means that mating insects often go through a considerable variety of contortions. The simplest way to achieve a successful mating seems to be for the male to alight on the female's back and curve his abdomen around to introduce the penis into the female's vagina. Some insects do mate in this way, although the males do not always have an easy time."[10] Without the lure of some sort of pleasurable sexual stimulation no insect would probably bother to undergo tortuous acrobatics which their love-making involves.

After reviewing many forms of love-making among animals and humans Briffault concludes that: "The congress of the sexes is assimilated by the impulse to hurt, to shed blood, to kill, to the encounter between a beast of prey and its victim, and all distinction between the two is not infequently lost. It would be more accurate to speak of the sexual impulse as pervading nature with a yell of cruelty than with a hymn of love."[11] Without being baited with sexual desire most animals would flee from their sexual partners and not be attracted to them with ardor, vehemence and persistence.

Linked to the bait of sex as a means of reproduction is the lure of youth in Sisyphean cultures. In ancient Greece, modern Europe, North America and other separant cultures, the cherishing of youth (which in some instances is close to worship) may be linked to its procreative potential and creative vigour. In Tantalic cultures (traditional Judaism, oriental and pre-communist Far Eastern societies) the male elders are revered as the proponents of sacrificial normativeness and religious revelation.

We note that the Gnostics, who regarded the spatiotemporal world as evil, saw love and sex as the sinister lure which seduces man to procreate and hence to continue the abject slavery of existence in the world. Jonas comments on Gnostic thought as follows: "The main weapon of the world in its great seduction is 'love'. Here we encounter a widespread motif of gnostic thought: the mistrust of sexual love and sensual pleasure in general. It is seen as the eminent form of man's ensnarement by the world: 'The spiritual man shall recognize himself as immortal, and love as the cause of death'. He who has cherished the body issued from the error of love, he remains in the darkness erring, suffering in his senses the dispensations of death."[12] The snare of man which effects reproduction and hence perpetuates the existence of Man in this world is the mystery of love.

Schopenhauer, who deplored spatiotemporality and the existence of man in it for different reasons, points at woman the culprit who allures man into reproduction. Says Schopenhauer:

With young girls Nature seems to have had in view what, in the language of the drama, is called a *striking effect*; for a few years she dowers them with a wealthy of beauty and is lavish in her gift of charm, at the expense of all the rest of their lives; so that during those years they may capture the fancy of some man to such a degree that he is hurried away into undertaking the honorable care of them as long as they live — a step for which there would not seem to be any sufficient warrant if only reason directed man's thoughts

... Here, as elsewhere, Nature proceeds with her usual economy; for just as the female ant, after fecundation, loses her wings, which are then superfluous, nay, actually a danger to the business of breeding; so, after giving birth to one or two children, a woman generally loses her beauty; probably, indeed for similar reasons.[13]

Schopenhauer continues as a remarkable precurser of modern socio-biology and states that:

... every lover will experience a marvelous disillusion after the pleasure he has at last attained, and will wonder that what was so longingly desired accomplishes nothing more than every other sexual satisfaction; so that he does not see himself much benefited by it. That wish was related to all his other wishes as the species is related to the individual, thus as the infinite to the finite. The satisfaction, on the other hand, is really only for the benefit of the species, and thus does not come within the consciousness of the individual, who, inspired by the will of the species, here served an end with every kind of sacrifice, which was not his own end at all. Hence, then, every lover after the ultimate consummation of the great work, finds himself cheated; for the illusion has vanished by means of which the individual was here the dupe of the species.[14]

We do not share Schopenhauer's misanthropy and we regard his woman baiting as the most serious blemish on his otherwise exquisite system of thought. Yet he is probably the only modern thinker who realized fully the snaring nature of sex and love which bait human beings to reproduce.

It is rather disconcerting to realize that the love of women which produced the *Song of Songs*, the poetry of Petrarch, the lovers' sculptures of Rodin as well as the multitude of novels, tunes and soap operas, were prompted by the same dynamics as the courting buzzes of bugs. Indeed curves of subcutaneous fat of the human female under a rustling piece of cloth which would seem rather neutral to a male chimpanzee or a lizard, fire the imagination and phantasies of the human male to unusual heights. For a man in love the senseless rambling of his beloved seems to him imbued with obscure yet profound meanings like a text by Heidegger. Beauty and desire are, no doubt, in the eyes of the infatuated viewer whereas the beautiful beloved is the trigger and many times an inadvertant catalyzer of the baiting desire and the luring love. The nature of the sexual bait is apparent in the momentary waning of the desire for the sexual partner right after orgasm but it surges up again with a subsequent excitation and rises to a crescendo after a period of sexual deprivation.

11
Display, Choice and Orgasm

Woman is so absolute and undeniable,
Man moves, his spirit flies here and there,
but you can't go beyond a woman.

Anne Smith: *Lawrence and Women*

The aims, techniques and rituals of courting differ widely between man
and woman. This stems from their different biological predispositions,
personality fixations and cultural role imprints. The male displays his
physical fitness and his charm in order to be admitted sexually and
accepted as a lover. He is not so much attuned to the results of his
sexual intercourse as to the intercourse itself. He is thus more inclined
to promiscuity and is less discriminate in the choice of his sexual mate.
This observation made by Williams in relation to the higher animals
generally seems to hold true also for Homo sapiens.[1] This fact is related
to the male's biological participant predisposition to seek entry within
woman as well as to an evolutionary atavism which allocated to the
male not very much more than the function of impregnating females.

The female, on the other hand, focuses right at the outset on her
offspring. She looks for a healthy (wealthy) and aggressively competitive mate who will be able to provide for her and their children a safe
and abundant existence. The male is more active in courting but the
female is the one who chooses and accepts. It is she who sets the
standards of male desirability because the final decision is hers to make.

With Man the blocking of direct sexual expression led to the longing
for the participant grace of mother-mate and its religious transformation into piety and purity. While examining the chivalric love and
poetry of the Middle Ages Huizinga says: "Love now became the field
where all moral and cultural perfection flowered. Because of his love,
the courtly lover is pure and virtuous. The spiritual element dominates
more and more, till towards the end of the thirteenth century, the
dolce stil nuovo of Dante and his friends ends by attributing to love the
gift of bringing about a state of piety and holy intuition."[2] Indeed, the
knights' tournaments in the Middle Ages are an exact replica of the

inter-male rivalry of other fauna, their display rituals and the choice of the victorious males by the females of the species. The direct sexual element in these tournaments was sublimated into "Pride, honour, love and art (which) give additional stimulus to the competition itself".[3] "Nowhere", says Huizinga, "does the erotic element of the tournament appear more clearly than in the custom of the knight's wearing the veil or the dress of his lady. In *Perceforest* we read how the lady spectators of the combat take off their finery, one article after another, to throw them to the knights in the lists. At the end of the fight they are bareheaded and without sleeves."[4] The participant religious sublimation of erotic display and inter-male rivalry inherent in the knights' tournaments are apparent in the pious pilgrimages of the chivalrous combatants to churches prior to the tournament and the dedication of their trophies to the Holy Virgin after them.[5]

Woman has been programmed to lure the male to court her aggressively and devote to her his undivided attention because this is *prima facie* evidence that he is interested in more than just a chance copulation. It indicates that he wishes to award her and their children security and protection. As a result the female is bio-psychologically predisposed to separantly manipulate the males and her physical environment in order to secure the continuity of her offspring and hence her species. The male, on the other hand, seeks more the direct and immediate expression of his sexual desire. He will strenuously compete with other males to achieve it. In human beings this inter-male competition is expressed by striving to prove to women that they are chivalrously more attentive to them, indicating that they are better providers and hence more worthy of their choice. The cultural sublimation of these display rituals and courting is usually expressed by love-drenched poetry, art and the Tantalic longing for religious grace. This model of a female-separant predisposition and the male participant anchor on sex changes drastically with female participant early oral fixations and Tantalic cultural imprints, or with male separant later oral fixations and the acquisition of Sisyphean cultural roles. But both in their original and transformed predispositions man and woman seem to have different expectations from their amorous encounters and they aim to implement these expectations by divergent means. Consequently love as subjectively longed for by each partner seems to be an impossible passion.

The Aggressive Display

Pulp magazine plots many times depict two best friends who swear brotherhood to each other. Then a *femme fatale* appears and the two

bosom friends fight over her with an "all is fair in love and war" vehemence. Another frequent phenomenon is that married couples do not
as a rule invite single women to socialize with them because the wives
object, fearing that their husbands might take a fancy to them and
there goes their love, attention and social status and security. Moreover,
even when some couples have been socializing together for quite a
while, once a couple is divorced the ex-wife is very likely not going to
be invited any more to the group for the same reasons. It seems that
whenever a sexual element is present in the intra-gender relationships
of human beings a conflict ensues; whereas the inter-gender relationship
is dominated by the dialectics of the bait of sex and the lure of love.

Tinbergen tells us that the female herring gull prostrates herself in a
submissive gesture of acceptance, signifying to the male that she is
ready for copulation.[6] There is a similar acceptance of the courting
man by the wooed woman, coupled many times by gestures and words
of submission. This could be reminiscent of the unconditional grace
and warmth of acceptance by the mother which is every longed for by
the adult male but never realized in his post-puberty years of strife.
The submission and acceptance by women is another lure of remem-
brance of the past graces of mother within the family fold.

Sex seems to be the prime separant tool of our programming. It
effects a physical separation between members of the same sex through
intra-sexual rivalry whereas its participant inter-sexual lures, both in
courting and intercourse, are illusory and serve as baits for the further
separation of reproduction.

The bio-evolutionary rationale for inter-male fighting is to display to
the females the greater fitness and survival potential of the male so that
the female who chooses a victor is assured of a better and therefore
stronger gene contribution to her offspring. For similar reasons a
woman is attracted to the more handsome (which many times is related
to better health), more intelligent and more successful man. Moreover
man and the males of other fauna actually seek out competitive situations in order to prove their superiority to the observing females so that
they have a better chance of being chosen by them.[7] Many coaches in
colleges know that one of the best methods of squeezing the best out of
a college team is to bring out the girls from the dormitories to watch
them play and cheer them to win.

The territoriality of males is related to their display tactics as well as
to their greater desirability as mates. The male seems to declare that he
is not only handsome and strong, but will also be able to provide for
her and their future offspring a sheltered space for breeding. It is
interesting to note in this context that with most species of birds,
males defend territories which initially attract the females.[8] This means
that the future abode of the family is also chosen by the female. This

is similar to humans where the choice of house usually rests with the wife. Thus both male competitiveness and inter-male fighting is sexually based and related to courting. It is a matter of conjecture how this competitiveness is related to the achievement motive and what proportion of sex and the protestant ethic is inherent in the rat race.

The aggressive show of the males of most animals is indeed a ritual display. They do not so much harm their opponents as let them know by threats and dance-like gestures how formidable and ferocious they are. When the opponent concedes his inferiority he is allowed to run away without harm. It seems as if the hens themselves do not take seriously the self-important inflation of the cocks. They know that they have the trump card because all the male fanfare and show of feathers is to impress them in the hope of being chosen and accepted as mates by the females. This male display of prowess and importance is apparent in the archaic announcements of kings, knights and warriors of the list of their titles and exploits, whereas the ritualized lightness in which woman takes the boisterous courting by man is apparent in her slightly mocking show of admiration of his performance and her elegant show of weakness and fragility.

It has already been pointed out that females are more psychologically aggressive whereas males are more physically aggressive.[9] Except for cases of a direct attack on her offspring when a mother becomes fiercely violent, the aggression of a woman is more subtly vicious and her cruelty more sophisticated than that of man. This is in line with her need to vicariously manipulate her environment with her lesser physical resources in order to secure the well-being of her family. Darwin noted the display of fitness by most male fauna and the choosing by females of this fitness as the prime mechanism of evolution.[10] In our context the display by men of their fitness, wealth and intelligence (as well as the show of prowess, colour, dance and song by males of other fauna) signify a participant quest of acceptance. The female is mostly the observer and the decision-maker in this slave market. It is the female who makes the separant decision in most species, including Homo sapiens, as to which male will be allowed to spurt his sperm into the sanctuary of her womb excluding, thereby, all the others. This separant admittance of one and the rejection of all the others is subsequently repeated by the participant race of the millions of sperm to reach the ovum and be incorporated by it.

The Manipulative Choice

The female chooses a male who appears to her to be a better breeder and a better provider. She bases her decision, *inter alia*, on the dominance of the male as apparent from his greater aggression and his larger size. There is abundant evidence establishing the link between dominance and reproductive success.[11] Male dominance is also apparent in more vigorous courting which is also one of the positive criteria for the females' choice of male mates.[12] The more dominant male as apparent from his size, vigour, perseverence and aggression is bound to bring to the match a more vigourous and hardier genetic potential and hence is assured of a greater number of female choices and a higher number of matings.[13] Conversely, sick and deformed males are rarely chosen by females.[14]

There thus seems to be a high correlation in the eyes of the choosing female between the health and fitness of the courting male and his sexual attraction. This is obviously programmed to assure that healthy and not deformed parents will be assured higher chances of transmitting their genes to their offspring. The female seems to have been appointed as a sentinel against genetical deformations by her tendency to avoid sick, undersize and malformed wooers. Indeed, females are programmed to infer that if a male is healthy and a vigourous courter, then he possesses a desirable genetic potential. Moreover, the very fact that a male of the higher animals has to have an erection in order to be able to copulate necessitates a minimum level of health, development and coordination, that is a certain standard of physical and mental fitness without which he would be technically disbarred from acceptance by the females. Some mytho-empirical hints supporting this premise include the figure of Zeus, ever ready to mount any female around him, whose powerful sexual drive led him to sire personally a great many dwellers of the Olympus; King Solomon with his thousand wives; and the dictum of Judah, the second century patriarch of Judea, that the greatness of a man is measured by the fierceness of his passions.

The feigned helplessness of woman and her studied gentility as evolved in the age of chivalry which reached its peak with the salon ladies of middle and upper class nineteenth-century Europe, catered for man's longing for the participant graces of mother. The helpless fragile look of women was all the rage at the time of Keats who sang: "God! she is like a milk-white lamb that bleats for Man's protection." Yet then and now woman urges her suitor overtly or by clandestine cues to fight over her and implies coyly that she is going to be the prized trophy of the victor. This facade of feeble gentility caches a separant manipulative incitement of ritualized male combat in which woman is the referee with the power to decide who is to become the father of her children. Guilt laden Judeo-Christianity is also a prime medium through which the bride and the wife manipulate the participant guilt of their bridegrooms and husbands in order to achieve their wishes within the family, although outwardly they seem powerless.

The superiority of woman in the age of chivalry and her idolization as a supreme image of grace, and hence as a symbol of power in Christian society, permeated the whole of occidental culture. The knight and gentleman, whom all men of lesser stature and descent tried to imitate and emulate, worshipped his beloved lady in participant self-effacement and with a Tantalic tortuous longing for self-sacrifice to his perfect love. "The knight and his lady," says Huizinga, "that is to say, the hero who serves for love, this is the primary and invariable motif from which erotic fantasy will always start. It is sensuality transformed into the craving for self-sacrifice, into the desire of the male to show his courage, to incur danger, to be strong, to suffer and to bleed before his lady-love."[15] This romantic and brutally self-effacing participant love is imbued with competition. Says Huizinga, "A more vehement stimulus is added to the primary motif: its chief feature will be that of defending imperilled virginity — in other words, that of ousting the rival."[16]

The servile submission of the mediaeval gentleman to his beloved lady is lauded in the following commendable description of a gentleman: "He served all, he honoured all, for the love of one. His speech was graceful, courteous and diffident before his lady."[17] This worshipful idolation of the lady could be interpreted in our context as the concurrence of "pure" love with the participant longing for the grace of partaking in unity. In the absolutism of Christianity in the Middle Ages, this Tantalic equivalent of love and the longing for grace seems to have been sanctioned by the socionormative system. The violent competition for the lady's heart and her ritualized choice of the victor who showed not only courage but mainly an abject devotion to her is depicted in the following scene from the thirteenth-century *Des Trois Chevaliers et del Chainse*:

> The wife of a nobleman of great liberality, but not very fond of fighting, sends her shirt to three knights who serve her for love, that one of them at the tournament which her husband is going to give may wear it as a coat-armour, without any mail underneath. The first and the second knights excuse themselves. The third, who is poor, takes the shirt in his arms at night and kisses it passionately. He appears at the tournament, dressed in the shirt and without a coat of mail; he is grievously wounded, the shirt, stained with his blood, is torn. Then his extraordinary bravery is perceived and he is awarded the prize. The lady gives him her heart.[18]

The choice of males by females seems to be determined by the complementarity of his attributes to hers,[19] and by some of the male's extreme traits which may enhance genetic polymorphism.[20] In humans this could involve a diversification of genes as well as the combination of complementary personality and other acquired traits which could enhance the coping with a wider scope of familial concerns and domestic tasks. We may add here that many times women are attracted to different and interesting men. This could be related to the diversification of the genetic potential of their offspring but it might also be linked to the woman's separant insight that creative innovators are many times bizarre in their outlook, uncommon in their behaviour and non-conforming in their creative methods.[21] Hence the choice of mates may be influenced by the woman's separant intuition that the bizarre oddball of a boyfriend might indeed have some ingenious creativity in him.

Mirror, Mirror, on the Wall . . .

As the function of mate choice is so central in woman's life, her being desired, loved and courted is her main concern. Conversely, if a woman is not wooed, pursued and loved, or worse if she is left by the man of her choice, her whole *raison d'être* is shaken. This is why women are much more hurt by their desertion by men than vice versa. Being courted and desired is so important for women and necessary for their self-esteem and confidence, that if a certain male in whom they are interested does not pay attention to them they are liable to brand him in self-defence as impotent or as a homosexual.

Woman is predisposed biologically and is socialized to separantly lure man so that she may choose him as mate. As her outward appearance determines, initially at least, her bait value she is very much concerned with the shape of her body, its odour, the cosmetics for her skin and the fashion of clothes which cover it. Not that men do not care about their external appearance. It is, however, a matter of degree: women do seem to be more concerned with external appearances because their more separant object relationship makes for their need to achieve a *modus vivendi* with their surroundings. They aim more for an immediate favourable impression on their human environment to accentuate their initial bait value. With men outward appearance is indeed an integral part of their display dynamics but intelligence, power and wealth which are very important components of man's display potential, are not immediately related to external appearances. With women, on the other hand, external appearance determines their initial luring value. Hence they have engaged in accentuating and augmenting it from times immemorial. Mothers, sisters, finishing schools and the mass media have perennially implanted into girls and women the current "proper" manner in which they should talk, walk, dress and make-up themselves so that they are more desirable to potential suitors.

The image of the attractive woman changes drastically with time and place. Feet binding in China was probably meant to accentuate the gentle helplessness of women, while big breasts were idolized in later orally fixated Sisyphean cultures such as ancient Greece and the U.S. In ancient Egypt all the hair of the women's body was removed and a rectangular wig covered the shaven head. The beauties of Lucas Cranach are narrow shouldered with small breasts, protruding bellies and wide hips while the renaissance favoured full voluptuousness in women. If Rubens represented the taste in women of his age it must have been close to heavy obesity. Papuan males are turned on by the long noses of women whereas the Hottentot ideal of feminine beauty is centred on their protruding buttocks. Whatever the fashion of women's body shape, hairdo, dress and make-up their aim is to lure as many suitors as possible to enable them to choose a mate from a wide range of choices. The initial purpose of woman's beauty is primping. Yet, sex being the anchor on which human core vector quests both separant and participant are focused, woman's and to a lesser extent man's pre-occupation with external appearance is a lifelong involvement.

The Trump Card

Woman determines the attributes of the ideal type man and he strives participantly to comply with this image in order to be chosen and accepted by her. The good looking, strong and healthy image of men is lauded by women due to its better bio-genetic potential. Man's aggressiveness and competitiveness are preferred by women because the more ambitious and successful a husband is the more he is likely to be a better provider and the greater likelihood of securing a higher social status for his family. "The good Jewish boy", "the clean faced devout Catholic American youth" and "the perfect gentleman" are images of men coveted by women because they are likely to be kinder and more considerate mates.

We are well aware that many factors are involved in crystallizing the images of the "ideal" man at a given time, place and culture. Mass communication media, fads, fashions, religion, socioeconomic and political conditions and ideologies are just some of the influences. The major influence, however, is the fact that from the crucial oral phase of development onwards, the mother implants in her children, both male and female, by a powerful non-verbal communication, the "proper" roles of boys and girls. Through the later stages of development in which these roles are reinforced both by the mother and other socializing agencies, the boy is encouraged to develop some traits which are later further reinforced by his girl friends and wife. These desirable male traits are, per force, projected onto culture and serve as a basis for whatever variations on the theme the mass communication media may add to them. The father provides more of the role models in the participant focal concerns of socionormativeness, religion and ideology than the mother, but as for the desirable masculine traits in relation to external appearance, competitiveness and attitudes towards women, the tone giver is woman.

The externally tough and internally soft (especially when he is with his sweetheart) masculine movie idol might not have been invented by women, but its popularity and durability has been sustained and reinforced by the projected feminine ideal of a man who is hard on his competitors but gentle to women. The trump card of women is most apparent in sex. To be a good lover a man must have the right kind of erection and make sure that his sexual partner also reaches orgasm. The news that a man is impotent or is a lousy lover spreads like wildfire. If a woman chooses to hide her frigidity she can still feign orgasm, but an erection cannot, alas, be feigned. Man has to perform sexually in a more exacting manner than woman. Moreover, in most of the cases the sole judge as to whether or not a man's performance was satisfactory is his sexual partner. Consequently the self-image of masculinity is more vulnerable than woman's feminine self-image. Man's masculine self-esteem is also much more dependent on woman's judgement than vice versa.

Woman absorbs the sperm, carries the foetus, gives birth and takes care of the children in their most crucial formative years. Woman has therefore to be more separantly attuned to her immediate environment not only because of her greater parental investment, but because of her greater need to be practically manipulative vis-a-vis her objective environment to assure the survival of her offspring.[22] What seemed to women baiters like Schopenhauer, Strindberg and Nietzsche as woman's pragmatic egocentrism is related to her greater share in the organism's programmed *raison d'être*, namely reproduction and the successful breeding of future generations. Hence a woman tends to be more pragmatic and resourceful even in the most adverse situations. Man, on the other hand, might tend in adverse situations to brood more over the injustice of his personal misfortune (woman being more separantly pragmatic believes less in the participant notions of justice to begin with).

The ideal of sexual fidelity is preached more by women than by men because it serves more their separant aims of domestic and social security. Man, say the sociobiologists, is only a reluctant monogamist. The coy retreat of women when courted and their bashful virtuous evasion of their suitors' advances serves as woman's primary line of defence to admit only those suitors whose serious intentions are apparent in their perseverence in wooing in spite of their paramours' reluctance to yield to their advances. This apparent teasing of the male suitors by their deceptively coy paramours serves the latters' aim to make a "better" choice of mate, that is one who is interested in marriage and a family and not just in sex or in a fleeting amorous adventure. This is also the reason why women usually shun a direct masculine approach and reject it as vulgar, preferring the indirect and rather lengthy courting which allows her to determine "what kind of a person that fellow is", and whether he is ready to award her his undivided attention, love and/or matrimonial assurance before she makes a final decision.

It is interesting to note that similar mechanisms are present in the courting techniques of fauna, and are especially apparent in the display and courting of fiddler crabs. The female in some of the species of this crab may at first be very timid and refuse the vigorous courting of the outsize claw-waving male. Only when the female is sure of the males' species specificity and his desirability as mate does she yield to his rather prolonged display and strenuous wooing.[23]

The "Right" Mate within the "Right" Species

Courting and the choice of mate involves two consecutive separant processes: first the prevention of inter-specific mating and second the assurance of maximum variability of intra-specific mating. This double-decked separant mechanism assures first the accentuation of differences between groups of flora and fauna, and then the maximization of differences within the specific groups. Here again we see that separant growth and separant variability seem to be programmed together. It is rather amazing to what extent our programming went in order to assure species specific mating. Smells, noises, physique and the locks and keys of genitalia combine efforts to secure mating within the species. The courting behaviour which is peculiar to each species is the main process through which the reproductive isolating mechanisms (RIM) are effected. It has been observed in many species that males are not too discriminate in their courting behaviour and many times display themselves to and chase females of species other than their own. It is the females who seem to "bear the burden of maintaining species integrity".[24] The female of the species that asserts her primary role as the guardian of proper separant reproduction and growth.

Within the species Homo sapiens both ascribed and achieved ethnicity, religion, nationality as well as socioeconomic status serve as artifacts to form further separate mating groups. The women usually supervise the courting of the young and try to confine it within the right groups. "Are you out of your mind! Who is going to date you after the neighbours have seen you go out with this black", "In our family nobody married a Catholic before", "My boy is never going to marry a shicksa", are only some of the exhortations by which mothers have induced their eligible offspring to court and mate within the "right" group. It should be stressed that whereas inter-specific isolating mechanisms in most species are physiological, anatomical, seasonal and behavioural, the reproductive isolation within the species Homo sapiens are psycho-cultural only. Once the species specific isolation has been secured another separant mechanism operates to secure maximum diversification within the species. This mechanism is the complementarity in the choice of mates. It has been observed that the females of many fauna tend to choose the extreme and rarer types of males as measured by some of their conspicuous physical and behavioural characteristics, in this way producing a greater diversity in their offspring.[25]

In Darwinian terms this diversity secures greater viability, but for our context this provides further evidence from the females more prominent role in securing the separant growth of her species. In human beings the proscription of incest in all its innumberable variations provides an additional powerful barrier against inbreeding and a mechanism for separant diversification. We should recall that in our model the origin of this separant proscription of incest is feminine. Finally, we pointed out earlier that the oral fixations of both daughter and son make for complementary orientations towards their parents which also influences choice of mates. This might explain the attraction of opposites which has been observed in human courting and which enhances the greater separant diversity of human mating, reproduction and offspring.

Orgasm

"After intercourse all animals are sad", says the Latin proverb. Is it because the pitifully short bait of ecstatic orgasm has vanished and the participants in intercourse are re-confronted with their separant state of existential drudgery and misery? With the human male there is an abrupt post-orgasmic loss of sexual tension and a momentary loss of erotic interest in his partner. Although woman are slower in their post-orgasmic loss of stimulative susceptibility and many are capable of multiple orgasms, Masters and Johnson established that there is a marked similarity between man and woman's post-orgasmic resolution phases.[26] As for animals, the males of the species do experience varying kinds of orgastic ecstasies during ejaculation but it is an open question to what extent female fauna experience orgasm.[27] Nevertheless, most female fauna do disregard the display, courting and sexual approaches of males after a copulation by which they have been presumably fertilized, while most female insects even stop the secretion of sexually attractive pheromones after mating.[28] Although some of the following observations by Briffault are outdated, most of them have been supported by subsequent research:

> With a large proportion of mammalian species the association between the male and the female does not extend beyond the primary purpose for which the sexes come together — the fecundation of the female. After that function is fulfilled there appears to be, as a general rule, an actual repulsion between the sexes. "As soon as pairing is over", says Brehm, speaking of mammals generally, "great indifference is shown towards one another by the sexes." Among most carnivora cohabitation of the male with the female takes place for a short time only during the rutting season, and in many species there is no cohabitation at all. Weasels continue together during the mating season for a week or more, then separate completely. Bears do not cohabit after sexual congress; "no one yet has found two adult black bears in one den; mother and half-grown cubs have been taken together in the same winter quarters, but never two old ones". "I have never seen the two (male and female) together at any time of the year," says an experienced observer of the species; "they meet by chance and again separate." The same is reported of the Indian, and of the polar bear. The jaguar cohabits with the female during one month of the year only; and the cougar during a few weeks. The leopard male and female live entirely separate.[29]

The conclusion is that after copulation and mating, which will presumably bring forth reproduction, the baiting of orgasm and its instantaneous glimmering of participant bliss have fulfilled their purpose and are hence unnecessary any more. The males have impregnated the females and the species is hooked on its task to reproduce. From this point on our programmer seems to lost interest in the moods, ecstasies and sexual attraction of the parents. Its interest is already fully concentrated on the foetus and the future generations. Orgasm is a short-lived exposure to a subjective peak experience of participant bliss cleverly manipulated to serve the purposes of our programming which are unknown and unknowable by the sexual partners.

The Spanish call orgasm *La poca muerta*, hinting at its participant and annihilating nature of longing to fuse with the sexual partner. Karen Horney realized the greater participatory significance of the nature of orgasm for the male than for the female. Man, she says, secretly longs for extinction through sex as a surrogate wish for reunion with woman-mother, whereas for a woman sex is only the initiation of a new cycle of procreation.[30] The more separant role of woman in sex has thus been recognized by one of the pioneers of psychoanalysis. The participant component of orgasm is apparent in its temporary blunting of separate awareness and the feeling of union with one's environment bringing about a transitory sense of non-being. The Tantalic nature of the participant longing for orgasm is apparent in the physical and emotional build-up towards it. When the climax is reached and a flicker of a sensation of union is experienced the orgasm is terminated and the ecstatic participant revelation is over almost before it has begun. The longing for participation is the prime mover of orgasm because actual union with the object is, of course, not achieved. There is a marked similarity between the rhythmic movements of the devout in a participant mood of prayer and the pelvic thrusts striving towards orgasm. This might lend a serious hue to the "wise guys about Jerusalem" who observe that the Wailing Wall is a very sexy place because men move to and fro in front of it, and the women behind their partition groan in ecstasy.

Ferenczi envisaged the participant craving of man in orgasm as brought about by his identification with his penis, which itself identifies with the sexual partner in penetration; in ejaculation the identification is transferred to the semen which permeates the woman's body.[31] Individuals with a weak ego boundary may experience in orgasm a participant loss of body contour and a crumbling down and melting of the partition between themselves and their surroundings including their sexual partners. This may account for the reluctance of individuals who have anxieties about their ego boundaries and body image to reach orgasm. For them to experience a participant melting down of their ego boundaries is tantamount to madness, for in their daily existence they relate a dissolution of their shaky ego boundary to just this. The enormity of orgasm and its overpowering effects on the senses have made people impute divinity to it. Indeed, the Greeks denoted genitalia as *aidoion* (inspirers of holy awe).[32] Many religions frown on the pleasures of sex and most of them condemn sexual activity which is geared only towards pleasure. Such condemnation seems to stem from the religious sanctioning of our programming to reproduce. Our programmer and his religious guardians feel cheated if we enjoy our sexual experiences without reproducing.

The separant component of sex is the epitome of Sisypheanism. Ego's craving to overpower and "swallow" alter through intercourse may be phantasied during the short span of orgasm, only to be confronted immediately with the post-orgasmic reality. Yet the separant ego is sure to resume his pursuit of more sex and more orgasms, culminating in identical Sisyphean failure followed by the inevitable renewed effort to overpower the sexual partner through the peak imagery of orgasm. We should remind ourselves at this point that the separant-participant components of orgasm constitute a continuum with women biologically predisposed to be nearer its separant pole, whereas men are nearer biologically to its participant pole. These biological predispositions are the results of many factors and may be shifted to smaller or greater extents by oral fixations and later cultural imprints.

The separant nature of the human female orgasm is not so much related to the vaginal or clitoral excitation which leads to it but to the orgasmic platform which develops at the outer third of the vagina and contracts rhythmically at the onset of orgasm embracing and containing the penis, and absorbing its flow of semen.[33] The more participant nature of the human male's orgasm is inherent in the penetration and ejaculation of the penis spurting out spermatozoa to be absorbed by the ova (although some male orgasms may occur without ejaculation).

Subjective phantasies involving both body image and object perception in orgasm are initiated at first by a participant blurring of the contours of self and partner by both men and women. The voluntary control of body movements is felt to be impaired together with a feeling of "emptiness" and an internal "void",[34] as well as a diffuse "floating and flying sensation".[35] Both Kinsey et al., and Masters and Johnson have reported a temporary lapse of reality contact during orgasm. Kinsey and his associates have stated that:

All of our evidence indicates that there is a considerable and developing loss of sensory capacity which begins immediately upon the onset of sexual stimulation and which becomes more or less complete, sometimes with complete unconsciousness, during the maximum of sexual arousal and orgasm. At orgasm some individuals may remain unconscious for a matter of seconds or even for some minutes. There are French terms, "La petite mort" (the little death) and "La mort douce" (the sweet death), which indicate that some persons do understand that unconsciousness may enter at this point.[36]

The above is precisely our conception of a temporary participant diffusion of the ego boundary and body image. After this initial participant baiting inherent in the orgasm of both males and females, we may note the following marked differences: women see in intercourse and orgasm just the first phase of reproduction. Consequently, even their phantasies at sexual arousal, intercourse and orgasm are related to the link between sex and reproduction, whereas men focus more during intercourse on their immediate sexual gratification.[37]   This indicates that even in the throes of orgasm woman does not lose awareness of her separant programming to reproduce. Kinsey et al., reported that women find more satisfaction during intercourse in their separant sensation of receiving whereas men found their psychological rewards and satisfaction mostly in their participant feeling of penetrating.[38] Of special importance is Kinsey's report that:

> The slower responses of the female in coitus appear to depend in part upon the fact that she frequently does not begin to respond as promptly as the male, because psychologic stimuli usually play a more important role in the arousal of the average male, and a less important role in the sexual arousal of the average female. The average male is aroused in anticipation of a sexual relationship, and he usually comes to erection and is ready to proceed directly to orgasm as soon as or even before he makes any actual contact. The average female, on the contrary, is less often aroused by such anticipation, and sometimes she does not begin to respond until there has been a considerable amount of physical stimulation.[39]

The more object oriented woman needs substantive tactile stimulation to be sexually aroused, whereas the more participant abstract male may be easily aroused sexually by erotic phantasies and imagery. The more down to earth functions of woman seem to permeate right through her need to be more directly and physically manipulated in order to be sexually aroused and satisfied. As woman is more firmly aware of her bodily contours and boundaries she is also bound to have more anxieties of being, that is of losing her body image during orgasm.[40] This again shows the more accentuated separant anchor of woman on her body and objective surroundings and her reluctance to lose her sense of concreteness even for the lures of orgasm. Thus many more women than men display anxiety of losing their bodily image during orgasm.[41] The more separant woman needs a firm anchor on her objective surroundings and if these fade in orgasm she is liable to be frightened.

Masters and Johnson report that their female subjects felt during orgasm a feeling of receptive opening whereas the male feels at the onset of orgasm the inevitability of his penetrating ejaculatory thrust.[42] This again vindicates our portrayal of the more separant Sisyphean role of woman and the more participant Tantalic role of man in sex and orgasm. Man and woman are predisposed to seek different aims in sex and orgasm. These aims can never be achieved and even their baited imagery are diametrically opposed. Sometimes the latter are complementary but mostly they are not.

12
Courting, Marriage and the Least Interest Principle

He who loves the more is the inferior and must suffer.

Thomas Mann: *Tonio Kröger*

Courting

As woman is entrusted by our programming with the more crucial functions of reproduction and the separant evolutionary selection and growth, she has to be very careful and choosy with whom she mates. Courting is a prerequisite and condition precedent before mating to allow the female of the species to evaluate her suitor both genetically and socially, and to ascertain whether he is only after the bait of sex or is also willing to commit himself to matrimonial duties and familial cares. Women shun the direct masculine approach which rushes to grab the trophy without trying first to win the match. Courting favours the more indirect and ritualized approach which allows woman ample time and opportunity to examine the intentions of her suitor, to determine whether he is willing and worthy to be a mate and a father. A girl or woman who submits indiscriminately to a direct masculine approach is deemed in most societies to be foolish or shameless. Even our own permissive culture, despite some vociferous lip service to sexual freedom, is uneasy about indiscriminate pre-martial sex by girls. The squandering of a girl's most valued asset (separant bait), without securing its reproductive and socionormative rewards, is considered by many to be a crime.

In many societies a girl has to be a virgin in order to be marriageable. If the bridegroom finds his bride to have been already deflowered, the marriage may be annulled. A boy in these societies may refuse to marry a girl on the grounds of her not being a virgin even if he was the one who was responsible for it. The rationale of this being that her consent to have pre-marital sex shows her irresponsible behaviour. This is because in some Mid Eastern and North African societies a girl who becomes pregnant out of wedlock has to be killed by her family in order to expiate the disgrace wrought on them.[1]

Virginity in many societies is guarded and cherished not only as a participant vestige of the longed for pure-mother-mate, but mainly as an asset to be bartered after a rigorous and ritualized courting for a home, security and status. Woman's separant interests are against promiscuity whereas man's biological predisposition and socionormative roles are all for it, provided there is no scandal. Here again religion and the cultural system recognize and sanction the primacy of woman's separant role in reproduction and in the provision of a proper context for the rearing of children. Man's promiscuity, on the other hand, is more acceptable as an atavism of his remote ancestors' display of fitness and prowess. In occidental societies man's promiscuity is usually more clandestine because of its rather peculiar development of monogamy and the chivalrous notions of loyalty to one's lady and spouse.

The more successful Casanovas are those who pay close attention to the slightest whim of their current sexual target and are a patient and intelligent audience for the recital of her personal and emotional problems. They know that they should not even hint at having sex on their first encounter because if they do it would take them farther away from their goal of having her in bed. Although many times a girl or a woman may be sexually attracted to a suitor, she is programmed to yield to his indirect courting so that his direct sexual approach is likely to turn her off. Woman may tease their suitors and hold back their consent in order to better examine the nature and intentions of these suitors. They may also practice to a fine art a brinkmanship of refusals firm enough to whet the appetite of the suitor and prolong the courting in order to better assert the nature and aims of the lover, but not too harsh in order not to completely discourage him. Then at the critical moment (sensed intuitively by most women) they say "yes" and the bells are quite likely to ring in matrimonial bliss.

Female fauna, like women, are always on the alert to test the suitability, moods and goals of their lovers. They test these by the nature, intensity and duration of the suitors' attentions as well as by the symbolic and material value of the gifts they bear. The male tern, for instance, catches a fish and presents it to his lady tern in a show of courting chivalry like a well-bred Jewish boy presenting his date with a gourmet package of lox. A male penguin who presents a lady penguin with a coloured pebble has a greater chance of being chosen by her as a mate than one who presents her only with a plain pebble.[2] The *Empidae* male fly packs an insect in a gift package of silk which it secretes from its body and presents it to the female who first starts sucking it and then allows the gift bearing male to copulate with her.[3]

Some female birds will absolutely refuse to mate without first receiving a gift of food from the courting mate.[4] These food gifts signify to the female that her suitor is a good provider, worthy to be chosen as a mate and father.

Of even greater significance are the courting practices of the male wren and bower birds who build spectacular and elaborate nests, decorating them with stones and flowers. Yet all these efforts are meant only to impress the female with the seriousness of the males' intentions and his devotion. They serve as a test of his perseverance and artistic excellence because once the female has chosen him she builds another nest in which she raises her young.[5] The main function of courting, as determined by the female of the species based on their more central role in reproduction and the care of the young, is to enable the female to choose a better provider and a more considerate husband and father; and not just a philanderer who is willing to savour the bait of sex but not to be harnessed into domestic and matrimonial duties.

The Least Interest Principle

The model of the least interest principle in amorous relationships operates along the following dynamics. A separant ego whose inclusive amatory and erotic aim is to engulf, possess, overpower and dominate his enamoured, is bound to feel his Sisyphean striving waning if the enamoured alter submits participantly to his courting. For the separant Casanova the Sisyphean dialectics to seduce and dominate his erotic target is the focus of his concern in his amatory involvement. Once this is felt to be achieved the libidinal energy of the Sisyphean suitor expends itself, he loses interest and rushes to another target. *Per contra,* the participant suitor (whose aim is to be accepted by his beloved alter) will also lose his amorous tension if he feels securely cuddled in his lover's lap. However if he feels a reluctance on the part of alter to accept him the agitated suitor will invest all his emotional resources to induce his beloved to receive and embrace him.

The least interest principle also operates, in the initial phases of encounter at least, between lovers who are both separant or participant. Consider a case where the similar goals of the partners to the dyad are coupled by diametrically opposite expectations from their encounter due to the operation of the least interest principle. This situation of opposite expectations may induce ego to perceive the adverse attitude of alter as a reluctance to accept him, heightening thereby his amatory craving and erotic desire with a corresponding augmentation in the vigour of his courting. This may, however, decrease and wane once ego realizes that his partner will not or cannot provide what he (ego) desires. This brings us to the curvilinear nature of the least interest principle. Some reluctance and partial non-acceptance heightens the courting vigour of the suitor, but a total rejection and a harsh rebuff will discourage him completely and he may turn his amatory interests to less reluctant quarters. The least interest principle thus serves a dual purpose. First the coy retreat of the lady and cocquettish reluctance to submit to the suitor's courting allow the female of the species enough time and exposure to evaluate the worth of the suitor and the seriousness of his intentions.[6] Second, this cocquettish rebuff and ritualized non-submission increases the courting vigour. But because a too harsh rejection may injure the suitor's participant ideals of love and honour the ladies usually do not make their refusals too final. The least interest principle seems to be another useful mechanism in the service of our separant programming to effect a successful mating and a viable reproduction.

One implication of the least interest principle is a rule of thumb which states that the party who is less involved in an affective dyad is stronger within the emotional context of it than the party who is more involved. This rule is starkly simplistic yet applies to a wide range of instances and is of unusual potency. Also when one party is more intensely involved in the dyad the other would likely be less so and vice versa. Consequently the one who terminates a love affair usually suffers less from its disruption than the party who was more involved in it. Furthermore the more separant predisposition of woman and her sense of worth being dependent on her being wooed and courted makes it more painful to her than to man when she is the deserted party of the dyad. The least interest principle might also have contributed to the masculine image of the tough guy who does not show his emotions. Apart from the strength which is represented by toughness and is evidence of greater competitive viability, the outward reluctance to show emotions might be a feigned demeanour to attract women by the least interest principle. This might be a partial account for the tough and silent movie idols à la Gary Cooper who utter half a dozen monosyllables during an entire movie.

Another painful correlate of the least interest principle is that an intense show of emotions by one party might frighten and repel the other unless both experience the same or a very similar intensity of affective emotions towards each other which is very rare indeed. An extreme example of a disruption of the amatory dyad due to uneven emotional involvement was the love stricken Van Gogh who held his hand in the flame of a table lamp and begged to see his beloved Kee Van Stricker "for as long as I can keep my hand in the flame".[7] We shall have more to say about the disruptive effects of an uneven emotional involvement on an amatory dyad in the final chapter.

Willard Waller who formulated the least interest principle stated that "there is always one who loves and one who permits himself to be loved", meaning that the latter has the upper hand within the affective dyad because he is less emotionally involved than the former.[8] Moreover if in addition to being more involved ego insists on showing his emotions and displaying them intensively he is liable to annoy the less involved alter, and in consequence is more likely to be rejected by him. Thus the more ego strives to gain the heart of alter the less he is likely to achieve his aim. Paradoxically in order to win one's beloved one is better off feigning some indifference towards him/her. We have stressed *some* indifference because as we have pointed out earlier, the least interest principle is curvilinear. A display of a total disinterest might lead the other party to conclude that the dyad has no chance of viability. The studied indifference of a John Wayne or a Humphrey Bogart is very appealing to women, and the *femme fatale* disdain of a Marlene Dietrich causes males to flock around her. Yet this indifference might not be feigned but real cold-bloodedness or downright frigidity. Because of these vicissitudes of the least interest principle one or both parties to the emotional dyad would be wary to "open up" because of their fear of being hurt, manipulated or taken advantage of by their less involved partner to the dyad.[9]

Girls and women encourage courting because it is of the essence of their separant self-esteem and programmed *raison d'être* to be able to chose the "right" mate biologically and socially from a range of wooers. A girl or woman might spread the news that so and so a much sought after date has made advances to her and invited her for dinner even if she has never met him in order to increase her bait value. Worse still a girl might imagine that men make advances to her even if they had no intention of doing so. This is the need to assert her bait value running paranoiacally wild. A similar technique serving the display purposes of man is the bragging to the boys at the bar about how many women he bedded lately. With men the number of seductions is a crucial factor fulfilling the need to display prowess on a competitive basis.

Another factor which reinforces the least interest principle is the mechanism of cognitive dissonance which induces the party who invests more in the dyad to impute to his partner greater worth. If ego persistently courts alter in spite of cold shouldering and being rejected time and again, he inflates alter's worth and desirability otherwise how could he justify (subjectively) the investment of so much emotion and effort in courting her/him. The gist of the least interest principle as stated by

Waller is: "The one who cares less can exploit the one who cares more".[10]

Finally, in love-making a too intense emotional involvement may hamper the performance especially that of the male. Here too the least interest principle is curvilinear. Some emotional involvement may heighten the enjoyment and enhance sexual performance but a too stormy emotional infatuation may hamper both enjoyment and the reciprocal build-up towards orgasm. Another impeding element in this context is that the party who is too much conerned with the sexual enjoyment of the partner (because of an intense infatuation) may experience a higher level of anxiety of failing. This may initiate a positive feedback cycle of a self-fulfilling prophecy, and the tense and anxious sexual partner might indeed fail to deliver the goods. Here again the paradox is that in order to be a good sexual partner one has to be, alas, somewhat of an egoist. '

Marriage

We have seen that the choice of mate by the female, her efforts to ascertain that he is biologically fit and likely to be a good provider, serve her separant programming and cultural imprints to reproduce and raise a viable family. This explains the greater desire of woman than man for matrimony.[11] Briffault says:

> The mating instinct being primarily a feminine instinct and subserv-
> ing feminine interests, the desire of the female to retain the male is
> biologically far more fundamental than the desire of the male to
> retain the female. The primary object of feminine jealousy is similar
> to that of primitive male jealousy, namely, not to lose the male who
> is desired by the woman as an economic assistant and protector in
> view of her functions.[12]

One of the main theses of our present work is that the proscription of incest, unlike Freud's stance, is ingrained into the children by the mother. We have, however, adopted the Freudian contention as to the link between the proscription of incest and the formation of the human nuclear family. Indeed there is ample evidence as to the major role of women in the enforcement of the incest proscriptions. This supports our general theory as to the central role of woman in the creation of the human family which is the main medium and channel for the dual separant goals of procreation within the context of cultural growth and creativity. Briffault has described the enforcement of the rules against incest by both the mother and the elder sisters who, in savage societies, share vis-a-vis their younger sisters and brothers, the maternal authority.[13] There is also mytho-empirical evidence from Germanic mythology as to the promulgation of the rules against incest sanctioned by the curse of the mother. This maternal curse against incest was regarded by the Germanic tribes as the only curse the effects of which could never be avoided.[14]

The maternal proscription of incest is linked to the formation of the nuclear family in which woman is more separantly concerned. She more than man is programmed to bring about successful reproduction and it is she who, in the main, cares for the health of the offspring. Consequently she is the one who has taken upon herself to guard against the adverse effects of inbreeding. Some classic accounts of arranging exogamous marriages in primitive tribes before their customs were too contaminated by occidental influences, stress the fact that negotiations for exogamous marriages were conducted only by women. This stems mainly from the fact that at that time inter-tribal contacts which were not conflictual were rare. A member of another tribe was a stranger and hence almost automatically an enemy. Consequently any male who tried to cross over to another tribe even for the purpose of negotiating a marriage, endangered his life. Women, however, were not actively engaged in war and did not constitute a direct threat to the other tribe. This was a pragmatic reason for the virtual monopoly which women had for negotiating exogamous marriages.[15]

Whatever the additional cultural reasons for woman's central role in assuring exogamous marriages her role of proscribing incest at the oral stage of the development of her children and her separant predisposition to assure the viability of her offspring and hence prevent inbreeding, qualify her for arranging proper (i.e., not inbred, not incestuous and not endogamous) marriages. Moreover there is ample evidence from many primitive societies that the mother or maternal relatives are entrusted with the choice of mate and with the actual arrangement of the marriage. In many instances mothers select brides for their sons without consulting them.[16] Among the Bushmen and the Hottentots in South Africa, before the ravages of Victorian prudery and the obscenities of apartheid played havoc with their tribal customs, the mothers of the courted girls chose their husbands.[17] These examples, which were purposely taken from primitive tribes whose archaic customs were not too much exposed to European disrupting influences, provide an initial anchor to our contention as to the major role of women in arranging mating and forming the nuclear family. The maternally based human family seems to have evolved as a suitable medium for the rearing of the slowly growing and developing offspring as well as for the transmission of the separantly manipulative skills and achievement motivated cultural goals spurred by maternal reinforcement and encouragement.

The maternal separant influence on the institution of marriage and its practical socioeconomic aspects were overtly apparent and formally sanctioned almost universally up to the present century. Among the ancient Romans and Greeks marriage was mostly a contract between families concluded for socioeconomic and political advantages for both parties, the amorous inclinations of the bride and bridegroom being hardly relevant.[18] In England a marriage between parties below the age of twenty-one without parental consent was considered void as late as the eighteenth century. In France until the First World War marriages were settled mainly by the family councils of both parties. The young couple were rarely consulted and were usually faced with the *fait accompli* that they were to become man and wife. In Renaissance Italy marriages among the upper classes were concluded by the families for power and monetary considerations even while the bride and bridegroom were still children. The first time they ever saw each other was usually on their wedding day.[19] The same held true for the Chinese, the American Indians, the Australian Aborigines and the Germanic tribes amongst whom marriages were arranged by the families mostly out of political, social and lucrative considerations which were assumed to be advantageous to the married couple as well.[20]

The separant lucrative nature of marriage is apparent also in the dowry, bride-money and wedding presents which are meant to provide the initial economic basis for the household. In many agrarian, nomadic and primitive societies the bride-money is collected from the whole extended family or tribe of the bridegroom and distributed among all the members of the bride's family. The manipulative managerial and investive nature of marriage is also evident from the institution of the professional matchmakers, the skills of whom (from the modern computerized matrimonial institutes to the folkloristic Jewish *Shadchan*) are centred on their ability to sell the social and economic assets of a potential mate. These go-betweens are an institutionalized extension of the original display dynamics of the male and the choice tactics of the female.

The gist of our present premise is that woman's separant predispositions and roles make her the senior partner in marriage and the family, with man as a junior partner. This is based first of all on the more central role in reproduction of the female. Humans share the growth dynamics of other fauna in which the basic reproductive unit is only the mother and her offspring,[21] with the males playing an auxiliary role. The care, protection and the rearing of the children in the formative years are also mainly in the domain of the mother. The maternal incest taboos and the enforcement of exogamy are linked, as we have pointed out earlier, to the formation of the nuclear family. Thus, the family is a corollary and a sequel to the ingrained maternal sexual restrictions. Moreover the separant cultural and achievement goals implanted by the mother in the children as a sublimation of incest, can only be promulgated in the early formative years in the family. These goals are then reinforced and realized through the family. The mother thus has higher stakes not only in the formation of the family, but in its maintenance. This is why women are more reluctant than men to break up a family with small children.

Woman's need for subsistence and protection during childbirth and child-rearing has evolved into the vast manipulative interests inherent in the separant arrangements of marriages. Finally, the normative structure of society which is based on an intricate mesh of its smallest social units (i.e., nuclear families) exerts a greater pressure on women than on men to marry and fulfil thereby her bio-psychological programming and sociocultural roles. A full cycle is thereby closed; woman's central role in the formation of the human family pressures her more than men through the normative system of society to realize her matrimonial role and fulfil within it her biological programming.

As marriage is a separant institution which is linked, apart from its mating and reproductive functions, to a wide range of socioeconomic transactions and political arrangements between families, tribes, social aggregates and governments, it is obvious that a participant *Weltanschauung* and creeds would be against it. An extreme instance is the Gnostic Saturninus who preached that marriage and generation stem from Satan and have to be rejected. Tatian, another Gnostic sage, called marriage corruption and fornication.[22] It might well be that the celibacy oaths of monks and nuns are also partially linked to a participant rejection of marriage reinforced by an intense longing to partake in unity.

13
Agony, Petrification and Rebellious Longing

Pleasure comes as a reward only to the man
who doesn't make it the goal of his life.
When a man makes it his goal in life,
the opposite always happens.

From a letter of Tolstoy to his son Misha

Agony

In *The Violence of Silence: The Impossibility of Dialogue* we expounded at length our thesis that whenever two people engage in a dialogic encounter both of them expect to achieve a deeper level of communication than they actually achieve.[1] There will always be a gap between the aspired and achieved levels of encounter as defined by each party to the dyad. The different biological predispositions personality fixations and cultural imprints of ego and alter make it statistically very remote or well nigh impossible that both parties to the dyad aspire to reach the same or similar level of encounter, let alone to be able to achieve it. Moreover, there are bound to be fluctuations of the willingness and ability to enter into a deep encounter of both ego and alter varying with place and time.

Love is a special case and to be sure an extreme one of dyadic encounter. Precisely this extremity of emotions and goals which in many instances is nothing less than a longing for the fusion of body and soul, makes the differences of the expectations from the amatory dyad between the parties to it far reaching indeed. The resultant discrepancies between aspirations and levels of achievement of emotional communion as sensed by the lovers is bound to be correspondingly more pronounced in the amatory dyad than in other types of encounter. This may account both for the emotional violence inherent in the amorous dyad, and its greater vulnerability and liability of rupture. The different expectations on the Sisyphean-Tantalic continuum between the parties to an amatory dyad are also bound to be initially greater because the primary predisposition of woman is to contain her lover in a Sisyphean manner, whereas man is predisposed to be Tantalically contained. The initial anticipations of man and woman from their encounter of love are bound to be complementary in form yet contradictory in content. We have already pointed out the adverse and disruptive effects which the least interest principle is liable to have on the dyad of love. An amorous encounter is liable to be fragile, precarious and agonizing. In the words of the folksong: "there are no happy loves".

All the configurations of factors which make for different expectations from the parties to the amatory dyad may also lead to a different intensity and display of emotions of these parties to each other. The resultant discrepancy of emotions would be an optimal arena for the vicissitudes of the least interest principle – a vigorous, intense or sincere show of emotions is bound to turn off and repel the party who is emotionally less involved in the dyad. When the amorously infatuated ego declares with a Dostoevskyesque heaviness his eternally tortured love to his not so responsive beloved, the latter might not be impressed so much by ego's passionate emotions. Alter would quite possibly feel compassion or even pity for the tortured ego but is more likely to feel harassed, nagged or angry because ego seems to force himself on her/ him.

Unequal involvement in an emotional dyad may sometimes result in cases where the lovelorn ego may try to control his torrential emotions to be more palatable and acceptable to the less involved alter. The relationship may proceed for a while in a socially sanctioned ritual, rather like a stylized minuet, but then the tortured ego will more often than not burst out with a torrential lava of passion and the less enamoured alter is liable to retreat in confusion, embarrassment or dismay. Alter expected a subdued and pleasantly soft hued presentation by an Ingre, but was exposed to a nerve racking shriek of a Munch. If ego wishes to reach a deeper level of amatory encounter than alter is ready or willing to reach he exposes, in the process, his innermost sensitivities and is liable to be hurt by the lack of alter's response, indifference and sometimes callous exploitation. We paraphrase Sartre's closing lines in his play *No Exit* and apply them to our context: an emotionally less responsive alter is the loving ego's hell.

One of the most painful effects of the romantic agony is that language is a very obtuse and inadequate means of communicating the elaborate, subtle or torrential amatory emotions felt by ego towards alter. Worse still, the more ego is emotionally involved the less articulate he becomes so that his frustrations and suffering augment with each new failure to convey to his beloved the enormity and tenderness of his feelings. Many times the fear of being hurt causes ego to assume a facade of toughness and indifference. The more sensitive ego is and the more he senses his vulnerability in an emotional encounter, the harder the front he may present. In some cases he may be rude and coarse as a reaction-formation to his excessive sensitivity. These barriers to an emotional rapport may be augmented by various role models found in some cultures according to which males have to be hard, tough and unyielding; whereas women are supposed to be fragile, soft, weak and sentimental. This fear of exposure as well as some culturally sanctioned stereotypes of erotic attitudes might also impede realization of the expectations of the parties to an amorous dyad.

A disruption of an emotional dyad may also occur because both parties to it have conflicting aims. Two separant lovers, for instance, aim to "take" emotionally (and many times materially) but not to "give" of themselves to each other. The result is liable to be that with a reluctance to "give" there is nothing much to "take" so that each separant party to the dyad would eventually seek more generous pastures. In a dyad composed of a separant and a participant, the submissiveness of the latter might be exploited by the former. Tenderness of one party in an emotional dyad is indeed liable to be perceived as weakness by the other and taken advantage of accordingly. The separant exploiter might, however, go just one step too far and the submissive participant might throw him off in rebellious defiance. In a few cases the submissive ego would carry on his masochistic abject yielding to the bullying alter because his overt or covert goals are self-destructive. In these cases the emotional dyad is liable to be disrupted by the breakdown, madness or even death of the participantly self-destructive party, or by the final loss of interest of the separant bully in his downtrodden victim.

Sartre has already pointed out that in amatory relationships there is always one who subjugates and the other who is subjugated.[2] In our context this would mean that in the dyad of love the one who is more involved has power over the one who is less enamoured. We have pointed out earlier that because of bio-psycho-social factors and contextual considerations, ego is bound to have different expectations from an amatory dyad and to be differently involved in it than alter. Consequently ego is always either more intensely or less intensely involved in the dyad than alter. This in itself has the seeds of disruption which are bound eventually to break up the dyad. The more involved ego will demand reciprocation from alter but because of the least interest principle he is liable to get less reciprocity of emotions, precisely because he longs for it and displays his intense quest for it. The less involved alter is liable to feel bored or fed up with ego's imposing emotions and disengage himself either abruptly or gradually from the dyad. The less involved separant alter might also feel that the over eager ego is already gained so that further targets for conquest have to be sought.

A durable love affair and a theoretically continuous one may be envisaged between partners who fully complement each other in their Sispheanism and Tantalism, and in their biological predispositions, personality fixations and cultural imprints. This, fortunately or unfortunately, is impossible; any discrepancy between the mutual expectations from the dyad due to a disjuncture between the relevant complementarities of the parties is bound to augment with time and be instrumental in disrupting the amatory liaison. If the two parties are separant, the amatory dyad is liable to be short-lived because each one would aim to emotionally engulf the other while they are both reluctant to be so engulfed. If both parties are participant they would wish to be immersed in each other while being averse to becoming receptacles of such an immersion. Even if the parties are separant and participant, but differ in the intensities of their emotions and their sensitivities, the disruption of the dyad may be due to the separant's greater insistence on the participant party's submission more than the latter is able or willing to comply with. In like manner the participant party might long to be immersed within the emotional lap and halo of the separant party more than the latter might care for. Discrepancies between expectations and differences between the sensitivities of the parties to an emotional dyad are liable eventually to sour, stultify or break up the relationship.

As intersubjective communication is impossible ego may assume from his presentation of himself and his behaviour that he wishes to be treated as a participant ideal of a "pure" asexual love, whereas in reality he is after prurient sex. Another instance of a miscommunication which is liable to break-up a love affair or even prevent it from being initiated is ego's erroneous perception of alter's expectations from him in the context of their emotional encounter. Ego being involved in the dyad proceeds to comply with his mistaken perception of alter's expectations from him with tragicomic and sometimes disastrous results which usually end in the break-up of the love affair.

We have already pointed out that the disruption of an amatory dyad due to miscommunication is a special case, albeit an extreme one, of the breakdown of any human encounter due to a lack of or biased communication. The disruptive effects of miscommunication on an amatory dyad are bound to be harsher and more painful because of the intensity of the emotions involved and the higher initial expectations from the dyad of one or both parties to it. Because the expectation of lovers is for the deepest level of encounter leading to communion, the likelihood of frustration and disenchantments are so much higher than with an encounter the expectations from which are relatively shallow. Furthermore, mistaken cues may be perceived by ego through non-verbal communication which emanate from the external appearance of alter but which have very little to do with his actual moods, emotions and expectations. A sultry looking woman emanating sensuousness might really be reserved and frigid, whereas a distant and cold looking man might be searing with pent-up passion.

The gist of our present premise is that the agony inherent in the amatory dyad is liable to lead to its disruption. This stems from the fact that each of the parties is bound to have different expectations from the dyad and, therefore, both would be disenchanted depending on the nature and the intensity of their expectations. Ego is bound to project on his beloved alter his Sisyphean quests or Tantalic longing expecting alter to fulfil them. This alter cannot or will not do. More-over as there is no intersubjective communication alter may not even be aware of the nature and intensity of ego's emotional or other expecta-tions. When alter inevitably fails to fulfil ego's projected expectations, ego feels cheated, betrayed and disenchanted; yet ego rarely realizes that it was not alter but his (ego's) own projected expectations concern-ing alter that have betrayed him.

Each party to the amarous dyad projects on the other expectations which the other not only cannot fulfil but more often than not cannot be aware of. This is the main reason for love being mostly a self-defeating passion. Those who have read the fascinating correspondence between Nietzsche and Lou Andreas Salomé witnessed the way the enamoured Nietzsche projected on Lou his dreams of a super man/woman and fell in love with his own projections. Lou, with her superb intuition, sensed that Nietzsche was in love not with her but with his own ideal of perfection but she failed to realize that this is the nature of the self-defeating dynamics of love itself and not the esoteric hangups of a Nietzsche. The painful disenchantment of Nietzsche was inevitable. He accused Lou, and not his own projections on her, of betraying him.[3] The essence of Don Juanism is precisely this infatua-tion with projected expectations on one's beloved; when such expecta-tions fail to materialize, which they invariably do, one focuses one's Tantalic longings on another love-object *da capo*. Indeed, at the heights of our emotional involvement we hang on to every twist of our beloved's eyebrows and anchor on each minute change in the hue or glow of his/her eyes as proof and reinforcement that ones projections are well placed and are being fulfilled. The disjunctures, alas, sooner or later become evident. The cracks widen and the ruptures cannot be patched up any more. A marriage may go on and the family thrive and multiply with children, grandchildren, feasts and rituals; a certain rather durable friendship may even develop between the former lovers, but their love is dead.

Some variations on the theme of the romantic agony may occur as a combination of the least interest principle and the discrepancies between the participant exclusionary aims and the separant inclusionary goals of the parties to the amorous dyad. In cases where the separant ego achieves the participant submission of alter he loses interest and seeks other conquests. But if alter rejects the advances of ego it is bound to kindle ego's separant passion for amorous conquests and he is likely to vigorously woo alter. A participant ego, on the other hand, who aims to immerse himself into total submission to alter would feel cheated of his Tantalic trials if immediately accepted by the latter. Moreover, an easily complying alter does not fit the ideal image of a strong and superior lover who is worthy of ego's total submission. This is why a participant lover may still be infatuated with a beloved who rejects or is indifferent to him/her, whereas the separant lover relates to his/her beloved in a curvilinear manner. Some rejection may spur his amatory interest but a total rejection would convince the realistically separant lover that his chances of making a conquest are very meagre and it would be more expedient for him to invest his efforts in more promising hunting grounds.

Falling Apart

The infatuation of love, says John Money, may last at most around two years but usually it wanes much earlier.[4] Like all life processes a love affair is conceived, erupts and grows, blooms, flowers, dims and may die a natural death. But mostly it breaks down violently because of the fierce emotions it invokes. Because of gender, personality type and cultural role differences the amatory goals as anchored on the core vectors of the lovers are bound to be conflictual to begin with so that the violent disruption of the dyad is even more inevitable.

The bait element of love induces us to anchor the quests of our core vectors on our beloved. We hold that a considerable part and intensity of our infatuation with our beloved is that we are programmed to envisage him/her as a means through whom our dreams both of Sisyphean conquest and Tantalic revelation are bound to materialize. The concentration of emotions focused on the beloved are so fierce and fervent that the infatuated ego feels that the only important essence in his life is the beloved alter; all other issues become irrelevant or trivial. The main cravings and longings of ego's core vectors have been immersed, integrated and projected on the beloved alter as an integral part of ego's emotions. However, as with sex, our programming seems to lose interest after fertilization has presumably been effected, so with love the infatuation seems to wane after it has led presumably to pair bonding, mating and reproduction.

After the infatuation wanes, the dynamics of which we have described earlier, the Sisyphean quests and Tantalic longings which were cathected onto the beloved alter revert back to ego's core vectors; the magic dims and ego starts asking himself in amazement what did he ever see in alter. Ego in love is a different person from ego the disenchanted lover; and alter without the hallowed projections of ego's emotions is just another Tom or Mary. Love makes ego selectively blind when all the cravings of his core vectors are projected on the beloved alter. Ego does not see alter's crooked legs nor does he notice alter's lisp. When the love of a director of a play for one of the actresses in the cast fades away he cannot understand how he could ever have thought that this mumbling mediocrity was a great actress and how on earth he had given her the lead in his play. When a student emerges from her amatory trance for her professor she wonders what came over her, and how the shallow tautologies of a bore previously appeared to her as the august wisdom of a Spinoza, a Freud or a Heidegger.

One of the most disrupting effects on the amatory dyad stems from the lack of synchronicity between the infatuation curves of ego and alter. The different expectations of man and woman; the different cognitive gestalts at a given time and place due to the uniqueness of each individual's bio-psycho-cultural configuration; the least-interest principle which makes for ego being cooler when alter is warmer and vice versa; and the fundamental difference in attitudes due to separant or participant personality types – all cause one party to the dyad to be more or less infatuated than the other at any given time. Thus when alter reaches his peak, ego's feelings have already waned into mild affection, indifference or even disgust. His stoic reaction to alter's fiery advances are probably that "it is too late". The curse of the amorous dyad is that it is almost always "too late" or "too early".

In some cases ego is so fervently infatuated with alter that he may "sweep her up in his love". This many times involves alter being enamoured in ego's love of her. Willard Waller has expressed this dynamic as follows: "The purest type of feminine love is a sort of reflected narcissism. The woman loves the man who loves her."[5] What it amounts to is that alter becomes enamoured in her own idealized image as radiating from ego. The amorous dyad is thus centred on alter's idealized image as processed by ego's projected infatuation and readily reinforced by alter. The fragility, precariousness and vulnerability of this amorous dyad becomes apparent when we realize that it all rests on the intensity of ego's infatuation with alter's ideal image and his perseverence in constantly projecting this image over to alter. Ego has to constantly feed the amorous fire while alter is a rather passive consumer. Once ego falters or is temporarily engaged in concerns other than his burning love, the pitch of his infatuation lowers and the amorous flame perishes because alter will not or cannot feed it. Its sole source is ego; alter provides only a reflector image of it. When the flame is extinguished its mirror image is blotted out with it.

The clever baiting of our quest to overpower the object and our longing for the return to pantheistic early orality through our programming to love our beloved, contains its own self-destructing mechanism. This is inherent in our amatory infatuation being based on our Sisyphean core quests and Tantalic longings which are projected on our beloved long enough to effect pair bonding, mating and reproduction. When this is brought about and we realize that our beloved cannot possibly implement our projections, matrimony (and reproduction) is well on its way or has already taken place; the bait of love has fulfilled its purpose and our programming seems to have lost interest both in us and in our loves. This is more or less the time when we start wondering or complain vociferously about our beloved not implementing our expectations. In our disenchantment we rarely ask ourselves what right we had to emburden any person with the realization of our core vector dreams and ambitions. The language of love is not inferential, alas, especially if it leads to self incrimination. This was learned the hard way by Nietzsche whose infatuation with Lou Andreas Salomē involved precisely this projection of his own image of perfection, expecting her to become the superwoman of his dreams. "I had the best intentions", declared Nietzsche, "of remaking her into the image I had formed of her."[6] This is the archetypal self-defeating projection of love. Nietzsche assigned Frau Lou the impossible mission of delivering Zarathustra the lonely recluse isolated on the top of a mountain from the rarified air of his miseries. When she failed to do so the relationship soured and Nietzsche felt betrayed. Yet even an Olympian of the stature of Nietzsche did not realize that he was enamoured with is own projections and that their failure to materialize had hardly anything to do with the deeds or omissions of Frau Lou.

When ego projects on alter his core vector quests and longing in the form of love, and expects alter to fulfill them, ego not only expects alter to perform a hopeless task but also emburdens their relationships with a strain which eventually kills the love and disrupts the amorous dyad. Ego's resentment against his seemingly betraying lover is misplaced because the lack of an intersubjective communication means alter cannot be aware of the form and contents of ego's projected expectations from him, and even less be able to implement them. Many loves may thus be modelled on the dynamics portrayed by Don Quixote's projections on Dulcinea of his dreams of chivalric glory and grace. This hilariously painful story highlights the projections of all lovers on their misinformed paramours.

John Money has remarked that some people perceive marriage as a long term incarceration.[7] Our hunch is that many more people may feel that monogamous marriages "do not work" yet they are quite often reluctant to admit it to themselves and much less to others. Although the study of the development of monogamy is outside the scope of the present work we note that monogamous marriages are mostly of European origin, and have been sustained and reinforced by the chivalrous ideals of the "pure" mother-woman archetypically linked to the grace of unity and the Mother-of-God.[8] We claim that the rigid adherence to monogamy is a compulsive concretization of man's Tantalic longing for partaking in unity and/or his quest to possess the mother-object, depending on his early or later oral fixations. We have already discussed the link between the maternal proscription of incest and the formation of the human family. In the present context we shall try to argue that the oppressive nature of monogamy stems from the insistence of the occidental religion-based normative system that the familial institution embody and fulfill its inclusive separant expectations and/or participant exclusionary ideals, according to the social character of a given society.[9]

Monogamy, as an institution, more than polygamy, aims to concretize and anchor one's participant longing for unity on the nuclear family through tying up the individual, his mate and their children into a tightly knit unit. Monogamy involves, normatively and ideally, a total commitment of love and loyalty to one's mate with a corresponding claim to the mate's love and loyalty — until death do them part. A mate with a separant predisposition may try to realize his craving for possessiveness by domineering his mate and children. As the possessive ego sees the lives of his children as an extension of his own he would try to realize his failed or insufficiently implemented ambitions by driving them or emotionally blackmailing them into over-achieving. If ego is of a participant disposition he would constantly efface and deprecate himself in order to be accepted by his mate. Many times this participant mate would artificially lower his intelligence and conceal his superior education in order to be acceptable to an ignorant unintelligent mate. The participant idea of the family places family honour, cohesion and unity above the well-being and dignity of its individual members. The epitome of the participant strain imposed by monogamy is mostly apparent in the occidental bourgeois family. The unrealistic imposition on the bourgeois family of absolute participant ideals, norms and sexual standards has led to the typical bourgeois hypocrisy of double moral standards in domestic relationships and almost universal sexual infidelity. Bourgeois hypocrisy in domestic and sexual matters serves as a safety valve to keep the unity of the family from bursting at its seams; it helps maintain the facade, the illusion and the paying of lip-service to graceful motherhood, the innocence of children and the inseparable family unit.

The institutionally more separant polygamous families, on the other hand, impose a less stringent normative strain on the family members and do not emburden them with lofty core vector ideals which are unachievable by definition. The women have their separant predispositions for reproduction fulfilled as well as almost exclusive freedom in the rearing of their children in their early years. The care, protection and material necessities are provided by the husband sometimes with the woman's active participation, while the women have dominion over the household. The availability of other wives has its advantages when one wife is either unable or unwilling to have sexual intercourse because of periods, pregnancies and childbirth. Husbands are also provided with a greater variety of sexual outlets to satisfy their greater predisposition to promiscuity. The belief held by occidental moralists and anthropologists is that polygamous marriages are oppressive to women has been found on closer scrutiny to be largely unfounded. The classic studies by Briffault, the essentials of which have not so far been refuted, are that there is a relative lack of jealousy and rivalry among polygamous wives and that the number of a man's wives is usually increased at the express instigation and request of the women who are the main upholders of polygamy. Briffault states that:

. . . the economic position of a wife in a polygamous family, in primitive and uncultured societies, is not endangered by the relations of the common husband to his other wives. On the contrary, since primitive women are workers, the accession of new workers in the family promotes the very object which is the biological purpose of the mating instinct in the female. Among the agricultural populations of Africa the accession of new wives not only facilitates the work of each, but increases the general wealth and well-being of the family, and thus forwards the aims of both the maternal and the derivative mating instincts of the women.[10]

This is in line with our conception of the separant economic considerations of women in pair bonding which are optimally expressed in the primitive agricultural polygamous families. Polygamy was also held to be good for natural selection and better breeding because " . . . he who has most wives is considered the best hunter, being obliged to provide for them by his own industry. In Africa polygamists are usually hard workers and aristocrats; men who by virtue of hard work and royal blood are able to work and support a number of wives. In other words, where a savage state of society obtains polygamists are, as a rule, the best type of men and the most staunch upholders of tribal life and customs."[11] The best hunters, the hardest workers and more successful members of the tribe (i.e., the better breeders and providers) have more wives and hence, father more children, who are fitter genetically. Briffault concludes his survey by stating:

> The grounds upon which the European conception of monogamous marriage is founded are, however, peculiar to European social development, and are without application or existence in any other society. None of the considerations which are urged by European sentiment against polygamy has any application in the conditions of uncultured society. Monogamy was favoured by early Christian moralists, who accounted marriage a necessary evil, as a reduction of that evil to a minimum, and on grounds of chastity and continence; but chastity and continence for their own sakes are not regarded as meritorious in uncultured societies. Monogamy is the only form of marriage which is in accordance with the sentiments of exclusive attachment which are assumed in European tradition to be the antecedents and foundations of the union; but such exclusive sexual attachment is not the antecedent of marriage in primitive societies, and is not understood.[12]

This passage highlights the unrealistic strain which the participant-Tantalic ideals of monogamy exert on the Christian based European family.

Petrification

Ego's petrification of alter and vice versa in an amorous dyad may be regarded as a special case of the inevitable mutual stultification inherent in interpersonal relationships as illustrated by Sartre. The works of Sartre which are relevant to our present context are some passages in the hardly intelligible *Being and Nothingness*,[13] and in his play *No Exit*[14] which is crystal clear, honed to perfection and one of the peaks of twentieth-century drama.

In the chapters of *Being and Nothingness* dealing with "The Existence of Others" and "The Concrete Relations with Others", and in the section on "God faith" (*mauvaise foi*), Sartre expounds his thesis that alter can never be but an object to ego because the only subjectivity that ego can be aware of is his own. Because of this alter defines and delimits ego's subjectivity for him and may even usurp it. This happens when ego internalizes alter within himself either as a "generalized other" or as a specific "relevant other". Yet in the latter case alter does not cease thereby to be an object for ego. Moreover, the internalized alter who is now part of ego but still an object to him regards and scrutinizes ego with an objectifying Medusa's stare. Alter thus subjugates ego from within and petrifies his subjectivity. In any dyadic relationship one party is bound to be weaker than the other at any given time. In consequence the subjugation by petrification of this party by the stronger would be more imminent. This is especially the case in a dyadic love relationship when emotions are intense and the operation of the least interest principle more severe. This duality of myself-for-myself and of myself-for-others, and the intense attunement of myself to the other and vice versa in the amatory dyad, make for the more participant or the weaker party to the dyad to internalize the objectifying expectations of the other and hence be subjugated by the other. The end product is that in many relevant aspects ego does not regard himself any more with his own awareness but with the petrifying awareness of alter which has been internalized by him. The vulnerability of ego to alter becomes extreme because alter does not control ego from without but most effectively from within by becoming part of ego's interactive, normative and especially affective self.

In *No Exit* Sartre depicts two women and a man in one room in hell.[15] One of the women, a lesbian, tries to woo the other who craves for the man. The lack of communication, the different expectations and the conflicting desires bring about the subjugation, petrification and torture of each member of the triad by the other two. The outward facade of Garcin is of a revolutionary hero, with the inner reality of a traitor and a coward. He sublimates his failure to achieve his revolutionary goals by totally crushing and subjugating his wife who is a habitual willing victim. Garcin tries to convince Inez that he is not a coward, but by his need to convince her to see him in a different way than she really sees him he holds him in bondage. The part of Inez, internalized by Garcin, judges him to be a coward. This verdict by the internalized relevant other is inescapable; "I'm watching you," hisses Inez to Garcin, "everybody's watching. I'm a crowd all by myself. Do you hear the crowd? Do you hear them muttering, Garcin? Mumbling, Coward! Coward! Coward! that's what they're saying . . . It's no use trying to escape".[16] The verdict of the internalized other is harsh, cannot be appealed and does not recognize extenuating circumstances. The third character of the triad is Estelle who married an older man for money and social position. When she became pregnant by her lover she drowned the new-born baby. Estelle is enslaved by the subjugating gaze of Inez who offers her pupils as the only viable mirrors in hell. Estelle realizes her bondage to the stare of Inez as internalized by her: "You scare me," exclaims Estelle.[17] Inez then asserts her mastery over the captive Estelle: "You know the way they catch larks — with a mirror? I'm your lark-mirror, my dear, and you can't escape me."[18]

When ego judges himself with the eyes of alter who was internalized to become part of ego's cognitive system the cycle of subjugation is complete. The fiercely separant and possessive Inez bases her emotional relationship with others on her need to subjugate them. Yet it is precisely this need that makes her dependent on these others. The bonds between the torturer and the tortured make them inseparable. The agonies of the least interest principle are also portrayed in the play: when Estelle is craving for Garcin he does not pay attention to her and when he tries ardently to court her she seems to be interested in something else. The expectations from the emotional dyad are also different. When Estelle begs to be loved, Garcin asks for her trust which she is not prepared to grant him. Estelle then portrays the essence of the disrupting effects of divergent expectations from the amatory dyad by each of its partners, by declaring that she is always inclined to do the opposite of whatever is expected of her. The indication is that in an emotional dyad each one tortures the other even if he does not want or intend to do so. The infernal component of the amarous dyad is not provided by intentional torture; for the most part the lovers torture each other inadvertly and inflict pain on each other without actually intending to do so.

The play ends with Garcin urging the others "Let's get on with it", implying that they should initiate another cycle of emotional subjugation and torture. In our context this would mean that whatever pain and suffering one incurs in one's amorous encounters, one is baited to ever engage in them by the Sisyphean desire to possess or by the Tantalic longing to be possessed by love.

Rebellious Longing

If love is agonizing, painful, frustrating, unattainable, illusory, subjugating, petrifying and well nigh impossible, what then kindles its fires? What induces us to indulge *da capo* in the amorous cycles of involvement, infatuation and disenchantment? We claim that our yearning for love, be it the Sisyphean covetousness of possessing our beloved or the Tantalic longing to fuse with him/her, is the essence of love. The process of involvement kindles our amorous fires and not the attainment of our love goals, which are as unachievable as the aims of our participant and separant core vectors. Nietzsche laments not so much his lost love for Lou as the destruction of his illusions of love and his ability to long for it.[19] Plato describes this yearning for union in love as follows:

> For the intense yearning which each of them has towards the other does not appear to be the desire of lover's intercourse, but of something else which the soul of either evidently desires and cannot tell, and of which she has only a dark and doubtful presentiment. Suppose Hephaestus, with his instruments, to come to the pair who are lying side by side and say to them, "What do you people want of one another?" they would be unable to explain. And suppose, further, that when he saw their perplexity he said: "Do you desire to be wholly one; always day and night to be in one another's company? for if this is what you desire, I am ready to melt you into one and let you grow together, so that being two you shall become one, and while you live share a common life as if you were a single man, and after your death in the world below still be one departed soul instead of two — I ask whether this is what you lovingly desire, and whether you are satisfied to attain this?" There is not a man of them who when he heard the proposal would deny or would not acknowledge that this meeting and melting into one another, this becoming one instead of two, was the very expression of his ancient need. And the reason is that human nature was originally one and we were a whole, and the desire and pursuit of the whole is called love.[20]

The essence of love is not the attainment of unity but the longing for it. Which one of us did not experience the thrill, the elation the quickening of the pulse when revisiting the place of our first kiss and embrace. The yearning for an amorous encounter is enough to fill our hearts even though its realization is remote or even impossible. The craving for love takes us out from our daily routines and drudgeries and lends a dimension of elation to our Sisyphean quests and infuses revelation into our Tantalic longing. This independent potency of the yearning for love which has an essence and a dynamic of its own irrespective of the object of love might well be the reason for our being baited by it to mate and reproduce. Love songs, tales, myths and drama are anchored on the yearning for amorous union and not on the processes of mating, reproduction and growth. Camus succeeded in capturing the essence of this yearning by describing "The Adulterous Woman" who exudes a free floating longing for love towards no specific object, but radiates this longing in all directions to the earth, sky, sea and stars, to be borne along by the evening breeze.[21]

Man is in love with love. The objects of our amorous involvement, however, are transitory. What is permanent throughout our life is our yearning to love and be loved. The Tantalic longing for love has been projected onto religion as the pure mother-of-God and the graceful

Sophia and Shechina. The timelessness of love is a function of the longing for it. A sacred love is a love for an inaccessible object. The rebellion of the participant lover is to immerse himself into his longing for his beloved, however unattainable he or she may be and however impossible the love might be. The rebellious lovers' motto is to love at all costs and to hell with the consequences. Adele H. carries on her Tantalic love irrespective of the indifference of her beloved, oblivious of his rejection of her. The professor in *The Blue Angel* carries on his debasing love affair with the cabaret dancer although he is fully aware that he is being destroyed by it. In a similar ideational context but in a different setting Beatrix, in Claude Grote's film *The Lace Embroidery*, can only achieve a pure and perfect love in the total isolation of an asylum for the insane.

Kierkegaard performed his metaphysical rebellion together with his renunciation of the consummation of his love for Regina Olsen. By so doing he elevated his love to a stature of permanence. He extruded it from the precariousness of spatiotemporality and made it timeless. He also prevented it from souring and waning through the levelling down and petrifying routines of matrimony. He renounced a love object and gained a permanent love-longing. To yearn for a love irrespective of the possibilities of its realization, and even being certain that it is unattainable, is to render it absolute. By the same logic but for diametrically opposite ends Sade aimed to destroy the longing for love and annihilate, thereby, love itself. Sade realized that the prime mover of love is the yearning for it. Hence the destruction of the longing for love will bring with it as a necessary corollary the extinction of love. This fits Sade's radical nihilistic design of killing sex through boredom by repetitive perversion. Sade wished to be society's ultimate executioner because without a yearning for an amorous encounter and a longing for an emotional dialogue man enters a state of indifference and loneliness and hence a lack of empathy and desire for involvement with his human surroundings. Without the longing for union the act of sex becomes a mere banality which eventually destroys the erotic passions. Without the Tantalic longing for grace and the Sisyphean dreams anchored on sex the contours of flesh, the texture of skin, and the glow of eyes lose their bait value and love peters out. By killing erotic desire and the yearning for love which sustain the human core vectors, Sade meant to halt reproduction, dissolve the human family and disrupt the normative system which he hated. Sade knew that by depriving man of the longing for love, human life which he despised and aimed to annihilate would become not only unbearable but totally meaningless and hence not worth living. Sade's negation highlights the basic assertion of life inherent in the longing for love.

The mutual longing of lovers for an emotional dialogue and encounter provides a framework, a context and a scaffolding for their love. Two lovers holding hands on a moonlit shore of the Mediterranean, the Atlantic Ocean or the North Sea might have different expectations and be on the opposite poles of the participant-separant continuum, yet their mutual longing for love provides them with a channel through which their divergent Tantalic revelations and Sisyphean aspirations may flow out and provide them and their offspring with some sort of a viable future. Only the longing for love can provide the human being's "throwness-unto-death" with a silver lining of grace.

Notes

Bible quotations are taken from *The New English Bible.*

INTRODUCTION

1. The other four are: S.G. Shoham, *Society and the Absurd* (Oxford: Basil Blackwell, 1974); S.G. Shoham, *Salvation Through the Gutters* (Washington D.C.: Hemisphere Publications, 1979); S.G. Shoham, *The Myth of Tantalus* (St Lucia: University of Queensland Press, 1979); S.G. Shoham, *The Violence of Silence: The Impossibility of Dialogue* (London: Science Reviews Ltd., to be published 1982).
2. E. Erikson, "The Problem of Identity", *Journal of the American Psychoanalytic Association* 4 (1956): 56-121.
3. Shoham, *Myth of Tantalus.*
4. Shoham, *Myth of Tantalus,* chapter 2.
5. This is the height of sexual excitement phase in both male and female just prior to orgasm as described and documented by W.H. Masters and V.E. Johnson in *Human Sexual Response* (Boston: Little Brown & Co., 1966).
6. G. Bermant and J.M. Davidson, *Biological Bases of Sexual Behavior* (New York: Harper & Row, 1974), p. 9.
7. Shoham, *Violence of Silence.*
8. C.J. Avers, *Biology of Sex* (New York: J. Wiley & Sons, 1974), pp. 4-5.
9. S. Michelmore, *Sexual Reproduction* (New York: The Natural History Press, 1964), p. 111.
10. G.C. Williams, *Sex and Evolution* (Princeton: Princeton University Press, 1975), p. 112.
11. A. Capellanus, *The Art of Courtly Love* (New York: F. Ungar, 1959), p. 30.
12. Shoham, *Myth of Tantalus*; Shoham, *Salvation Through the Gutters.*
13. Cited in Bermant and Davidson, *Bases of Sexual Behavior,* p. 258.
14. Kurt H. Wolff, *The Sociology of Georg Simmel* (New York: The Free Press of Glencoe, 1964), p. 128.
15. Capellanus, *Art of Courtly Love,* p. 28.
16. Shoham, *Myth of Tantalus,* chapter 2.
17. Shoham, *Violence of Silence,* chapters 1-3.
18. H.S. Gvetzkow and P.H. Bowman, *Men and Hunger: A Psychological Manual for Relief Workers* (Elgin, Ill.: Brethren Press, 1956).

19. F. Heider, *The Psychology of Interpersonal Relations* (New York: Wiley, 1968), p. 198.
20. See the introduction to S. G. Shoham and A. Grahame, eds., *Israel Studies in Criminology*, Vol. 5. (Tel Aviv: Turtledove Press, 1979).

CHAPTER 1

1. J. Maynard Smith, "What use is Sex?", *Journal of Theoretical Biology* 30 (1965): 319–35. Compare G. C. Williams, *Sex and Evolution* (Princeton: Princeton University Press, 1945).
2. E. D. Carr: *The Sexes* (New York: Doubleday, 1970), p. 11.
3. E. Mayr, *Animal Species and Evolution* (Cambridge, Mass.: Harvard University Press, 1963).
4. G. Bermant and J. M. Davidson, *The Biological Bases of Sexual Behavior* (New York: Harper & Row, 1974), pp. 15–16.
5. J. Crane, "Basic patterns of display in fiddler crabs Ocypodidae (genus Uca)", *Zoologica* 42 (1957): 69–82.
6. J. E. Lloyd, "Studies on the flash communication system in Photinus fireflies", *Miscellaneous Publications Museum of Zoology, No. 130* (Ann Arbor: University of Michigan, 1966).
7. Bermant and Davidson, *Bases of Sexual Behavior*, pp. 20–27.
8. J. Sheffer, *Incest* (Cambridge, Mass.: Harvard University Press, in press).
9. *Encyclopedia Brittanica*, 15th ed., s.v. "Sexual and non-Sexual Reproduction".
10. W. F. Loomis, "The Sex Gas of Hydra", *Scientific American* (1959): 145–56. See also A. Burnett and N. Diehl, "The Nervous System of Hydra III. The initiation of sexuality with special reference to the nervous system". *Journal of Experimental Zoology* (1964): 237–50.
11. S. Michelmore, *Sexual Reproduction* (New York: The Natural History Press, 1964), pp. 98–99.
12. N. T. Spratt, *Developmental Biology* (Belmont, California: Wadsworth Publishing Co., 1971).
13. S. G. Shoham, *Salvation Through the Gutters* (Washington D.C.: Hemisphere Publications, 1979), pp. 2–11; S. G. Shoham, *The Myth of Tantalus* (St Lucia: University of Queensland Press, 1979), chapter 8.
14. Michelmore, *Sexual Reproduction*, pp. 110–11.
15. S. Weitz, *Sex Roles* (New York: Oxford University Press, 1977), pp. 15–25.
16. D. Lack, *The Natural Regulation of Animal Numbers* (Oxford: The Clarendon Press, 1954), p. 157.
17. R. C. Friedman, ed., *Sex Differences in Behavior* (New York: John Wiley & Sons, 1974).
18. Ibid., p. 339.
19. C. J. Avers, *Biology of Sex* (New York: John Wiley & Sons, 1974), p. 23.
20. E. O. Wilson, *Sociobiology* (Cambridge, Mass.: Harvard University Press, 1976), pp. 320–21.
21. R. Briffault, "The Origin of Love", in *The Making of Man*, ed., V. F. Calverton (New York: The Modern Library, 1931), pp. 487–88.
22. Michelmore, *Sexual Reproduction*, p. 167.

23. K. Roeder, *Nerve Cells and Insect Behaviour* (Cambridge, Mass.: Harvard University Press, 1963).
24. Bermant and Davidson, *Bases of Sexual Behavior*, p. 187.
25. Weitz, *Sex Roles,* p. 30.
26. Bermant and Davidson, *Bases of Sexual Behavior,* p. 36.

CHAPTER 2

1. S. Freud, *An Outline of Psychoanalysis: Standard Edition* (London: Hogarth Press, 1940), p. 188.
2. S. G. Shoham, *Salvation Through the Gutters* (Washington DC.: Hemisphere Publications, 1979).
3. S. G. Shoham, *The Myth of Tantalus* (St Lucia: University of Queensland Press, 1979).
4. Shoham, *Salvation Through the Gutters.*
5. We mainly rely on the sources in F. R. Tennant, *The Sources of the Doctrine of the Fall, and Original Sin* (New York: Schocken Books, 1968).
6. S. Fisher, *The Female Orgasm* (New York: Basic Books, 1973), p. 153.
7. Shoham, *Myth of Tantalus,* chapters 1 and 2.
8. R. Fairbairn, *Psychoanalytic Studies of the Personality* (London: Tavistock Publications, 1966).
9. Ibid.
10. Shoham, *Myth of Tantalus,* final chapter.
11. J. J. Bachofen, *Myth, Religion and Mother Right* (Princeton: Princeton University Press, 1967), p. 73.
12. M. Eliade, *The Myth of the Eternal Return,* trans. W. R. Trask (New York: Harper & Row, 1959).
13. C. G. Jung, *Psychological Types* (London: Kegan Paul, Trench, Trubner & Co., 1944), pp. 241, 615.
14. Shoham, *Salvation Through the Gutters.*
15. *Selected Papers of Karl Abraham* (London: Hogarth Press, 1928), p. 407.
16. Cited by Tennant, *Sources of the Doctrine of the Fall,* p. 140.

CHAPTER 3

1. H. Vital, *Sefer Ha'likutim Parashat Vayishlah 22/A* (Jerusalem, 1913).
2. G. G. Scholem, *Major Trends in Jewish Mysticism* (New York, 1961), p. 13. Some Kabbalist systems regard infinity as the equivalent to Keter the Sephira. See J. Gikatila: *Shaare Orah* (Jerusalem: The Bialik Institute, 1970), p. 138.
3. I. Tishby, *The Doctrine of Evil and the "Kelippah" in Lurianic Kabbalism* (Jerusalem: Schocken, 1942), p. 28.
4. Ibid., p. 31.
5. Ibid., p. 22.
6. F. Lachover and I. Tishby, *The Wisdom of the Zohar: Texts from the Book of Splendour,* vol. 1 (Jerusalem: 1971), p. 319.

7. Tishby, *Doctrine of Evil*, p. 15.
8. S. G. Shoham, *Salvation Through the Gutters* (Washington D.C.: Hemisphere Publications, 1979).
9. Tishby, *Doctrine of Evil*.
10. H. Jonas, *The Gnostic Religion* (Boston: The Beacon Press, 1963), p. 141.
11. Ibid., p. 301.
12. J. Doresse, *The Secret Books of the Egyptian Gnostics* (London: Hollis & Carter, 1960), p. 162.
13. Cited by Tishby, *Doctrine of Evil*, p. 24.
14. See the arguments presented in Tishby, *Doctrine of Evil*, p. 64.
15. Ibid., p. 40.
16. Jonas, *Gnostic Religion*, p. 227.
17. Ibid., p. 76.
18. Ibid., The Epilogue.
19. Shoham, *Salvation Through the Gutters*, Part 1.
20. Tishby, *Doctrine of Evil*, p. 29.
21. Ibid., p. 27.
22. Ibid.
23. Ibid., p. 45.
24. Ibid., p. 58-59.
25. Ibid., p. 46.
26. Ibid., p. 24.
27. H. Vital, *Etz Haim* (Jerusalem, 1913), chapter 4, p. 38.
28. Ibid., p. 12.
29. Vital, *Sefer Ha'likutim*, Scholem, *Major Trends in Jewish Mysticism*.
30. Vital, *Sefer Ha'likutim*, part 8.
31. Tishby, *Doctrine of Evil*, p. 46.
32. H. Vital, *Shaar Ha'kelalim* (Jerusalem, 1913), chapter 2, p. 4.
33. Vital, *Etz Haim*, chapter 4, p. 3.
34. H. Vital, *Sefer Mevo Shearim* (Jerusalem, 1913), chapter 2, p. 3.
35. Vital, *Sefer Ha'likutim*, chapter 2, p. 2.
36. Scholem, *Major Trends in Jewish Mysticism*, p. 267.
37. E. Conze, *Buddhist Texts Through the Ages* (Oxford: Bruno Cassirer, 1954); J. Hastings, ed., *Encyclopaedia of Religion and Ethics* (New York: Scribners & Sons, 1951).
38. M. Eliade, *Birth and Rebirth* (New York: Harper & Row, 1965), pp. 8-9.
39. Scholem, *Major Trends in Jewish Mysticism*; Tishby, *Doctrine of Evil*.
40. G. Widengren, *The Principle of Evil in the Eastern Religions* (Evanston: Northwestern University Press, 1967), p. 48.
41. Ibid., p. 46.
42. Ibid., p. 47.
43. E. Neumann, *The Great Mother* (Princeton: Princeton University Press, 1972).
44. Ibid., p. 42.
45. Ibid.
46. Ibid.
47. Widengren, *Principle of Evil*, p. 47.
48. Ibid., p. 27.
49. Scholem, *Major Trends in Jewish Mysticism*, p. 236.
50. Hesiod, *Theogony* (Harmondsworth: Penguin Books, 1977).
51. Jonas, *Gnostic Religion*, p. 228.
52. Neumann, *The Great Mother*, chapters 10 and 11.

53. Tishby, *Doctrine of Evil*, p. 19.
54. Neumann, *The Great Mother*, p. 168.
55. Ibid., p. 170.
56. F. R. Tennant, *The Sources of the Doctrine of the Fall, and Original Sin* (New York: Schocken Books, 1968).
57. Doresse, *Secret Books of the Egyptian Gnostics*, p. 101.
58. Shoham, *Salvation Through the Gutters*, chapter 1.
59. F. Leboyer, *Birth Without Violence* (London: Wildwood House, 1975).
60. Ibn-Tabul, "Drosh Heftziba", cited by Tishby, *Doctrine of Evil*, p. 24.
61. Ibid., p. 35.
62. Vital, *Sefer Mevo Shearim*, part 2.
63. Tishby, *Doctrine of Evil*, p. 33.
64. R. M. Grant, *Gnosticism* (New York: Harper Brothers, 1961), pp. 75, 81, 82.
65. Widengren, *Principle of Evil*, p. 47.
66. Genesis 3:16.
67. Shoham, *Salvation Through the Gutters*, Part I.
68. Tishby, *Doctrine of Evil*, p. 125.
69. Jonas, *Gnostic Religion*, p. 52.
70. Ibid., p. 60.
71. R. Graves, *The White Goddess* (New York: Vintage Books, 1948), p. 539.
72. Doresse, *Secret Books of the Egyptian Gnostics*, p. 113.
73. Jonas, *Gnostic Religion*, p. 59.
74. Neumann, *The Great Mother*, p. 396.
75. See Mario Praz, *The Romantic Agony* (London: The Fontana Library, 1950), p. 231.
76. Ibid., p. 323.
77. Ibid., p. 50.
78. S. Giora Shoham, "Separant and Participant Personality Types of Suicides", in *Israel Studies in Criminology*, vol. 7, ed. S. G. Shoham and A. Grahame (White Plains: Sheridan House, to be published 1982).
79. Shoham, *Salvation Through the Gutters*.
80. S. G. Shoham, *The Myth of Tantalus* (St Lucia: University of Queensland Press, 1979), chapters 2 and 3.

CHAPTER 4

1. S. G. Shoham, *The Myth of Tantalus* (St Lucia: University of Queensland Press, 1979), chapter 1.
2. C. J. Avers, *Biology of Sex* (New York: J. Wiley & Sons, 1974), p. 4.
3. *Talmud Yevanot* 61:2.
4. For negative attitudes of other cultures towards menstruation see S. Weitz, *Sex Roles* (New York: Oxford University Press, 1977), p. 30.
5. The source of this myth is mainly the Homeric Hymn to Demeter. For other sources and references see R. Graves, *The Greek Myths*, vol. 1 (Harmondsworth: Pelican Books, 1955).
6. *Talmud Yoma* 77/A.
7. C. G. Jung and C. Kerenyi, *Introduction to a Science of Mythology* (London: Routledge & Kegan Paul Ltd., 1951), p. 150.

8. E. Neumann, *The Great Mother* (Princeton: Princeton University Press, 1972), p. 307.
9. Jung and Kerenyi, *Science of Mythology*, p. 171.
10. See for instance, W. Lotto, "The Meaning of the Eleusinian Mysteries", in *The Mysteries*, ed. J. Campbell (New York: Pantheon Books, 1955), p. 14.
11. H. Rahner, "The Christian Mystery and the Pagan Mysteries", in ibid., p. 351.
12. For a classic and brilliant exposition of this premise see S. Ranulf, *The Jealousy of the Gods and the Criminal Law in Athens* (Copenhagen: Levin & Munksgaard, 1933).
13. Jung and Kerenyi, *Science of Mythology*, p. 193.
14. Paul Schmitt, "The Ancient Mysteries in the Society of Their Time, Their Transformation and most Recent Echoes", in Campbell, *The Mysteries*, p. 101.
15. See Hans Leisegang, "The Mystery of the Serpent", in ibid., p. 237.
16. E. A. Wallis Budge, *Legends of Our Lady Mary* (London: Martin Hopkinson & Co., 1968), p. 27.
17. Ibid., pp. 52-3.
18. Marcello Craver, *The Life of Jesus* (New York: Grove Press, 1970), p. 17.
19. Budge, *Legends of Our Lady Mary*, p. 32.
20. Ibid., p. 28.
21. R. Graves, *The White Goddess* (New York: Vintage Books, 1948), p. 535.
22. B. Blanshard, *Reason and Belief* (London: George Allen & Unwin, 1934), p. 462.
23. R. M. Grant, *Gnosticism* (London: Thames and Hudson, 1969), p. 324.
24. H. Jonas, *The Gnostic Religion* (Boston: The Beacon Press, 1963), p. 231.
25. S. G. Shoham, *Salvation Through the Gutters* (Washington D.C.: Hemisphere Publications, 1979), p. 221.

CHAPTER 5

1. S. G. Shoham, *Salvation Through the Gutters* (Washington D.C.: Hemisphere Publications, 1979), pp. 124-25.
2. S. G. Shoham, *The Myth of Tantalus* (St Lucia: University of Queensland Press, 1979); Shoham, *Salvation Through the Gutters*.
3. W. R. D. Fairbairn, *Psychoanalytic Studies of the Personality* (London: Tavistock Publications Ltd., 1966), p. 33.
4. F. R. Tennant, *The Sources of the Doctrine of the Fall, and Original Sin* (New York: Schocken Books, 1968), pp. 149-50.
5. Ibid., p. 243.
6. Romans 5:12.
7. H. Jonas, *The Gnostic Religion* (Boston: The Beacon Press, 1963), p. 62; I. Tishby, *The Doctrine of Evil and the "Kelippah" in Lurianic Kabbalism* (Jerusalem: Schocken, 1942), pp. 110, 118.
8. *Genesis Raba* 22B.
9. Tennant, *Sources of the Doctrine of the Fall*, p. 197.
10. Ibid., p. 194.
11. H. Vital, *Sha'arei Kedusha* (Jerusalem, 1913), chapter 1, p. 8a.
12. *Genesis Raba* 22B.
13. *The Book of Adam and Eve* 19:3.

14. Ibid., 21:7.
15. Ibid., 7:7.
16. Ibid., 9:2.
17. Ibid.
18. Ibid., 7:2.
19. Tennant, *Sources of the Doctrine of the Fall*, pp. 196-97.
20. Genesis 3:20.
21. H. Vital, cited in Tishby, *Doctrine of Evil*, p. 95.
22. Shoham, *Myth of Tantalus*, chapters, 1, 2, 3.
23. *Genesis Raba* 38B.
24. *The Book of Adam and Eve* 19:3.
25. *Talmud Shabbat* 146 A; *Talmud Yevamoth* 103 B; *Talmud Avoda-Zara* 22 B.
26. Genesis 3:1.
27. G. Widengren, *The Principle of Evil in the Eastern Religions* (Evanston: Northwestern University Press, 1967), p. 30.
28. C.G. Jung, *Symbols of Transformation* (London: Routledge & Kegan Paul, 1956), p. 102, 103.
29. P.E. Slater, *The Glory of Hera* (Boston: The Beacon Press, 1968), p. 82.
30. E. Neumann, *The Great Mother* (Princeton: Princeton University Press, 1972), p. 144.
31. C.G. Jung, *Symbols of Transformation* (New York: Harper & Row, 1965), p. 102.
32. K. Abraham, *Selected Papers* (London: The Hogarth Press, 1927), p. 333.
33. M. Klein, *Mourning and its Relation to Manic-Depressive States* (London: The Hogarth Press, 1948).
34. Fairbairn, *Psychoanalytic Studies of the Personality*, p. 33.
35. *Talmud Sota* 18 B.
36. Gikatila, "The Secret of the Snake and its Trial", in G. Scholem, *Major Trends in Jewish Mysticism* (New York: 1961), pp. 405-406.
37. Hesiod, *Theogony* (Harmondsworth: Penguin Books, 1977), p. 32.
38. Neumann, *The Great Mother*, p. 104.
39. *Genesis Raba* 43 B.
40. *The Book of Adam and Eve* 26.
41. Neumann, *The Great Mother*, p. 10.
42. Genesis 2:25.
43. Genesis 3:10.
44. Klein, *Mourning and its Relation to Manic-Depressive States*.

CHAPTER 6

1. See S.G. Shoham, *The Myth of Tantalus* (St Lucia: University of Queensland Press, 1979), chapters 1-3.
2. W.R.D. Fairbairn, *Psychoanalytical Studies of the Personality* (London: Tavistock Publications, 1966), p. 154.
3. M. Klein, *Contributions to Psychoanalysis* (London: The Hogarth Press, 1948), p. 202.
4. Ibid., p. 378.
5. S.G. Shoham, *Salvation Through the Gutters* (Washington D.C.: Hemisphere Publications, 1979), part 2.

6. Ibid., p. 378.
7. Fairbairn, *Psychoanalytical Studies,* p. 25.
8. Ibid., p. 31.
9. See G. Bermant and J. M. Davidson, *Biological Bases of Sexual Behavior* New York: Harper & Row, 1974), p. 261.
10. P. E. Slater, *The Glory of Hera* (Boston: The Beacon Press, 1968), pp. 135–36.
11. See P. Watzlawich, "A Review of the Double Bind Theory", *Family Process* 2 (1963): 132–53.
12. D. Levy, *Behavioural Analysis* (Springfield, Mass.: C. C. Thomas, 1958).
13. J. Bowlby, *Attachment* (New York: Pelican Books, 1972).
14. K. S. Winter, "Characteristics of Fantasy while Nursing", *Journal of Personality* 37 (1968): 58–71.
15. N. Newton, *Maternal Emotions* (New York: Paul B. Hoeber, 1955), p. 103.
16. R. R. Sears, E. E. Maccoby and H. Levin, *Patterns of Child Rearing* (Evanston, Ill.: Row, Peterson, 1957).
17. S. Fisher, *The Female Orgasm* (New York: Basic Books, 1973), p. 153.
18. Fairbairn, *Psychoanalytic Studies,* p. 144.
19. Karl Abraham, *Selected Papers* (London: Hogarth Press, 1927), p. 395.
20. Ibid., p. 265.
21. Fisher, *Female Orgasm,* p. 153.
22. Abraham, *Selected Papers,* pp. 254–65.
23. Ibid., p. 265.
24. Ibid., p. 334.
25. Hesiod, *Theogony* (Harmondsworth: Penguin Press, 1977), p. 28.
26. E. Neumann, *The Origins and History of Consciousness* (Princeton: Princeton University Press), p. 64.
27. R. Graves, *The Greek Myths,* vol. 1 (Harmondsworth: Pelican Books, 1955), p. 53.
28. Slater, *The Glory of Hera,* p. 346.
29. R. Briffault, *The Mothers* (London: George Allen & Unwin, 1927), pp. 667–68.
30. Abraham, *Selected Papers,* p. 335.
31. Slater, *The Glory of Hera,* p. 64.
32. Shoham, *Salvation Through the Gutters,* part 1.
33. Shoham, *Myth of Tantalus,* chapter 1.
34. Shoham, *Salvation Through the Gutters,* pp. 141–42.
35. Abraham, *Selected Papers,* pp. 396, 404.
36. Klein, *Contributions to Psychoanalysis,* p. 269.
37. Fairbairn, *Psychoanalytic Studies,* p. 144.
38. Slater, *The Glory of Hera,* p. 206.
39. F. R. Tennant, *The Sources of the Doctrine of the Fall, and Original Sin* (New York: Schocken Books, 1968), p. 207.
40. Klein, *Contributions to Psychoanalysis,* pp. 312–13.
41. Fairbairn, *Psychoanalytical Studies,* pp. 23 et seq.
42. "The Book of the Dead", cited in E. Neumann, *The Great Mother* (Princeton: Princeton University Press, 1972), p. 161.
43. C. G. Jung and C. Kerenyi, *Introduction to a Science of Mythology* (London: Routledge and Kegan Paul Ltd., 1951), p. 163.
44. Ibid., pp. 176–77.
45. J. Money and A. A. Ehrhardt, *Man and Woman, Boy and Girl* (Baltimore: Johns Hopkins University Press, 1972), pp. 18–19.

46. A. Macfarlane, *The Psychology of Childbirth* (Cambridge, Mass.: Harvard University Press, 1977).
47. Fisher, *Female Orgasm,* p. 104.
48. Hesiod, *Theogony,* pp. 28–29.
49. S. Shoham, et al., "The Etiology of Middle Class Delinquency in Israel", in *Israel Studies in Criminology,* vol. 3 (Tel Aviv: Gomeh Publishing House, 1970), pp. 121–22.
50. Klein, *Contributions to Psychoanalysis,* p. 363.
51. Hesiod, *Theogony,* p. 28.
52. Richard Friedman et al., eds., *Sex Differences in Behavior* (New York: John Wiley & Sons, 1974), p. 157.
53. Hesiod, *Theogony,* p. 28.
54. Graves, *The Greek Myths,* vol. 2, p. 90.
55. E. Neumann, *The Origins and History of Consciousness* (Princeton: Princeton University Press, 1970), pp. 50–51.
56. S. Freud, *Totem and Taboo* (London: Penguin, 1938).
57. R. Graves, *The White Goddess* (New York: Vintage Books, 1948), pp. 51–52.
58. J. Bachofen, "Das Mutterrecht", in *The Making of Man,* ed. F. Calverton (New York: Random House, 1931), pp. 162–64.
59. S. G. Shoham, "The Isaac Syndrome", *The American Image* 33 (1976).
60. B. Malinowski, *Sex and Repression in Savage Society* (London: Routledge, Kegan Paul, 1953), p. 138.
61. Genesis 3:15.
62. Genesis 3:16.
63. Genesis 3:17–19.

CHAPTER 7

1. For a full exposition of the separant and participant core personality dynamics and the Sisyphean and Tantalic cultural imprints, see S. G. Shoham, *The Myth of Tantalus* (St Lucia: University of Queensland Press, 1979), chapters 1, 2, and 3.
2. S. Michelmore, *Sexual Reproduction* (New York: The Natural History Press, 1964).
3. E. H. Erikson, "Sex Differences in the Play configuration of Pre-Adolescents", cited in S. Fisher, *The Female Orgasm* (New York: Basic Books, 1973), p. 69.
4. Ibid., p. 70.
5. Ibid., p. 71.
6. Ibid., p. 71.
7. E. G. Pitcher and E. Prelinger, *Children Tell Stories – An Analysis of Fantasy* (New York: International University Press, 1963), S. Fisher, *Body Experience in Fantasy and Behaviour* (New York: Appleton Century Crofts, 1970).
8. Fisher, *Body Experience in Fantasy.*
9. Fisher, *The Female Orgasm,* p. 177.
10. S. G. Shoham, *Salvation Through the Gutters* (Washington D.C.: Hemisphere Publications, 1979), Part 2.
11. Shoham, *Myth of Tantalus,* chapters 1 and 2.

12. Fisher, *Female Orgasm*, p. 77.
13. E. Neumann, *The Great Mother* (Princeton: Princeton University Press, 1972), chapter 10.
14. Ibid., p. 171.
15. P. E. Slater, *The Glory of Hera* (Boston: Beacon Press, 1968), p. 76.
16. J. Gikatila, *Shaare Orah* (Jerusalem: The Bialik Institute, 1970), p. 10.
17. Cited in S. Weitz, *Sex Roles* (New York: Oxford University Press, 1977), p. 210.
18. Ibid., p. 210–17.
19. Ibid., p. 221.
20. R. Friedman et al., eds., *Sex Differences in Behavior* (New York: John Wiley & Sons, 1974), p. 72.
21. M. Diamond, "A Critical Evaluation of the Ontogeny of Human Sexual Behaviour", *Quarterly Rev. of Biology* 40 (1965): 147–75.
22. J. Money and A. A. Ehrhardt, *Man and Woman, Boy and Girl* (Baltimore: John Hopkins University Press, 1972), p. 12.
23. Ibid., p. 18.
24. J. L. Hampson and J. G. Hampson, "The Ontogenesis of Sexual Behaviour in Man", in *Sex and Internal Secretions*, vol. 2, ed. W. Young (Baltimore: Williams & Wilkins, 1961), pp. 1401–32.
25. S. Goldberg and M. Lewis, "Play Behaviour in the Year Old Infant, Early Sex Differences", *Child Development* 40 (1969): 21–31; J. Kagan and M. Lewis, "Studies in Attention in the Human Infant", *Merrill-Palmer Quarterly* 2 (1965): 95–127.
26. L. Kohlberg, "A Cognitive Developmental Analysis of Children's Sex-role Concepts and Attitudes", in *The Development of Sex Differences*, ed. E. MacCoby (Stanford: Stanford University Press, 1966), pp. 82–173.
27. A. Katcher, The Discrimination of Sex Differences by Young Children, *Journal of Genetic Psychology* 87 (1955): 131–43.
28. Goldberg and Lewis, "Play Behaviour in the Year Old Infant".
29. Fisher, *Female Orgasm*, p. 80.
30. M. Kay Martin and B. Voorhies, *Female of the Species* (New York: Columbia University Press, 1975), p. 44.
31. J. Kagan, "Acquisition and Significance of Sex Typing and Sex Role Identity", in *Review of Child Development Research*, ed. M. L. Hoffmann and L. W. Hoffmann (New York: Russel Sage, 1964), p. 143.
32. Fisher, *Female Orgasm*, p. 80.
33. S. Goldberg and M. Lewis, "Play Behavior in the Year Old Infant".
34. R. Friedman et al., *Sex Differences in Behavior*, p. 154.
35. D. C. McClelland, "Wanted: A New Self Image for Women", in *The Women in America*, ed. R. J. Lifton (Boston: Houghton Mifflin, Co., 1964), p. 176.
36. Ibid., p. 181.
37. Ibid., p. 176.
38. Martin and Voorhies, *Female of the Species*, p. 55.
39. S. G. Shoham, *The Violence of Silence: The Impossibility of Dialogue*, (London: Science Reviews Ltd., to be published, 1982), chapter 9.
40. R. Friedman et al., *Sex Differences in Behavior*, p. 158.
41. S. G. Shoham et al., "Separant and Participant Personality Types of Suicides", in *Israel Studies in Criminology*, vol. 7, ed. S. G. Shoham and A. Grahame (White Plains: Sheridan House, to be published 1982).
42. S. G. Shoham et al., "Personality Core Dynamics and Predisposition towards Homosexuality", in *Israel Studies in Criminology*, vol. 5, ed. S. G. Shoham and A. Grahame (Tel Aviv: Turtledove Publishing, 1969).

43. J. Money, J. G. Hampson and J. L. Hampson. "An Examination of More Basic Sexual Concepts: The Evidence of Human Hermaphroditism", *Bulletin of the Johns Hopkins Hospital* 97 (1955): 301-99; J. Money, "Sex Reassignment as related to Hermaphroditism and Transexualism", in *Transexualism and Sex Reassignment,* ed. R. Green and J. Money (Baltimore: Johns Hopkins Hospital Press, 1978).

44. G. S. Klein, "The Personal World Through Perception", in *Perception: An Approach to Personality,* ed. R. R. Blake and G. G. Ramsey (New York: Ronald Press, 1951), pp. 328-55; H. J. S. Guntrip, *Schizoid Phenomena, Object Relations and the Self* (New York: International Universities Press, 1964); D. W. Winnicott, *The Maturational Processes and the Facilitating Environment* (London: The Hogarth Press, 1965); R. Fairbairn, *Psychoanalytic Studies of the Personality* (London: Tavistock Publications, 1966) pp. 162-79.

45. Fairbairn, *Psychoanalytic Studies.*

46. A. Kinsey, W. B. Pomeroy and C. E. Marin, *Sexual Behaviour in the Human Male* (Philadelphia: Saunders, 1948).

47. L. Ovesey and E. Person, "Gender Identity and Sexual Psychopathology in Men", *Journal of American Academic Psychoanalysis* 1 (1973): 53-72.

48. Shoham, *Myth of Tantalus.*

49. H. Miller, *Sexus* (New York: Grove Press, 1965), p. 181-82.

50. Norman Mailer, *An American Dream* (New York: Dial, 1964), p. 45.

51. J. Genet, *Our Lady of the Flowers* (London: Panther Books, 1968), p. 114.

52. M. Praz, *The Romantic Agony* (New York: Meridan Books, 1956), pp. 205-206.

53. Cited by K. Davis in *Human Society* (New York: MacMillan, 1949), p. 176.

54. R. Graves, "Real Women", in *Masculine and Feminine,* ed. B. Roszak (New York: Harper Colophan Books, 1969), p. 33.

55. R. Binion. *Frau Lou* (Princeton: Princeton University Press, 1968), p. 231.

56. R. Shatz-Uffenheimer, *Contemplative Prayer in Hassidism in Studies in Mysticism and Religion* (Jerusalem: Magnes Press), p. 216.

57. O. Wilde, *De Profundis* (London: Methuen, 1950), p. 22.

58. F. Harris, *Oscar Wilde* (New York: Dell, 1960), pp. 131-32.

59. Cosima Wagner, *Die Tagebucher,* vol. 1, ed. G. Dellin and D. Mack (Munich: Piper, 1976).

60. S. Freud, "Contributions to the Psychology of Love, The Most Prevalent Form of Degradation", in *Collected Papers,* vol. 4, p. 203.

61. J. Money, "Dirt and Dirty in Sexual Talk and Behaviour", in *MIMS Magazine* (September 1978).

62. See J. M. Allen, *Candles and Carnival Lights, The Catholic Sensibility of F. Scott Fitzgerald* (New York: 1978).

63. J. Genet, *The Thief's Journal* (New York: 1964), p. 91.

64. Praz, *The Romantic Agony,* pp. 42-44.

65. "The Odyssey of Homer, Book X", in *The Complete Works of Homer* (New York: The Modern Library).

CHAPTER 8

1. E. Rostand, "The Last Night of Don Juan", in *The Theatre of Don Juan,* ed. O. Mandel (Lincoln: University of Nebraska Press, 1963), p. 601.

2. G. Casanova, *History of my Life,* vol. 1 (New York: Harcourt, Brace and World Inc., 1966), pp. 25-26.
3. F. Marceau, *Casanova ou l'Anti Don Juan* (Paris: Editions Gallimard, 1948).
4. Casanova, *History of my Life,* vol. 1, p. 227.
5. Ibid., p. 145.
6. As for the mechanisms of fixations relevant to the present context see the introduction to the present volume and S. G. Shoham, *The Myth of Tantalus* (St Lucia: University of Queensland Press, 1979), chapters 1-3.
7. *The Memoirs of Casanova* (New York: Bantam Books, 1968), p. 1.
8. Casanova, *History of my Life,* vol. 1, pp. 157-8.
9. Ibid., p. 245.
10. *Memoirs of Casanova,* pp. 67-8.
11. Casanova, *History of my Life,* vol. 1, p. 7.
12. Ibid., vol. 3, p. 236.
13. Ibid., vol. 1, p. 257.
14. Ibid., vol. 1, p. 157.
15. Ibid., p. 156.
16. *Don Juan* (Paris: Obliques Editions Borderie, 1978).
17. See Mandel, *Theatre of Don Juan.*
18. Cited in A. G. Bragaglia, *Pulcinella* (Rome: G. Cassini, 1953), p. 527.
19. C. Lazare, trans., "Don Juan, Eine Fabelhafte Begenbenheit, die sich mit einem re senden enthusiasten Zugetragen", in Mandel, *Theatre of Don Juan,* p. 323.
20. C. D. Grabbe, "Don Juan and Faust", in Mandel, *Theatre of Don Juan,* p. 322.
21. Tirso de Molina, *El Burlador de Seville Y Convidada de Piedra Obras, Theatre of Don Juan,* p. 90.
22. J. Zorrilla, Y. Moral, *Don Juan Tenorio Obras* in Mandel, *Theatre of Don Juan,* p. 516.
23. G. Flaubert, "Une Nuit de Don Juan", cited in Mandel, *Theatre of Don Juan,* p. 540.
24. Tirso de Molina, "The Playboy of Seville", in Mandel, *Theatre of Don Juan,* p. 96.
25. E. T. A. Hoffmann, "Don Juan", in Mandel, *Theatre of Don Juan,* p. 323.
26. A. de Musset, "Namoura", in Mandel, *Theatre of Don Juan,* p. 450.
27. Grabbe, "Don Juan and Faust", p. 328.
28. Ibid., p. 375.
29. Zorrilla and Moral, "Don Juan Tenorio", p. 524.
30. Ibid., p. 537.
31. Moliere, "Don Juan, or the Libertine", in Mandel, *Theatre of Don Juan,* p. 154.
32. "The Don Juan version of the Commedia dell'Arte", in Mandel, *Theatre of Don Juan,* pp. 108-109.
33. Rostand, "The Last Night of Don Juan", p. 611.
34. T. Shadwell, "The Libertine", in Mandel, *Theatre of Don Juan,* p. 195.
35. Cited in ibid.
36. Rostand, "The Last Night of Don Juan", pp. 591-2.
37. Ibid., p. 592.
38. Mandel, *Theatre of Don Juan,* p. 452.
39. Rostand, "The Last Night of Don Juan", p. 615.
40. Casanova, *History of my Life,* vol. 3, p. 85.
41. Ibid., vol. 3, p. 262.

42. Ibid., vol. 5. p. 58.
43. *Memoirs of Casanova*, p. 115.
44. Casanova, *History of my Life*, vol. 3, p. 185.
45. Ibid., vol. 3, p. 190.
46. Ibid., vol. 1, p. 291.
47. Ibid., vol. 3, p. 242.
48. *Memoirs of Casanova*, p. 121.
49. Casanova, *History of my Life*, vol. 1, p. 290.
50. Tirso de Molina, "The Playboy of Seville", p. 57.
51. Moliere, "Don Juan, or the Libertine", pp. 124–5.
52. Rostand, "The Last Night of Don Juan", p. 601.
53. Ibid., p. 603.
54. Ibid., p. 603.
55. Ibid., p. 605.
56. Casanova, *History of my Life*, vol. 1, p. 267.
57. Ibid., vol. 5, p. 47.
58. Tirso de Molina, "The Playboy of Seville", p. 57.
59. Casanova, *History of my Life*, vol. 5, p. 71.
60. *Memoirs of Casanova*, p. 64.
61. Ibid., p. 72.
62. Ibid., p. 65.
63. Casanova, *History of my Life*, vol. 3, p. 264.
64. Ibid., vol. 8, p. 22.
65. Ibid., vol. 5, p. 19.
66. Ibid., vol. 1, p. 269.
67. Ibid., vol. 3, p. 199.
68. Ibid., vol. 1, p. 33.
69. Mandel, *Theatre of Don Juan*, p. 324.
70. Grabbe, "Don Juan and Faust", p. 343.
71. Mandel, *Theatre of Don Juan*, p. 343.
72. Ibid., p. 355.
73. Ibid., p. 377.

CHAPTER 9

1. S.G. Shoham, *The Myth of Tantalus* (St Lucia: University of Queensland Press, 1979), chapter 8.
2. Y.A. Cohen, *The Transition from Childhood to Adolescence* (Chicago: Aldine, 1964), p. 105.
3. E. Wellish, *Isaac and Oedipus* (London: Routledge & Kegan Paul, 1954), pp. 95 et seq.
4. Shoham, *Myth of Tantalus*, chapter 8.
5. Francis Bacon, *Study after Velasquez's Portrait of Pope Innocent X* (1953). New York, collection of Mr and Mrs A.M. Burden.
6. J. Money, "Sexual Dictatorship Dissidence and Democracy", *The International Journal of Medicine and Law*, No. 1 (1978): 11.
7. R. Graves, *The Greek Myths*, vol. 1. (Harmondsworth: Pelican Books, 1955), p. 91.
8. Deuteronomy 32.

9. Euripides, "Iphigenia in Aulis", in *The Complete Greek Drama*, vol. 2 (New York: Random House, 1938), p. 323.
10. Ibid., p. 334.
11. H. R. Tottman, *Albert Camus* (Doubleday, 1979).
12. Proverbs 14:34.
13. S. Freud, *Modern Sexual Morality and Modern Nervousness* (New York: Eugenics Publishing Co., 1931), pp. 16-17.
14. M. Drabble, *The Ice Age* (Harmondsworth: Penguin Books, 1978), p. 128.
15. R. L. Trivers, "Parental Investment and Sexual Selection", in *Sexual Selection and the Descent of Man*, ed. B. Campbell (Chicago: Aldine, 1972), p. 137.
16. Ibid., pp. 142-43.
17. Ibid., p. 173.
18. Ibid.
19. E. O. Wilson, *Sociobiology* (Cambridge, Mass.: Harvard University Press, 1976), p. 326.
20. Trivers, "Parental Investment and Sexual Selection", p. 164.
21. R. Sadleir, *The Ecology of Reproduction in Wild and Domestic Mammals* (London: Methuen, 1967).
22. Wilson, *Sociobiology*, p. 320.

CHAPTER 10

1. G. B. Bermant and J. M. Davidson, *Biological Bases of Sexual Behavior* (New York: Harper & Row, 1974), p. 61.
2. C. J. Avers, *Biology of Sex* (New York: John Wiley & Sons, 1974), p. 23.
3. Cited in S. G. Shoham, *The Myth of Tantalus* (St Lucia: University of Queensland Press, 1979), p. 79.
4. S. Zweig, *The World of Yesterday*, trans. Phyllis and Trevor Blewitt (London: Cassell, 1939).
5. M. Nordau, *The Accepted Lies of Human Culture* (Tel Aviv: Mizpah Publishing Co., 1930), pp. 236, 243, 244.
6. Mikhail Stern, "La Vie Sexuel en USSR", cited by *Time Magazine*, 23 July 1979.
7. S. G. Shoham and G. Rahav, *The Mark of Cain*, 2nd ed. rev. (St Lucia: University of Queensland Press, 1982).
8. S. Peele, *Love and Addiction* (New York: A Signet Book, The New American Library, 1975).
9. S. Michelmore, *Sexual Reproduction* (New York: The Natural History Press, 1964), p. 72.
10. Ibid., pp. 76-77.
11. R. Briffault, "The Origins of Love", in *The Making of Man*, ed. V. F. Calverton (New York: The Modern Library, 1930), p. 488.
12. H. Jonas, *The Gnostic Religion* (Boston: The Beacon Press, 1964), p. 72.
13. A. Schopenhauer, "Essay on Women" (New York: The Modern Library, 1928), p. 78.
14. Ibid., p. 49.

CHAPTER 11

1. G. C. Williams, *Sex and Evolution* (Princeton: Princeton University Press, 1975), p. 124.
2. J. Huizinga, *The Waning of the Middle Ages* (Harmondsworth: Penguin Books, 1979).
3. Ibid., p. 81.
4. Ibid., pp. 79–80.
5. Ibid., p. 81.
6. N. Tinbergen, *The Herring Gulls' World* (New York: Basic Books, 1960).
7. R. C. Friedman et al., eds., *Sex Differences in Behavior* (New York: John Wiley & Sons, 1974), p. 337.
8. D. Lack, "Pair Formation in Birds", *Condor* 42 (1940): 269–86.
9. M. K. Martin and B. Voorhies, *Female of the Species* (New York and London: Columbia University Press, 1975).
10. See R. L. Trivers, "Parental Investment in Sexual Selection", in *Sexual Selection and the Descent of Man*, ed. B. Campbell (Chicago: Aldine, 1972), p. 137.
11. Trivers, "Parental Investment and Sexual Selection", p. 160.
12. Ibid., p. 168.
13. Michelmore, *Sexual Reproduction* (New York: The Natural History Press, 1969), p. 178.
14. Trivers, "Parental Invesment and Sexual Selection", p. 169.
15. Huizinga, *The Waning of the Middle Ages*, p. 76.
16. Ibid., p. 76.
17. Ibid., p. 78.
18. Ibid., p. 80.
19. Trivers, "Parental Investment and Sexual Selection", p. 169.
20. A. C. Wilson, *Sociobiology* (Cambridge, Mass.: Harvard University Press, 1976), p. 319.
21. See S. G. Shoham and G. Rahav, *The Mark of Cain*, 2nd ed. rev. (St Lucia: University of Queensland Press, 1982).
22. Trivers, "Parental Investment and Sexual Selection".
23. J. Crane, 'Basic Patterns of Display in Fiddler Crabs Ocypodidae (genus Uca)", *Zoologica* 42 (1957): 69–82.
24. Bermant and Davidson, *Bases of Sexual Behavior*, p. 17.
25. Trivers, "Parental Investment and Sexual Selection", p. 171.
26. W. H. Masters and V. E. Johnson, *Human Sexual Response* (Boston: Little Brown & Co., 1966), pp. 286 et seq.
27. A. C. Kinsey et al., *Sexual Behavior in the Human Female* (Philadelphia: W. B. Saunders & Co., 1953), p. 629.
28. C. Butler, "Insect Pheromones", *Biological Review* 42 (1967): 42–87.
29. R. Briffault, "The Origins of Love", in *The Making of Man*, ed. V. F. Calverton (Random House, The Modern Library, 1931), pp. 490–92.
30. K. Horney, "The Dread of Woman", *International Journal of Psychoanalysis* 13 (1932): 348–60.
31. S. Ferenczi, "Thalassa: A Theory of Genitality", *Psychoanalytic Quarterly* (1938), p. 18.
32. G. R. Tayler, "Historical and Mythological Aspects of Homosexuality", in *Sexual Inversion*, ed. Judd Marmon (New York: Basic Books, 1963), p. 146.
33. Although some male orgasms may occur without ejaculation.

34. T. Agoston, "The Fear of Post Orgasmic Emptiness", *Psychoanalytic Review* 33 (1938): 197, 214.
35. E. Fried, *The Ego in Love and Sexuality* (New York: Grune & Stratton, 1960), p. 3.
36. A. C. Kinsey et al., *Sexual Behavior in the Human Female*, pp. 613-14.
37. T. Benedek, "Discussion of Sherfey's paper on Female Sexuality", *Journal of the American Psychoanalytic Association* 16 (1968): 424-48.
38. Kinsey et al., *Sexual Behavior in the Human Female*, p. 592.
39. Ibid., pp. 626-27.
40. S. Fisher, *The Female Orgasm* (New York: Basic Books, 1973), pp. 53-4.
41. Ibid., p. 52.
42. Masters and Johnson, *Human Sexual Response*, pp. 135, 216. ·

CHAPTER 12

1. See J. Ginat, "Illicit Sexual Relationship and Family Honor in Arab Society", in *Israel Studies in Criminology*, vol. 5, ed. S. Giora Shoham and A. Grahame (Tel Aviv: Turtledove Publishing, 1979), p. 179.
2. S. Michelmore, *Sexual Reproduction* (New York: The Natural History Press, 1964), p. 36.
3. Ibid., p. 39.
4. W. A. Calder, "Breeding Behaviour of the Roadrunner, Geococcyx Californi Anus", *Auk* 84 (1967): 597-8.
5. Michelmore, *Sexual Reproduction*, p. 46.
6. E. O. Wilson, *Sociobiology* (Cambridge, Mass.: Harvard University Press, 1976), p. 320.
7. A. J. Lubin, *Stranger on the Earth* (Frogmore, St Albans: Paladin, 1975), p. 78.
8. W. Waller, *The Family, A Dynamic Interpretation* (New York: Dryden, 1938), p. 191.
9. Ibid., p. 190.
10. Ibid., p. 191.
11. Ibid., p. 112.
12. R. Briffault, *The Mothers*, vol. 2 (London: George Allen & Unwin, 1927), p. 263.
13. Ibid., vol. 1, p. 256.
14. See sources cited in ibid., p. 251.
15. See sources cited in ibid., pp. 560-1.
16. See sources cited in ibid., p. 544.
17. See sources cited in ibid., p. 543.
18. G. Lowes Dickinson, *The Greek View of Life* (London: Methuen, 1941).
19. E. Radocanochi, *La Femme Italienne de la Renaissane* (Paris, 1891).
20. See sources cited in Briffault, *The Mothers*, vol. 1, pp. 524-25.
21. J. Avers, *Biology of Sex* (New York: John Wiley & Sons, 1974), p. 192.
22. R. M. Grant, "Gnosticism, Marcion, Origen", in *The Crucible of Christianity*, ed. A. Toynbee (London: Thames and Hudson, 1969), p. 324.

CHAPTER 13

1. S.G. Shoham, *The Violence of Silence: The Impossibility of Dialogue* (London: Science Reviews Ltd., to be published 1982).
2. J.P. Sartre, *Being and Nothingness* (New York: Citadel Press, 1965), chapter on "Bad Faith".
3. R. Binion, *Frau Lou* (Princeton: Princeton University Press, 1968).
4. J. Money and A.A. Ehrhardt, *Man and Woman, Boy and Girl* (Baltimore: John Hopkins University Press, 1972), p. 191.
5. W. Waller, *The Family, A Dynamic Interpretation* (New York: Dryden, 1938), p. 191.
6. Binion, *Frau Lou*, p. 69.
7. Money and Erhardt, *Man and Woman, Boy and Girl*, p. 188.
8. See R. Briffault, *The Mothers* (London: George Allen & Unwin, 1927); and J. Huizinga, *The Waning of the Middle Ages* (Harmondsworth: Penguin Books, 1979).
9. As for the relationship between the social character of a given society in relation to the separant-participant continuum see S.G. Shoham, *The Myth of Tantalus* (St Lucia: University of Queensland Press, 1979), chapter 3.
10. R. Briffault, *The Mothers*, vol. 2, p. 263.
11. Ibid., p. 265.
12. Ibid., p. 257.
13. Sartre, *Being and Nothingness.*
14. J.P. Sartre, *No Exit* (New York: Vintage Books, 1949).
15. Ibid., pp. 24, 25.
16. Ibid., p. 46.
17. Ibid., p. 21.
18. Ibid., p. 21.
19. Binion. *Frau Lou*, p. 75.
20. "The Symposium", in *The Dialogues of Plato* (New York: Random House, 1937), pp. 318-19.
21. A. Camus, "The Adulterous Woman", in *Exile and the Kingdom* (Harmondsworth: Penguin Books, 1961).

Index